Today everyone is talking about money: how to spend it, how to save it, and how to invest it. But how much of this wall-to-wall money talk really makes sense? And how does all of it affect you? Now America's best known and most trusted personal finance expert brings her down-to-earth style to a book for real people with real issues about money. Jean Chatzky wants you to grab a cup of coffee, pull up a chair, and start...

TALKING MONEY

"Finally, I have an answer to all those friends and relatives who are always asking me, 'Should I do this or that with my money?' I can just say, 'Buy Jean Chatzky's book. It's all there.' And it is."
—John Huey, editorial director, Time Inc.

"For good general advice on such abstruse matters as stocks, bonds, and asset allocation, TALKING MONEY fulfills its title promise....Covers small details of large issues in easy, well-organized doses."
—*BookPage*

"Talk is cheap unless you're talking money, and Chatzky talks up a treasure box full of practical advice on the subject, in this excellent seminar-like look at the strategies of personal finance."
—*thebooxreview.com*

TALKING MONEY

Everything You Need to Know about Your Finances and Your Future

by Jean Chatzky

WARNER
BUSINESS
BOOKS™

Published by Warner Books

An AOL Time Warner Company

Excerpts of this book have appeared in different form in *Money* magazine.

 Warner Business Books are published by Warner Books, Inc.,
1271 Avenue of the Americas, New York, NY 10020

Visit our Web site at www.twbookmark.com.

 An AOL Time Warner Company

The Warner Business Books logo is a trademark of Warner Books, Inc.

Printed in the United States of America
Originally published in hardcover by Warner Books, Inc.
First Trade Printing: January 2002

10 9 8 7 6 5 4

The Library of Congress has cataloged the hardcover edition as follows:

Chatzky, Jean Sherman.
　　Talking money : everything you need to know about your finances and your
future / Jean Chatzky.
　　　　p. cm.
　　ISBN: 0-446-52570-7
　　1. Finance, Personal. 2. Investments. I. Title.

HG179.C536 2001
332.024'01—dc21   00-044929

ISBN: 0-446-67810-4 (pbk.)

Book design by H. Roberts Design
Cover design by Brigid Pearson
Cover photograph by Brad Trent

To my parents, Chuck and Elaine Sherman,
whose names may not appear on this volume,
but whose commonsense wisdom is throughout it.

ACKNOWLEDGMENTS

I am very grateful to all of the people who helped me complete this book: First, the three crack researchers who worked diligently on the project: Elyse Mall, who poured her heart into the investment chapter (and many others), Anne Ashby Gilbert, who helped me round up the real people whose lives you read about in every chapter, and Jonathan Lesser, who whipped the Five Questions sections into shape. Next, the folks at Warner Books—the supportive (and always understanding) Rick Wolff, who edited the manuscript with style, Jamie Raab, who kept a close eye, Mari Okuda, who kept me on my grammatical toes, and Dan Ambrosio, who made sure every *i* was dotted and every *t* crossed. My agent, Robert Shepard, who worked tirelessly behind the scenes (and sometimes out in front) in every way imaginable. And finally, my friends and colleagues who read the manuscript when it wasn't in terrific shape and offered enormously helpful input: Ken Adler, Janine Rosenblum, and Denise Martin.

I also owe a huge debt to the experts who lent their knowledge to this project (and to so many of the articles I've reported through the years): financial planners extraordinaire Ric Edelman, Harold Evensky, Victoria Felton Collins, Joan Gruber, Dee Lee, Patricia Drivanos, Ross Levin, and Gary Schatsky; mortgage whiz Keith Gumbinger of HSH Associates; money therapist Olivia Mellan, author of *Overcoming Overspending;* financial counselor Karen McCall; my good friend David Landay, author of *Be Prepared;* Max Bazerman, author of *Smart Money Decisions;* Gary Belsky and Thomas Gilovich, authors of *Why Smart People Make Big Money Mistakes;* real estate guru Ray Brown, coauthor of *Home Buying for Dummies;* Scott Cooley and Eric Jacobson of Morningstar; Juliet Schor, author of *The Overspent American;* debt experts Marc Eisenson, Nancy Castleman, and Gerri Detweiler of the Good-Advice Press; credit card guru Robert McKinley of Cardweb.com; *Inside Flyer* magazine's Randy Petersen; Dan Rottenberg, author of *The Inheritor's Handbook;* Manhattan estate planning attorney Gideon Rothschild; Jeanne Salvatore of the Insurance Information Institute; Evan Kass of Northwestern Mutual Insurance; Dan Langan of the National Charities Information Bureau; Ron Passaro, founder of the American Society of Home Inspectors; consumer expert Edgar Dworsky; Beth Givens of the Privacy Rights Clearinghouse; matrimonial attorney John Fiske, elder care attorney H. Clyde Farrell; *Retire Early* author John Wasik; and fee-only insurance consultant Glenn Daily.

I am so fortunate to have three incredible professional families. At *Money* magazine, I want to thank Denise Martin, Craig Matters, Marion Asnes, Patrick Taylor, and Andrea Bennett for their friendship and overwhelming support—and the incredible Bob Safian, for luring me here in the first place. At *USA Weekend*, a huge thank you to Kathy McCleary and Marcia Bullard. And at *Today*, Jeff Zucker, Michael Bass, Betsy Alexander, and Patricia Luchsinger: You guys are the best!

Finally, to my friends and family—particularly my husband, Peter, and kids, Julia and Jake—who put up with months of me rising at 5:00 A.M. to complete this project (and sometimes falling asleep during dinner as a result), I love you guys.

CONTENTS

Kristin, a thirty-seven-year-old recently married freelance writer, is down on her money. It's not like she isn't making any. Actually, she's fairly successful. The problem, she says, is that she's not using her money to its full potential. She ticks off the symptoms: "I write down my checks but not my cash machine withdrawals. My husband and I don't have wills. Twice, AT&T has called offering me 7 cents a minute and I've said, 'I don't have my bill in front of me, would you call me back in a couple of days?'"

Marianne, a thirty-six-year-old researcher at a high-tech firm in Silicon Valley, is similarly distressed. Her cash reserve isn't where she wants it to be. She's overloaded with credit card debt. And, though she deftly unearths facts each day that would take ordinary people months to find, she candidly admits her company's stock purchasing plan has her baffled. "I e-mailed my company's human resources department to suggest that a Stock Options for Dummies class might be in order," she quips.

But deep down she feels this is no laughing matter. "I'm constantly finding out things I should have known about my money if only I was reading the stock pages every day," she says. "Even when I do make time to read the paper, I'll learn about something and say: 'I'm going to go out and do that. Maybe I'll even do it on my lunch hour.' But most of the time, I don't."

Then there's George, a seventy-year-old former clothing manufacturer in New York City. He has just one money goal: to make sure his six-figure nest egg lasts him through retirement. He turned to a financial adviser to help him develop a portfolio of mutual funds. The result: unending frustration. In less than a year, George found himself the owner of more than two dozen mutual funds. Monitoring them was difficult enough, but worse, he had no idea how to figure out whether they were the right funds to help him accomplish his goals.

Kristin, Marianne, and George are all out of control where their finances are concerned. It's like they're running a race they have no chance of winning—which makes perfect sense, because they don't even know what course they're on. They feel overwhelmed and confused. And not just about one particular problem—like Marianne's options—but about their money in general. "My husband can tell you to within $1,000 what he's worth," says Kristin. "I have no idea what I have." Not that she hasn't tried to remedy the situation. She even made a list of all the money chores she had to accomplish. It sat on a shelf over her desk for two years. She never crossed anything off.

Sound familiar? Have you ever felt your money was running you rather than the other way around? You are not alone. Far from it. I've given a lot of talks on the subject of money and whenever I ask this question, I see a lot of smiling, nodding, even hand raising throughout the room. Even more importantly: You are not the problem. The problem is all the so-called experts using buzzwords and lingo, and throwing around big numbers and making your money more confusing and frightening than it needs to be. They do this because it's profitable. They know that there's a better chance of getting you to pay for something if they can convince you that you desperately need it—even if you don't exactly understand what you need it for.

Take a car dealer. If he can get you to sign a lease that looks cheap on the surface, even though it's incredibly costly in the fine print, who profits? He does. If a credit card company can entice you to sign on the dotted line with a three- or six-month bottom-of-the-barrel teaser rate that you only later find out doesn't apply to balance transfers, it's going to make a mint. And if a broker or financial planner can get you to buy shares of stocks or mutual funds that really don't suit your needs, she still makes a commission. In fact, she makes it twice—once when you buy and then again when you figure out what the real deal is and sell.

You are not the problem. But—in the pages that follow—you'll see that you do hold the keys to the solution. And, on its face, the solution is fairly simple: You need to learn to talk about your money.

Think about that. What would it really mean to be able to talk about your money? It would mean that you could have a heart-to-heart with your spouse about buying that first house, a tearful conversation with your aging folks about their wills, or a blowout with your twenty-five-year-old who doesn't want to move out of the house (and still won't clean up his room), all without losing your nerve. It would mean that you'd feel comfortable interviewing potential home renovation contractors and feel competent negotiating for your new car. And it would mean you'd have the confidence to take on the rip-off artists in the financial services world, because you'd be able to discern the real deal from the baloney. Any decision that you make involving your money, whether you're saving it, spending it, investing it, or just planning what you'll do with it in the future, can be made easier, simpler, more straightforward with a good dose of money talk.

The good news is there's very little about money that can't be explained in terms of sixth-grade math and plain English. Which doesn't mean that talking about money is particularly easy. It's not. Psychologists like to say that the subject of money is *loaded*—and they don't mean rich. What they mean is that it's the last taboo. It's harder to talk about than sex or childhood trauma. That's why when the topic of money comes up in therapy it's like everyone's ghosts are sitting right there in the room.

But the fact is, if you can get yourself over those hurdles and learn to talk about your money, you can learn to manage it. Once you learn to ask the right questions, to get to the pertinent answers, to filter out the important information from the garbage—then all of a sudden you undergo an amazing transformation: You become more *confident* and more *competent* when it comes to actually dealing with it.

That's never been as critical as it is today. Our parents and grandparents could slide by without talking about their money. They didn't have to. They worked for one or two companies their entire careers, racked up a substantial pension, threw in Social Security, and knew they'd have enough to live on for the rest of their lives. Not us. We're living in a world ruled by three new financial realities:

Reality Number One: We are responsible for our own retirement—and we know it. We are the 401(k) generation, rather than a generation of pension-earners like our folks. That much we have absorbed. A 1998 survey from the Certified Financial Planners of America found that 67 percent of prospective clients consider their employers' financial plans their primary source for funding retirement goals. Want to guess how many people are counting on Social Security benefits? Three percent. Other research has shown that more Gen X'ers believe in UFOs than believe Social Security will offer them any sort of support in their golden years.

And yet—perhaps because we're frightened—we're not doing enough. Only 15 percent of Americans have $100,000 or more socked away for retirement. More than 40 percent of middle-class Americans (those making $35,000 to $50,000 a year in household income) have less—less!—than $10,000 put away. Even when we're getting our hands held, we don't do all that we can. Only about half of the financial planners surveyed said that their clients were socking the maximum into their 401(k) and other retirement accounts. Why are we making such bad choices?

Reality Number Two: Information overload. Have you ever walked into a bakery only to be so overwhelmed by the number of choices—the bagels, the Danishes, the donuts, scones, the filled pastries, not to mention dozens of different types of little cookies—that you left with just a cup of coffee? Despite the fact that you were hungry? That's what's happening in the world of money. There are 9,000-plus mutual funds. There are over 8,000 stocks. There are 1,400 money market funds. Even many local banks have a dozen different types of accounts.

And not only are there more entities from which to choose, but more information about making those choices. Not so many years ago, if you wanted to buy a stock, you'd call your broker. He'd pull the latest research his firm's highly paid research analyst had generated on the company and stick it in the mail. A few days later, when you received it—and read it leisurely over your morning coffee— you'd make a decision, call him back, and either pull the trigger or take a pass. If you were extremely motivated, maybe you'd head to the library, read the latest issues of *Value Line* or *Forbes*, and then make the call. Today, we have the Internet. Research reports, screening tools, calculators, and more advice (some totally useless, some not) shoot onto our screen the minute we care to type in a ticker symbol. Today we have CNBC, where over the course of a day you can hear a half dozen different opinions on the direction of the market alone, many more on individual stocks. It's no wonder so many people feel paralyzed when it comes to making a decision. And, to add insult to injury, there's . . .

Reality Number Three: We have no time. There aren't enough minutes in every hour or hours in every day to spend with your kids or write that new business proposal, let alone manage your money. Take a look at your life. If you're like most Americans then you're working more and sleeping less. You spend evenings working with your kids on homework, visit your parents on weekends, exercise a few times a week, and desperately try to find some time to relax and enjoy yourself with your spouse or friends.

For better or for worse, you're largely succeeding. According to Harvard economist Juliet Schor's calculations in *The Overworked American*, our average hours of work have risen about 10 percent in the last twenty-five years. Put another way: You're very likely putting in a month's more time each year at work than your folks did.

As a result, you may very well be pulling out your hair. A land-mark 1991 study, the Hilton Time Values Project, found that most of us would trade a day's pay to have an extra day off. A few years later, a University of Maryland survey repeated the study with similar results—45 percent of respondents said they'd take a day off without pay. Women age thirty-five to forty-four wanted the day off most of all.

How are these new financial realities affecting us? We're stressed. Since the mid-1980s, the National Center for Health Statistics has been collecting data on Americans' perception of stress in their lives. More than 30,000 people were interviewed in 1985 and again in 1990, and more than 20,000 in 1993. Between the first time the survey was taken and the last, the percentage of people reporting "a lot" or "moderate" stress in their lives jumped six full percentage points.

We're also scared. "I'm trying to pick some stocks that are good for the long haul, but at the same time trying to understand what's happening abroad and keep up with the Fed rates," Marianne acknowledges. "Sometimes I'm afraid to do the research because I'm afraid I'll find out I should have been doing something that would have helped a lot and I'll get upset because I haven't."

In other words, she's paralyzed. Many people are. Because when you put all that stress, all that fear, all those options together, the choice we often make—and yes, it is a choice—is to do nothing at all. Financial writer Gary Belsky and behavioral psychologist Thomas Gilovich, authors of *Why Smart People Make Big Money Mistakes*, have a name for this sort of behavior. They call it "decision paralysis." The higher the stakes, the more conflicted we feel. And for most people the stakes are never higher than when their choices involve their finances.

Learning to talk about your money is the solution. If you can talk about your money, then you can talk about your dreams, your goals, your hopes, your fears. Your entire life comes more clearly into focus.

What's involved? Well, it's a little like learning to speak a new language. First, you need to clear the hurdle money presents as a subject. That means breaking down some long-standing psychological barriers that make money a taboo subject. There were years when people didn't talk about sex, decades when it was thought to be rude to ask a person what he or she did for a living. Now both are matters of casual conversation. We'll talk about how to open up similarly when it comes to your finances.

The next thing you need to learn is how to listen. The world of money has become incredibly confusing. The sales pitch comes at you from all directions—from television and magazines, from Web sites and those annoying telemarketers. How do you take away the message without swallowing the pitch? I've been a reporter for fifteen years and I'll admit it isn't easy. Many people find it helps to paraphrase the information and repeat it back; it not only firms up the information in your own memory, it makes the speaker feel like he or she has been heard. That verbal pat on the back can result in more information coming at you, which of course is the goal. For me, being quiet has always worked best. The person I've been asking for information will often get so flustered that he'll just start spilling his guts. When that happens, you get every bit of detail you were looking for.

In fact, you'll probably get more. Which brings me to the vital third component of money talk: asking good questions. When it comes to your money, you have to be your own consumer advocate. There are too many terrible investments and deals out there for you to do otherwise. Making the right decisions for you means probing. What's the expense ratio on this mutual fund? Does this minivan have a five-star rating for safety? What benefit do I get, Ms. Insurance Agent, from spending $3,000 on a policy from you, when I can buy the same one for $2,000 on the Web?

You need to be able to separate the good information from the bad. So along with lists of crucial questions to get you started in more than a dozen different money conversations, I've given you some answers as well—not just the ones you want to hear, but the ones that are wrongheaded and off base. If they start to pop up as you're interviewing a broker or a real estate agent, for example, you'll know it's time to walk away.

Finally, you need a basic grasp of personal finance—some schooling in Money 101. Why? Have you ever tried to have a conversation about the latest Oscar winners without having seen the films? You may be able to get out a sentence or two, but say too much and everyone knows you're faking it. And you know that they know it. Your ears turn red. You want to go home. It's the same with money. In order to talk about your finances intelligently—and therefore to feel comfortable participating in the conversation in the first place—you need to be grounded in the subject. Much of *Talking Money* is devoted to bringing you up to speed.

How do all of these components work together? Take Chapter 2, which focuses on getting—and staying—out of debt, as an example. In the heart of the chapter are three debt reduction plans; you pick the one that's right for you depending on how much debt you're carrying and what it's doing to your psyche. There are sections devoted to teaching you how to find the best credit cards for your needs and how to use your cards to your best advantage (think frequent flyer miles). In other words, all the nuts and bolts. But you'll also get the talking points: the five questions you should be asking your credit card company and your credit bureau. They may look like a basic Q & A, but in fact, they're part of an overall strategy. If you can get yourself to start asking questions, to start incorporating talk about those cards into your everyday conversation, you'll become much more comfortable with your finances in general. You'll save money.

That's exactly what happened to Ellen, a career coach in Seattle. She racked up $15,000 of credit card debt when she started her own practice—so much, in fact, that she couldn't see a time in the future when she would be able to pay it off. She knew falling behind on her monthly payments could be disastrous for business—and she certainly wasn't ready to shut her doors. So she sat down at her desk and started working the phone. Ellen called each of her five credit card companies and started talking. "I explained that I was three years into a new business I had started without an emergency fund in case of trouble. I said, 'Gee, I have this really high interest rate. Can you do anything for me?' I talked to people straight."

It was time-consuming, Ellen remembers. And it was emotional. No one likes admitting that they're having money problems. But it worked. Almost every one of her creditors lowered its interest rate. Some only gave her a few points, some gave a lot. Two years later, she had only $4,000 left to pay, her business was going strong, and she was actually starting to save. And she's been much more conscious of her money ever since.

Admittedly, applying the concepts of *Talking Money* requires a change in attitude. It did for me. I first received a glimpse of how hard it can be to talk about your finances when I got over my head in credit card debt. I was a year or two out of college, earning $13,500 as an editorial assistant at *Working Woman* magazine, and living a pretty frugal existence. My rent in Brooklyn was $400 a month. I managed to eat, pay the utility bills, buy subway tokens, and even find a few bucks to go out with my friends. But when it came to extras—like clothes—I reached for my credit card. My balance was $3,000 and it was growing. Worse, I was paying interest at 18 percent.

Simultaneously, though, I had a small savings account. Whenever I wrote a freelance story or tutored a kid for his SATs, I tried to forget about that money. I put it directly in the bank. My balance there was about $4,000. Not much, but enough of an emergency cushion to make me feel a little safer. If I ever needed to flee New York for the calm of my parents' home in Peoria (yes, *that* Peoria), I had the cash for a ticket. And on that money I was earning a slim 4 percent.

One day, my roommate caught a glimpse of my credit card bill. A banker (a Citibanker, no less), she was horrified. "I know you have money in the bank," she said. "Why don't you just pay that off?" She ran a quick mental calculation. "You know, it's costing you hundreds of dollars a year to let it ride."

I changed the subject and left the apartment before she could ask me any more questions. Thinking back, I knew that running this balance wasn't particularly smart. I was embarrassed about the fact that I had it, and mortified that I couldn't bring myself to pay it off. And I had no intention of talking about it because I knew that as soon as I talked about it, I was going to have to do something about it. And part of me very much wanted to keep that money "safe" in the bank.

But my roommate wasn't what you'd call a wallflower, and she had no intention of letting me off the hook (after all, if I could free up some cash, we might be able to buy something for the apartment). So she kept after me and eventually we did talk about it. We even sat down at our kitchen table with a pencil and paper and figured that I'd been earning $120 a year keeping my money in the bank and spending $540 by running a $3,000 tab with MasterCard. By writing one big $3,000 check to erase my balance I'd actually save $420 annually. We could get a VCR for that.

Getting out of debt felt so good I found myself venturing into more money conversations. I boasted that the designer skirt I was wearing cost $12 at a sample sale. I talked to my friends about how they negotiated for raises (I desperately needed one, as you'll recall), to my parents about their retirement accounts, and to my journalist colleagues about which write-offs were acceptable come tax time. I found talking about money freeing and exciting—and fun.

I still do. When I went shopping for a new Dodge Durango and the salesman said to me—not once but twice—that he didn't think we could do any *real* negotiating because my husband wasn't there, I told everyone I could think of (and then I bought the vehicle from someone else).

And I'm not the only one for whom "talking money" has paid off. For years, Allison and Tom, a Colorado couple, blew off their money conversations. When they had free cash, they spent it. When they didn't, they went into debt. When the debts got big enough to force them into Chapter 11, they worried and they filed. But they never really *discussed* it.

Then, a few years ago—solidly back on their financial feet—they started thinking about moving to a bigger house. Their current home wasn't tiny by any means, but there were some days when Allison, who works from home, felt cramped; or at least that's what Tom thought. And there were days when Tom wanted a bigger backyard to stretch his legs; or at least that's what Allison thought.

So without really talking about it, they started planning to put the place on the market and look for something more spacious.

Then one evening, spurred by a couples seminar they attended, they took the leap into conversation. They talked in detail about what a move would mean to their financial situation. They talked numbers. They listened to what the other was saying. And what they discovered shocked them. Allison, as it turned out, didn't want to spend hundreds of thousands on a new house. She wanted to travel and to "have a life." Tom didn't want to move either. A new house wasn't as important to him as having some financial flexibility—and neither were the new cars and electronic gadgets they'd been spending so much money on for so many years. And they've been happier—and more in sync—with their money choices ever since.

That's what we all want when it comes to our money. We want to earn more, save more, invest wisely, and pay less. That's all. Talking—to our bosses, spouses, friends, colleagues, and the experts who are trying to help us—can help us achieve every one of those goals.

Think of this book as my conversation with you. Let's grab a cup of coffee and talk about our money.

TALKING MONEY

CHAPTER 1

Talking Goals

What do you want from your money? Think about that for a minute. It's a loaded question, a difficult question, a question with an infinite number of answers. But it's a question you need to address. You've already taken the first step: You picked up this book. That alone tells me you *know* that figuring out what you want from your money is something you're ready to do.

Some of it won't be easy. It's important that you understand that up front. Setting financial goals means making at least some temporary decisions (and I say "temporary" because you'll certainly revise them along the way) about not just your money but your life. It means thinking about how big a family you want to raise, how you wish to retire, and whether your aging mother should live with you or in a nursing home. It means dealing with the queasy subjects of who should be the guardians for your minor children and how and when you need to write a will.

But the payoff will be enormous. Just think about how good it would feel to have a plan in place to deal with all the "what-if" scenarios in your life (what if I lose my job, what if I get divorced, what if I become disabled . . .). And the rewards won't just be emotional. Once you leap in and get hold of your finances, there are a number of small moves you can make that'll pay off big in the wallet.

The key here is to relax. I'll talk you through all the issues, page by page, one by one. And we'll start back at the question I asked a moment ago: What do you *want* from your money? What do you *want* your money to do for *you?* Let's take a look at the answers some other folks gave to get us going.

My friend Susan, who recently married, can sum up the answer in one five-letter word: h-o-u-s-e. She and her new husband want to move out of his bachelor pad/apartment in New York City and into a house of their own, preferably somewhere in the suburbs of Westchester County, where she grew up. She doesn't know *exactly* what the place will look like, but she's got a specific enough list of prerequisites that she'll know it when she sees it. "It has to be old," she told me, "with lots of charm. But it doesn't have to be huge. I don't want bedrooms that are big enough to land a plane in. And I don't want so many rooms that I can't afford to furnish the place nicely all at once. And I don't need a ton of land either, just enough for a substantial garden."

Ken and Nancy, a couple nearing forty with two young kids, are crystal clear on the subject, too. They want an early retirement with plenty of free cash to travel the globe. When Ken was around thirty, he passed up a chance to spend six months in Asia roughing it with three friends. All three of these other guys were at career roadblocks. Not one of them really liked what he was doing. So they quit their jobs and went on an adventure to clear their heads.

Not Ken. He had been working at the same bank since college and was quickly rising up the ranks. Every time I spoke to him, it seemed, he had been given more people to manage. Taking time off to travel would have deadened his momentum. In hindsight, it was a good thing that he stayed. Shortly after his friends left on their trip, he met Nancy. A year later, they married. And nearly a *decade* later, he's still at the bank and he and Nancy have two kids and a house they designed themselves on a quiet cul-de-sac. They live well, but not lavishly. Instead, they sock every extra dollar into savings, so that once the kids are through with college, they'll be free to go on an adventure of their own when they retire—*at age fifty*. And this time they won't have to rough it.

As for me . . . in the short term, my husband, Peter, and I already have a house that we love. We've tackled the big-time structural fixes: new heating system, new roof, new air-conditioning. (It's seventy years old, and we knew it was a fixer-upper!) I'd like to see it fully furnished sometime soon, but we're taking it one room at a time. Long-term, our goals are fairly straightforward. We'd like our kids to go to the colleges of their choice with no financial worries. We'd love to—someday—add a beach house to our real estate portfolio. And though I, in particular, can't get a clear picture of my "retirement" yet (probably because I'm one of those people who doesn't believe I'll ever *really* retire), I know that as I get into my fifties or sixties, I'd like to be able to work a little less, play a little more, and have enough free time to exercise just about every day.

But that's me. What do *you* want? Clearly, if you're reading this book, then one of your goals is to gain a clearer understanding of your money in general. But what about the specifics?

- Do you feel you're not investing enough for retirement?
- Are you fighting about money with your spouse?
- Are you afraid you'll die leaving your family in a bind because you don't have the right insurance?
- Do you feel like everyone's making money in the stock market except you?
- Are you mired in credit card debt?
- Or do you feel like you simply need a good—that is, an *understandable*—introduction to money?

I could sit here and type questions like this page after page after page. And perhaps I'd never hit on what drove you to the business section of your favorite bookseller. But it's important to get a grip on what you want from this book—and what you want from your money in general—in order to be truly successful as you work toward your financial goals.

Most people, you should know, have absolutely no idea what their financial goals are. According to one survey from the Certified Financial Planner Board of Standards, *not setting measurable goals* is the number one mistake Americans make with their money. Fewer than one third of financial planning clients actually have an idea of what they'd like their money to do. (And remember, those are people who've *sought out* professional financial help. The percentage of the population at large that's setting financial goals must be slimmer still.)

Why is goal setting a big deal? Because research shows it works. Establishing benchmarks for your money is like setting goals on the job, or on your diet or exercise plan. Unless you have them—unless you know that you want to make manager in under a year, lose five pounds in four weeks, or run a 10K this fall—your accomplishments will be meaningless. You may achieve all of those things, but because you never set benchmarks, you won't have any means to measure your success. You'll never know when you've crossed the finish line. As a result, it'll be harder to keep going.

You also never get the emotional payoff that comes with having knocked an item off your list. I remember when my husband and I got our first wills. We already had an infant (yes, we should have done it before he was born, but we waited—like many people—until we were getting on our first airplane). And I was definitely nervous about sitting down in a lawyer's office and discussing all the issues that come up when you're making a will (we'll get to them in Chapter 7). But when the document finally arrived in the mail, all I can remember feeling was relief. We ran over to a friend's that day so we could sign in front of them as witnesses.

So that's the first thing we're going to talk about in this chapter: how to figure out what you want, and why you also need to revisit those desires every so often simply to make sure they haven't changed, and alter your plans if, as is likely, they have.

You may have noticed that earlier I didn't refer to just plain goals, but to *measurable* ones. Setting your benchmarks is one thing. But once you've set them—whether they include a new station wagon, retirement at sixty, or eliminating credit card debt—you have to figure out what they're going to cost you. Only then can you develop a schedule for stockpiling the assets you'll need in order to make those things happen.

Can you accomplish all of this yourself? Absolutely. You can do it with instruments as basic as a No. 2 pencil and a legal pad. Or you can install the latest version of Quicken or Money from Microsoft in your computer and let it walk you through the decisions. And if you're comfortable online, the Internet has more financial planning tools than I could ever describe in a book twice this size. (You can also hire a financial planner to help—we'll talk about that in a later chapter.)

Finally, none of this works unless you can make it happen—consistently—for weeks, months, or even years on end. Those of you who have seen me on television probably know I like to compare managing your money to exercising. The first day you hit the gym for Cardio Kickboxing (or whatever) it's brutal. Your thighs hate you. You can't breathe. Your muscles weren't made to work this way. Five minutes into the class, you're fantasizing about vegging out in front of Rosie. But if you can get yourself to stick it out, three times a week for a month, then all of a sudden you realize you can do it. You're kicking higher and punching harder. You have form. Now if you *don't* make class, you feel as if you're missing something. That dose of endorphins has become as indispensable as your morning coffee. It's a habit. It's part of your life.

Managing your money works the same way. The first day you save every receipt so that you can track your spending, it's a pain. The bulge in your wallet is annoying. You don't quite understand how knowing that you spent $6.95 on a cobb salad roll-up and a Diet Coke and $4.69 on film is going to make a difference in your retirement account. But if you stick with it for a few days, then a week, then a month, all of a sudden you experience the same sort of confidence-boosting flash of results. You've got $200 more in your bank account at the end of the pay period this month than you did last month. Your brokerage account is gaining weight. Over time, saving those receipts, following your money, taking pride in your growing account balances becomes a part of you. You don't understand how you could have ever done it any other way.

Setting Goals

So here we are again, back to the question I asked at the top of the chapter: *What do you want from your money?* The difference between what you have today and what you'll have months or years from now can be nothing—or it can be very substantial. If you'd like to see your assets grow, it helps immeasurably to have a road map, to set you on course. You can use it to become clear on your priorities, so that soon you'll know which investment accounts to fund, which credit cards to pay down, what you're saving for. Think of this planning exercise as making a financial to-do list—only this time, instead of a to-do list for the day, you'll be making one for the next couple of years (or if you're *really* clear, maybe the next couple of decades).

The Wish List

How do you start? Diving in is the only way. Pick up a pencil and a piece of paper, pull out your Palm (or other PDA) or take a seat at your computer, and let's make a list, a financial wish list. This is a time for thinking really big. In a few minutes, we'll attach numbers to the items on your list and decide what you can accomplish in the short term and what's a fantasy. But if you restrict yourself from the outset, chances are you're missing something that's important to you. So go ahead and dream a little.

I have no idea what's in your head (sorry) but here are some possibilities to get you started:

- I want to buy a home.
- I want to go back to school.
- I want to start saving for college for my kids.
- I want to get rid of my credit card debt.

- I want to buy a car.
- I want to retire in Phoenix.
- I want a time-share in Orlando.

Throughout this book, you'll find lists of questions: Five Questions to Ask a Financial Planner, Five Questions to Ask Your Life Insurance Company, Five Questions to Ask Before Buying a Stock. They're designed to help you figure out whether you're buying the right products, getting the best deal, working with an up-to-date (and on-the-level) professional. Perhaps no list of Five Questions, though, is more important than this one:

Five Questions to Ask Yourself (and/or Your Partner) About Your Goals:

1. What do I want to accomplish financially this year? Don't censor your answers. They can be anything from I want to spend winter break in Boca to I want to have $1,000 in my savings account to I want to pick better stocks. All are acceptable. Just be sure to list accomplishments that are possible to achieve in the next twelve months. *Red Flag!* Don't allow yourself to be wishy-washy. Specificity is key. Otherwise, a year from now you'll still be starting from scratch.

2. What do I want to accomplish with my money in the next ten years? Again, be very detailed. Perhaps you envision having $30,000 in your IRA or 401(k) by that time. Perhaps you can see yourself having zero in credit card debt. Or maybe you'd like to be working for a company that grants stock options. Knowing what you're striving for makes the path toward those goals easier to find—and therefore easier to follow.

3. What do I want to accomplish with my money far off in the future? These are your stretch goals. They may include retirement at age fifty-five, a second career in the Peace Corps, or the ability to leave your kids a sizable inheritance. One of my colleagues at

Money magazine, Jason Zweig, says his long-term investment time horizon is 100 years. No, he's not expecting to break the Guinness Book records for longevity, but he has children and he's planning to leave certain investments to them.

4. Am I willing to begin? There is only one thing standing in the way of achieving your goals—at the very least your short-term ones—and that's you. Are you willing to do it? Perhaps you decided you wanted to save an extra $1,000 this year. Are you willing to cut your spending by the $20 a week it'll take to accomplish that? Or to take on a freelance project or some overtime? Are you ready to do it today? When it comes to your money, procrastination can be a killer.

5. Do I know how to get started? Don't worry, that's what this book is here to teach you. But the key to beginning is to break that goal down into smaller chunks that you can wrap your hands around. Take that $1,000 example again. As one sum, it sounds like a lot of money. But when you realize saving it on a weekly basis only means socking away a $20 bill, it's manageable. If you want to buy a house five years from now and need to come up with a down payment, you're working with larger sums of money—but still they can be broken down into manageable parts. Put away $50 a month into Treasury securities at a 6 percent return, and you'll have $3,342 in five years after taxes (assuming a 28 percent tax bracket). If that's not enough, run the numbers for a $100 contribution (you'll have $6,684) and a $150 contribution ($10,026) and a $200 contribution ($13,368). That $200 may sound like a lot in one chunk but if you think of it as $50 a week it's much more reasonable.

As you go through this exercise, remember that it's okay if your answers are all over the map. Your first time through these questions should truly be a brain dump. Then go back over the items and organize them in terms of priorities. Which is more important to you, the home or the car? If you get rid of your credit card debt today, do you think you can stay out of debt tomorrow? If so, you should probably tackle your credit cards first and start stashing as much as possible into the retirement fund second. Putting all your money muscle behind a single financial task will often provide the biggest payoff (in the credit card case, for example, it's often impossible to beat the return you get by paying off an 18 percent card by investing your money another way). But there will be times when you can work on multiple goals at once. If your company has a tuition reimbursement program, for example, you *can* go back to school while you're paying off your Visa.

Note: It's fine to focus *much* of your energy on the expenses of tomorrow such as retirement and college, but you also need to have a life today. Ross Levin, a Minneapolis financial planner, had a client in his office who wanted to move his family to a neighborhood with better schools. But he was hesitant to do it *now*. Instead he wanted to wait three years, thinking he could use the time to rack up a really substantial balance in his retirement accounts before he started pouring money into a new residence. Levin talked him into reconsidering: "The reality is you want your kids growing up in this neighborhood, in these schools, with these playmates," he argued. "The impact of moving now on your family will be much more dramatic than the additional money you're putting away for later."

His point is an important one. There is such a thing as too much delayed gratification. Saving so much today that you're living unhappily isn't worth a few rounds of golf or even a few expensive vacations down the road. You have to find the middle ground. The key is to be as intentional about your spending as you are about your saving. When you plan for a kitchen renovation or a trip to Europe for your twentieth anniversary—just as you would plan to make your 401(k) contributions—then they don't play havoc with your future. You decide how much you'll need to make them happen, put the money aside, spend it, and move on to the next item on your list. Which brings us to . . .

Challenge Your Goals

Once you've set your goals and listed them, it's time to make sure you believe in them. Write a first draft. Put it away for a week or two and then revisit it. Have any of your goals changed? Have some begun to seem more or less important than they did when you first put pen to paper? The items that stick after two weeks are the ones you should work toward. If you're a couple, you'll each want to make separate wish lists, edit them, and only *then* merge them.

Things to avoid as you go through this process: "Brussels sprouts goals," items that end up on your list because you believe you *should* want them, whether or not you really do.

Take college saving, for example. It's likely to show up on many lists. But do you really want to put enough money aside to pay 100 percent of your child's expenses? Is that the best thing for you considering how many years you have until retirement? Is paying for college in full the best way to encourage your eighteen-year-old to stand on her own financial feet? Maybe. Maybe not.

Or take your retirement projections. Does your life revolve around your work? Is your work the impetus for your social life or the source of most of your friends as well as your financial support? Are you the sort of person who says (and truly means): "I *love* what I do"? If so, then quitting work cold turkey the day you turn sixty-five is highly unlikely. The numbers you plug into whatever retirement calculator you're using should reflect that.

Frame Your Goals

Now that you have a working list, you need two other pieces of information to make your goals real. The first is some idea of timing. When do you want to make these things happen? You also need to figure out what they'll cost. You'll be guessing a bit (particularly on things like how much it'll cost to rent that villa in Tuscany in the year 2007 for your twentieth anniversary). But that's okay. Getting close means you'll only have to put a small amount on your credit card or that you'll have a slight surplus. Either way, you'll be better off than if you hadn't saved at all.

What you'll have sitting in front of you at that point is a big number: $3,000 for the vacation, $22,000 for one year at private college, $25,000 for the down payment on your first house. Now you have to figure out how much you'll have to put away each month—or each pay period—in order to get there. There are plenty of calculators on the Internet to help you. But you can also get extremely close with pencil, paper, and a handheld calculator.

Let's work out the math for the biggest example above: the $25,000 down payment on a house. We'll assume you're already almost halfway there and say that you have $12,000 earning 5 percent in a money market fund. In two years, assuming you're in a combined 33 percent state and federal tax bracket, that $12,000 will be worth just over $12,800, so you'll still need another $12,200. How do you pull it together?

Start with a rough guess. Looking at your take-home pay, you think you can put away $400 a month. Again, that'll go into a money market account earning 5 percent. If you put away $400 a month for two years, you'll have saved $9,600. A simple interest calculation on that earns you $480, so even before you take taxes into account, you know that $9,600 in savings won't be enough. What if you increase your monthly contribution to $500 instead of $400? In savings alone, that'll get you to $12,000. You know that taxes zap a little more than one third off the top of the 5 percent interest rate your money will earn, bringing it down to 3.35 percent. Now multiply $12,000 times 1.0335 and you'll find that your total return is about $12,400. That's close enough for me.

Siphoning $500 or however many dollars you've determined it's going to take to reach your goal out of your spending money each month isn't always going to be easy. There will always be a ski trip or a Christmas list or a new suit that looks more immediately attainable—and therefore more attractive. That's why it's crucial to make saving as automatic as possible. Arrange with your bank to have the proper amount deducted every month from your checking account and moved directly into your money market (or other short-term investment) so that you don't have a chance to spend it.

It also helps to keep those long-term goals in sight. Post little reminders around the house where you're sure to see them to help you remember *why* you're not spending $98 on that skirt in the window of Banana Republic. For years now, my friend Jonathan has had a picture of a waterfront home in Rye, New York, taped to the refrigerator of his apartment in New York City. He cut it out of the real estate section of the *New York Times Magazine* when the home was up for sale. Never mind that it sold years ago. It's *like* the home he knows he wants. It's something to keep in mind as he heads off to work each weekday (and often on Sundays), putting in many more hours than a salaried employee would to get his start-up business off the ground.

Revisit Your Goals

In the fall of 1999, my family got together on a Friday night and heard some great news: My brother Eric and his wife, Gabrielle, were expecting a baby. Then the phone rang on Monday with some even greater news. It was *twins!*

Even though they were ecstatic, the good news threw their financial plan out of whack. They had figured on staying in their one-bedroom apartment in Manhattan for at least a year, maybe two. It had a small dining alcove that could easily fit a crib for the babies. Now it seemed they'd have to buy a two-bedroom place or house soon after the kids even arrived. And—not knowing how Gabrielle would feel about going back to work—they were only going to look at places they could carry on Eric's salary alone.

My point is this: Life is a moving target. You plan on spending $2,000 to repair the kitchen in your new home, when all of a sudden the roof goes, too. Or your aging parent needs to move in. Or your cat needs dialysis. Or you visit Santa Fe and decide, "The heck with the East Coast," and start packing your bags. Or, like my brother and sister-in-law, you have twins. It happens. (On my husband's side of the family, it happened to the same sister *twice!*)

The best way to rid your stomach of the butterflies this sort of a financial roller coaster brings is to sit down, once again, to talk about what these changes mean to your life and to run the numbers. Some people find numbers frightening. I find them very reassuring. It's nice to know that having a second baby doesn't double the charge for labor and delivery, it only raises it by a third, that buying a new dishwasher only costs *double* what it would cost to fix your old one (not five or six times the cost of the repair as you might have been imagining) or that even though you went insane with your gift buying at holiday time you can pay it off by April if you cut back on a few small nonessentials. Then you can sit back and live—even enjoy—your life.

You Can Do This! (Will You?)

A revelation: From a purely numerical point of view, there isn't anything *that* complicated about financial planning. You figure out how much money you need, what sort of savings and investment return it'll take to get there, and you make a plan that will get you to your goal. A handheld calculator is the only tool you may need. Especially when there are only a few items on your list, it's pretty easy to do the math.

But as your goals get a little more complicated—as you're trying to save for a car, invest for college, put money away for retirement, and pay down your mortgage simultaneously—you'll want help. The cheapest form of sophisticated help available is an off-the-shelf software package. I'm a big fan of Quicken; my husband and I have been relying on it to track our spending and our portfolios for years. But you'll find many of the same tools in Microsoft Money, or on the Web sites of just about any large financial institution. Using these tools, you can run through many of the same calculations that a financial planner would run either with you or for you. (Little-known fact: Many financial planners rely on similar computer aids—just like many tax preparers rely on souped-up versions of Turbo Tax, a software product you can buy yourself.)

The downside of doing it yourself? *You really have to do it yourself.* I'm not kidding. Gary Schatsky, a New York–based financial adviser, goes as far as to say that he "bets" most of his clients could do their planning on their own. The question is: Would they? "Most of them are so focused on their families or their own businesses that they don't have the time to do it," he says. "I have clients who manage portfolios for a living. They know small cap stocks like the backs of their hands—but their personal finances specifically, they don't have a lot of time to spend on."

Doing your own financial planning means taking the time to make sure your plan makes sense. Doing well by your money means revisiting that plan every six months to a year to make sure it still makes sense. And you'll have to commit to putting your plan in action, too: opening the accounts, buying the mutual funds, purchasing the insurance, working toward your goals. By far, more people do this themselves than hire someone to help them. It's completely possible—it doesn't even take *that* much time, just a day or

SEVEN WAYS TO MAKE A GOOD HABIT STICK

The way to make managing your money seem like a natural extension of the rest of your life is to make it habitual, a regular part of your routine. That's true whether we're talking about paying all your bills on time (which we'll do in Chapter 2), keeping track of your expenses (Chapter 3), or having regular money discussions with your spouse (Chapter 11). But how do you do that? If you've ever tried to adopt a new habit (and who hasn't?) then you know: Some stick but some vanish as soon as the next sun rises.

Study after study shows that you have to have patience. It takes twenty-one days for a daily behavior to become a habit. A weekly or monthly behavior takes even longer. The difference between successful attempts and failures is that people who are successful do the following:

1. Keep a record. For new habits, a daily journal is the best medicine, suggests Kelly D. Brownell, a professor of psychology at Yale University. If you like numbers better than words, a daily graph noting even the tiniest improvements often works as well.

2. Organize your environment to help—not hinder. You want to keep things that'll help you reach your goals nearby—and keep temptations as far away as possible. That may mean leaving your credit cards in a drawer at home if you can't think of a reason you'd need them that day. It also means setting up mechanisms to make your accomplishments come easier. For example, when Michelle and Adam, a Seattle couple, were trying to get themselves to stick with a budget, they kept a spending log on their pillow so they'd remember at the end of the day to write down every expense.

3. Don't set yourself up for a fall. If you've hated research since the time you were in junior high school, you're probably not going to love spending hours in the library (or even online) researching stocks. Don't fight this reluctance: Go with it. Instead of forcing yourself to pick a new stock or fund every time you have a few dollars to invest, schedule automatic monthly withdrawals from your checking account and have the money deposited into a mutual fund that you can stick with for the long term. Likewise if balancing your checkbook is what you dread, buy a software program that'll do all the actual figuring for you. You can thus make these tedious tasks nearly effortless.

4. Reward yourself for good behavior. Just make sure that your rewards don't work against your ultimate goals—for example, if you're trying to save money, your reward shouldn't be spending an extra $30 at the Gap, it should be something free like an extra-long soak in the tub. Likewise, don't punish yourself when you experience a setback. Let's just acknowledge right now that you will. A friend will come into town for a few days and you'll go on a little Visa bender. Give yourself a break and get back on the plan as soon as you can.

5. Seek out support. Sometimes working with another person—or group of people—can provide just the boost you need to get with the plan. It can be a group with similar goals, like an investment club filled with beginners who all want to learn the basics of research, or a single individual—perhaps a money therapist—who can help keep you on the right path through a series of well-tested suggestions. Some people find that quarterly trips to a financial adviser who can provide structure and encouragement are enough to keep them on the straight and narrow.

6. Keep going—even when you feel down (*especially* when you feel down). By actually doing something over and over again, you'll gain a feeling of accomplishment—even power. That's why it's so important that when you find yourself feeling frustrated and overwhelmed by something, you do just what will help you conquer what's getting you down. When you're feeling fat, you should hit the StairMaster instead of the refrigerator. And when you're feeling poor, you should sit down with a pad and paper and figure out just how much money your new habits are saving you. Two dollars a day saved by walking to work rather than taking the bus may not sound like much, but it adds up to more than $500 a year. Once you write it down, focus on how the accomplishment makes you feel. Concentrating on the change will make you feel energized. Think of it as insurance for how you'll behave tomorrow.

7. Trust yourself. Don't let your feelings of self-doubt get in the way. Whether you realize it or not, it took time and practice to develop your current habits. It'll take the same time and practice to develop the ones you want to adopt for the future.

so to get organized, then a couple of hours each month to stay that way. You just have to commit to it, like you'd commit to a job search or earning a degree. It's a matter of habit—and of making it stick:

THE BIG THREE: THINGS TO TAKE AWAY FROM TALKING GOALS

1. If you don't know where you want to go, you're never going to get there. So sit down with pencil and paper and rough out your long- and short-term goals. A legal pad is your best friend.
2. The next step is to understand financially what it'll take to achieve those goals on your list. That means doing enough research to attach actual numbers to your goals.
3. Accept the fact that none of this will happen overnight. But small habitual changes in the way you handle your money can have an enormous impact on your overall financial picture.

CHAPTER 2

Talking Debt

On the surface, Robert looked like another financial success story. The twenty-nine-year-old married bookkeeper and father of one had worked steadily for a civil engineering firm in New Jersey for a good half decade. His income was $39,000 and growing. His job was secure. He and his wife, a dental hygienist, traveled. They ate out several times a week. On the surface, life looked good. But just beneath was a growing mountain of credit card debt. And Robert realized that if he didn't do something about it—and soon—it was going to swallow him whole.

"I was totally overwhelmed," he says. "My family lives in California and Florida and we had paid for a lot of travel on my cards," he says. And those dinners out? They were killing him. They alone were costing him $300 a month, $3,600 a year.

By early 1998, his wallet was bulging with *nine* different credit cards. His total debt had topped $33,000—nearly as much as his take-home pay. The steady stream of overdue payments and late fees was driving him nuts. As if that wasn't enough pressure, Robert's wife was being phased out of her full-time job and into part-time status.

Clearly it was time for drastic measures. First, he sat down at his desk at home and shoved every card but one into a shoebox (and that one, he swore, he'd only use in a dire emergency). Next he called every one of his nine card companies and asked them to lower their interest rates. Three of them knocked 3 percentage points off without blinking. Another dropped its rate from 19 percent to 12 percent. Finally, he picked up the want ads and started looking for work he could squeeze in around his day job. Eventually he hit on this solution. He took a paper route. In the beginning it paid $150 a week. Now it pays double that. He also started freelancing as a computer consultant. And slowly but surely he started chipping away at that credit card debt, starting with the card with the highest interest rate and working his way down the list.

How's his progress? It's not as fast as he'd like, but it is steady. Between February 1998 and May 1999, he paid off $5,000 in high interest rate debt and got rid of two cards. His life's changed a bit with this new emphasis on frugality: He can't remember the last time he had dinner out, for example. But knowing that he's solving this problem on his own, without the help of a debt consolidation service or a bankruptcy attorney, has made him confident that he'll one day have a secure financial future. He's thinking about setting up an IRA. He wants to become a regular contributor to a retirement plan. "I know it's never too early," he says. "But it's also never too late."

There's little doubt about it: Skyrocketing consumer debt is our biggest barrier to financial success. Who can think about saving for college or investing for retirement when the Visa bill is looming large? Throughout the 1990s, Americans took on debt at record levels. By the year 2000, debt service as a percentage of disposable income was higher than it was during the early 1990s recession. We still pay, on average, about $1,200 a year to our credit card companies in interest and fees alone, not including principal. That's $100 a month. Many people, people like Robert, pay several times that.

The cost of that money is higher than it sounds. Consider the other things you could do with $100 each month. You could save it. Better yet, you could invest it. If you'd put that $1,200 into the Vanguard 500, an index mutual fund that mirrors the Standard & Poor's 500, every year from 1993 to 1998, it would have earned $3,690 and grown to $9,690 before taxes. The reason that I put this chapter on debt ahead of the one on saving is that being overloaded in debt makes it far too difficult to save. This is no chicken-or-egg situation. You have to get rid of your excessive debt before you can move forward financially.

Notice that I said "excessive." *All* debt is not evil or even expensive. Used wisely, debt can be a very powerful financial tool. It can help you afford assets like homes and college educations that may either appreciate in value or help you get ahead in other ways.

There's even a good side to plastic: It's convenient. I'm one of the growing army of people who use their credit cards for absolutely everything. I charge at the grocery store, the veterinarian's, in fact everywhere I can. It saves me a trip to the ATM (and a potential $1.50 to $2.00 surcharge if I'm not in the neighborhood of my own bank). It's valuable for tracking my expenses. When my husband and I enter our expenses into Quicken at the end of each month, the Visa and American Express bills make it very easy to follow the money. And, of course, there are the frequent flyer miles. By the time my kids are six and four, I'm going to use what will then be a huge pile of points to take the whole family to Disney World. The cost of this convenience is low: $49 a year in annual fees for my frequent flyer card, $35 for American Express. I don't pay interest because I pay off my credit card every month without fail.

Debt is a balancing act, to be sure. A basic thirty-year home mortgage can be a positive; a loan that allows you to take 125 percent of the equity out of your home (unless you're using it for major renovations), extremely dangerous. A home equity loan or line of credit can be a good investment if you use the money to increase the value of your home, but using the money for a trip to Europe that takes years to pay off can make that vacation a very expensive proposition. Even the fun of collecting frequent flyer points or miles can become a dangerous game; if you're not paying off your credit card balance with regularity, they can end up costing you much more than they're worth.

In the pages that follow we'll focus on how to walk that line. We'll talk about how to get out of debt. A quick quiz will help you figure out how much trouble charging has caused you. Then you can follow one of three targeted debt reduction strategies to work your way out. Even if you're carrying no liabilities on your personal balance sheet right now, there will come a time when you'll need to borrow again. So the second part of the chapter is devoted to helping you learn how to do it wisely. Finally, we'll talk about your credit rating: what it is, why it's more important than ever before, and how to keep it in shape.

Quick Quiz: How Debt Dependent Are You?

1. When the Visa bill comes each month you:

a) Pay it immediately and in full, maybe even using your computer to zap the dollars from your bank account to your card company directly.

b) Wait until the deadline approaches to pay the bill, then write a check for as much as you can. Some months it's just not possible to pay off the whole thing.

c) Usually pay just the minimum. That's what a credit card is for.

2. Your mailbox is bulging with catalogues of the new spring fashions. You really don't need yet another black suit—and the budget is a little tight this month—so you:

a) Give the catalogues a quick perusal, then stick them in the recycling bin.

b) Order a gray one at a good price. After all, the fashion magazines have *all* been saying that gray is the new black.

c) Stock up, telling yourself that even though you completely overspent this month, you'll be good the next month (and the month after that).

3. Your best friends just flew to Europe for free—business class—using their frequent flyer miles. You felt:

a) Fine, actually. You've already booked a trip to Barbados (for two) using yours.

b) A little peeved. You never seem to accrue enough miles to get you much more than a yearly upgrade or occasional coach ticket.

c) Green with envy. You charge as much as they do, and yet you've never earned a thing. What do they know that you don't?

4. You were shopping in Bloomingdale's and the salesman offered you a 10 percent discount on the day's purchases if you signed up on the spot for a credit card. You said:

a) "Thanks, but no thanks." You don't need another credit card in your wallet.

b) "Sure, why not?" But you vowed to stick this annoying piece of plastic in a drawer.

c) "Of course!" You don't really have the money to pay for the sweater you were buying anyway. Now you can put off actually paying for it for a month or two.

5. Your wallet:

a) Closes easily and slips into your pocket or the zipper compartment of your purse.

b) Is a little overstuffed, but mostly because you're a little anal about keeping each and every receipt.

c) Bulges at the seams because of the six or more credit cards you carry.

6. If you add up your total consumer debt it equals:

a) Less than 20 percent of your take-home pay.

b) 20 to 30 percent of your take-home pay.

c) 30 percent of your take-home pay or more.

7. Your credit rating is:

a) Absolutely fine, you check it once every year or so just to make sure.

b) Pretty good, you think. Although, come to think about it, you were late with the utility bill a few months back, so it may not be squeaky clean.

c) Abysmal. You got turned down for the last low-rate card you applied for (even though the notice you received in the mail said you were preapproved).

How'd you score? Give yourself one point for each "a" answer, two for each "b," and three for each "c." If your tally is:

7–9: You have a pretty rational view of your debt and you're not in over your head. Still, it would be nice to know you're getting the best deal possible from your credit card company. Follow Debt Relief Plan No. 1 below.

10–16: Debt may not be causing you sleepless nights, but it's occupying your daydreams. You're probably paying your bills on time, but one minor disaster—a new transmission for the car, a leak in the roof—could easily push you into the world of credit delinquents. Follow Debt Relief Plan No. 2. It starts on page 25.

17–21: You have serious debt problems (but you already knew that, didn't you?). Stop worrying. Follow Debt Relief Plan No. 3 to get back on track. It begins on page 27.

Debt Relief Plan No. 1

You're responsible with your plastic, paying off your bills on time, often even in full. Even if you're carrying a moderate debt load, you're *managing* it well. But you do have a problem—one you may not even be aware of. For model customers like you, credit cards are getting even more expensive. You've got *such* impeccable money habits that from the point of view of the credit card company, you're a nightmare. Particularly if you only charge occasionally, you're not making them any money.

Here's the way profitability shakes out for the card companies. Most bank cards make about 1 percent on every purchase you charge. That means if you charge $1,000 a year, the company makes $10. You charge $3,000, it makes $30. Everything else is made on interest (averaging right now about 17 percent), annual fees, and penalty fees (charged for things like paying late and going over your credit limit).

So let's say you shopped around for a credit card, settling on one that has no annual fee and a moderate interest rate. You don't care because you never pay interest anyway. The only money your card company is making on you is that slim 1 percent. Consider postage and the cost of printing statements and unless you're charging more than $250 a month ($3,000 a year) the company is making zero. Zilch. Nada.

You're the reason that credit card companies have gotten so aggressive with penalty fees. In years past, you could pay your bill a few days late and the card company would look the other way. Now, at many card companies if you're one day late you may find a $25 charge on your next statement (one large card issuer has recently started assessing late fees on payments that arrive after 10:00 A.M. on the *day* they're due!). Going over your limit can cost you another $25 (and by the way, it's up to you to keep track of just how close to that limit you are).

And then there's the GE Rewards card example. It charges you $25 a year simply for paying off all your bills in full and on time, in effect penalizing you for not paying any interest. What's the best way for a conscientious consumer to handle this sort of difficult environment? By getting even more aggressive.

• **Start with a great low-rate card.** In general, you want to have two credit cards. The first should be a low-interest, low- (or preferably no-) annual-fee, essentially bare-bones card. Simply stash it in your wallet for emergencies, just in case one day you do have to make a large purchase that you know you're not going to pay off immediately. Think of it as having a low-rate line of credit. It doesn't cost you much (if anything) but it could bail you out if you're in a jam. (Note: If you're the kind of person who charges only very small amounts, say less than $250 a month, or $3,000 a year, you'll want to take a different tack. A low-rate, low-fee card should be your primary charge card. At these low charging levels, you'll never earn enough in frequent flyer miles or other points to compensate for the annual fees rebate cards typically have.)

• **Add a perk card.** If you're an avid charger, the kind who loads purchases on a credit card for the sake of convenience and then pays them off each month, your primary card should be a perk card. It should give you something back—dollars toward buying a car, frequent flyer miles, points toward hotel rooms, or even cash. The goal is to pick a reward that you'll actually use. People let billions of miles expire each and every year. That translates into millions of dollars. So while dollar for dollar the cash-back deals aren't as sweet as the mileage ones, they can be more valuable if you rarely fly.

• **Do you need a third card?** Rarely. If you're very aggressive about earning points, and you charge thousands of dollars a year, you may max out whatever rewards a certain program is willing to give you each year. The trick is to use cards like these only until you reap the maximum reward, which means keeping track of your spending. Then switch to another perk card.

• **Read your statements.** Credit card statements are about as scintillating as junk mail, I know. But it's important to give them the time of day. In many cases the information printed there is the only notice you'll get of changes to your card program, which can be substantial. Interest rates can go up. New fees can be assessed. Reward programs can vanish into thin air, leaving you with a limited amount of time to use the points you've already amassed. And all of these changes may take effect in as few as fifteen days. Particularly in the case of an interest rate hike, that can cost you some serious money. Many state banking departments have laws that allow you to cancel the card and pay off your balance at the old rate. But if you use the card once you've received notice of the change, it's considered a de facto acceptance of the new rate. In other words, you're stuck with it.

DON'T HESITATE: AUTOMATE

With late payment fees on the rise—not just for your credit card bills but for other regular bills—you need insurance that your payments get to their destination on time every single month and here it is: Pay those bills automatically. You can preauthorize withdrawals from your checking account to pay your mortgage, car payments, insurance, utilities, even the health club—almost anything that's a fixed amount.

Debt Relief Plan No. 2

The appearance of your credit card bill each month in your mailbox is no longer a comfortable event. Perhaps you delay a day before opening it, because you know the number on the "new balance" line is going to be higher than you'd like it to be. The good news is that you're quite normal. In fact, in the scope of credit card customers, you're average. According to CardWeb, most households have thirteen cards in their combined wallets, including 5.5 bank cards (Visa, MasterCard, Discover, Optima). Here's how to break the habit:

• **Raid your savings account.** Do you have hundreds of dollars sitting in the bank earning 3 percent? Or thousands in a money market account earning a little more? Take that money out and use it to pay off your credit cards. You'll save considerable money. Say you take $3,000 out of a 3 percent savings account and use it to pay off debt on a credit card where the interest rate is 18 percent. In a year, you'll net $450 on the deal. That's a substantial start to your *new* emergency fund.

• **Pull out all your credit cards.** If you have more than two or three, you have too many. First separate those that you haven't used in a while. If you don't owe them any money, call the toll-free numbers on the back of the card and cancel them *right now*. They're cluttering up your wallet—and doing damage to your credit rating. Then, a month or two down the road, request a copy of your credit report (more on this momentarily) to make sure that all those canceled cards reflect that they were closed by you, the customer, and not by the institution—or as often happens, that they weren't closed 'at all.

• **Pay off the highest rate card first.** Next, look at the pile again and find the card with the highest interest rate. The fastest and cheapest route out of debt is to put all your extra cash toward paying off that card, while paying the minimum on the rest. When you've paid the balance down to zero, then cancel the card. Cut it up. Then move to the card with the next highest interest rate and repeat the process. If you're sitting with a portfolio of cards that all have high rates, you should also look at transferring your balances. These days, rates of 12 percent or less are fairly competitive. Anything higher should be shuffled around. Just make sure balance transfers aren't charged interest at a higher rate before you do the deal.

• **Eliminate department store cards.** These probably make up a good portion of the cards in your wallet and generally they're a rip-off. Their interest rates tend to be well above average and, to make matters worse, they're usually nonnegotiable. I know, they're tempting. Every time you make a major department store purchase, you probably get offered a card with a 10 percent discount on everything you buy that day. I would have saved $300 on a couch I was looking at in Bloomingdale's by signing on the dotted line. If I'd yielded to temptation but then canceled the card immediately, it would have been worth it. But that's another temptation you don't need. If my couch purchase was followed by a month where money was tight, then another and another, it would have cost me $600 in interest to let the couch sit on my card for a year.

• **Watch out for fees.** The way the credit card industry is piling on the fees these days, it's tough even for a fairly decent customer to avoid them. Late fees averaged $23 per payment in 1999, a 20 percent jump from a year earlier. Worse, they're just the starting point. Exhibit the same bad behavior—whether it's paying late, exceeding your credit limit, or not using your card enough—more than once or twice and many card companies use it as an excuse to raise your interest rate. Beware.

Debt Relief Plan No. 3

You've got some serious debt problems. Take heart in the fact that a lot of people do these days—1998 saw a record number of personal bankruptcy filings. The key to getting out from under is first to evaluate the situation you're in, and then to decide if you're willing to do what it takes to change it. Are you going to stop using the mall as your playground? If so, then you have a chance to get out of debt *without* resorting to bankruptcy. In fact there are many tactics to try before you even think of heading to a lawyer. Here they are, from the least drastic to the most. Try to work your way down the list.

• **Consolidate to a low-rate credit card.** If you can find a low-rate credit card that will allow you to transfer some or all of your outstanding balances, that's probably your best bet. But be *very careful.* Many of today's tempting credit card offers exclude balance transfers or are based on teaser rates (low initial rates that then go higher after, say, six months or even less). If you go this route, make sure you cut up your other credit cards, calling the issuer to officially close your accounts, and pay at least as much on that one low-rate card each month as you were on all your other cards combined. That's insurance that you'll be debt free in a shorter period of time.

• **Negotiate for lower interest rates.** Call your creditors (or if you're nervous on the phone write a letter) and ask for a reduction in your interest rate. Explain why you're having trouble dealing with your debts (you lost a job, you're caring for a sick spouse, or whatever it may be) but that it's very important to you to stay current with your creditors. In some cases, that alone will earn you a break. One thing to watch out for is the IRS. If you settle any debts for $600 or more less than you owed, that money has to be reported as income at tax time.

• **Sell a major asset.** Perhaps you can do without your second car, your boat, a piece of jewelry or valuable antique, or even a few shares of Yahoo!. For many people, the 1990s was a decade marked by making acquisitions. If you find yourself regretting some of your purchases now that you're paying for them, selling them may be the simplest way out. Even losing a little money on the deal may help significantly when it comes to sleeping at night.

• **Borrow from your life insurance policy.** Typically, you can borrow up to 90 percent of the cash value from whole, universal, and variable life policies. The big plus of this sort of loan (unlike a home equity loan, which comes later as a strategy in this debt relief plan) is that there are no closing costs. But understand, if you die while the money's out on loan, your death benefit is reduced by the amount you've withdrawn, which means your heirs receive less.

• **Borrow from your retirement accounts.** Borrowing from your 401(k) plan has become very popular—16 percent of 401(k) account holders who have the option have stepped up to the plate, according to the Employee Benefit Research Institute. That's because it's an easy loan, with no credit check. But there are some considerable disadvantages as well. First, while you've got money out of your retirement plan it misses out on any gains in the stock market. In years like 1997 and 1998, that can be quite substantial. Second, although the interest rate is likely just a point or two over prime, you'll be paying it back with after-tax money, which increases the cost of your loan. And finally, should you lose your job while the money is out on loan, you may be asked to repay it to your plan within sixty days. That could send you scrambling further down this list for other options. Traditional IRAs aren't made for borrowing, but the newer Roth IRAs are. Since you've already paid taxes on contributions, they may be withdrawn at any time, though of course any money you take out may significantly reduce the amount you have at retirement. If you converted a traditional IRA to a Roth you must wait five years before the converted funds may be withdrawn without penalty.

• **Consolidate with a personal loan.** Debt consolidation loans, also called unsecured personal loans, typically must be paid off in three to five years. These come at higher rates than mortgages and car loans because there's no collateral behind them—the lender is taking more risk because there's no underlying asset to repossess. Despite that, if you can find one of these loans at a rate that's substantially cheaper than your credit card rates, this can be a decent solution. Note: To be sure you'll keep up with the payments, arrange to have them automatically deducted from your checking account each month (in some cases, agreeing to do this can also earn you a break on the interest rate).

• **Borrow against your home.** If you've paid off a great deal of the debt on your home, refinancing your mortgage or taking out a second mortgage (i.e., a home equity loan) and taking out some additional cash to ease your credit card burden can be a smart way to go. The reason this option falls late on this list is because you'd be putting your home at risk—and such sources of cash can be expensive to boot. Watch out for hefty closing costs. And say "no thanks" to any credit card that's tied to a home equity line of credit (that's what got you into trouble in the first place).

• **Go for credit counseling.** All of the above are do-it-yourself suggestions, but you can also couple any or all of them with the help of a credit counselor. These are folks who will help you work out a payment schedule for your debts. In some cases, they'll negotiate with your creditors for interest rate breaks. Unfortunately, some counselors are much worse than others. Even the well-reputed National Foundation for Credit Counseling (www.nfcc.org), which has Consumer Credit Counseling Services offices scattered nationwide, is a mixed bag in terms of the quality of its counselors. Myvesta.org (www.myvesta.org) is a reputable organization, as is Debtors Anonymous, a twelve-step program for compulsive spenders modeled after AA. Any organization that asks for money up front is a rotten bet. Before signing up with any group in your area call your local Better Business Bureau (or go to www.bbb.org) to check it out.

• **File for bankruptcy.** If you're not going to be able to change your behavior enough to get your debts under control, then you may—at some time—have to resort to bankruptcy. Understand, it's not the panacea that some attorneys and debt counselors make it out to be. It will mangle your credit for nearly a decade and make it difficult for you to get a job, rent an apartment, and find a decent rate on auto insurance among other things. For a good primer on the subject, check out the Web site of Nolo Press, the country's largest self-help law publisher, at www.nolo.com.

WHEN COLLECTORS COME CALLING: KNOW YOUR RIGHTS

Calls from a collection agency can certainly make an already unpleasant situation much worse. Here are four ways they're not allowed to harass you:

1. **By calling you between the hours of 9:00 P.M. and 8:00 A.M.**
2. **By phoning you at the office.**
3. **By bothering your friends or relatives to try to collect your debt.**
4. **By being hostile or abusive.**

If you encounter any of this behavior tell the collector you'll be reporting the agency to the Better Business Bureau. Then do it.

Five Questions to Ask About Your Credit History

Credit bureaus, sometimes called credit reporting agencies, are the keepers of your credit history. They receive information from your creditors, digest it, sell it to other creditors—and will pass it to you, sometimes at a price.

1. Who sees my credit report? In years past, the only time anyone took a look at your report was when you applied for a credit card or some other loan. Not anymore. Now, when you try to rent an apartment, when you apply for a job, even when you purchase auto insurance, your credit report is used as a key indicator of how responsible you'll be.

2. Can I see it? Not only *can* you see your credit report—you *should.* It's a good idea to take a peek annually to check for unwanted inquiries that could mean mistakes or even fraud. If you live in Colorado, Georgia, Maryland, Massachusetts, New Jersey, or Vermont, you can get one free copy of your credit report a year from each of the three reporting agencies. Where credit reports aren't free, they'll cost you up to $8. Checking one should be sufficient unless you find major errors. In that case, you'll need to check all three. Call the credit bureaus at:

Equifax: 800-997-2493.

Experian: 888-397-3742.

Trans Union: 800-888-4213.

If you see something you don't understand, write to the credit bureau. It's required to respond within thirty days.

Red Flag! When you're checking your credit report, look for accounts that don't belong to you and any companies that have been looking into your report without your permission (i.e., when you didn't apply for credit). Report both immediately to the fraud departments of the credit bureaus and ask to add a "victim's statement" to your credit report so that you're contacted to verify all future credit applications. Two of the bureaus maintain separate lines for this purpose. The numbers are: Equifax: 800-525-6285; and Trans Union: 800-680-7289; Experian's is the same: 888-397-3742.

3. What's my credit score? This is a computer-based determination of the risk you pose to your creditors. In fact, it's calculated differently for each lender using those particular parts of your credit report that are thought to be the most telling. According to Fair, Isaac & Co., a leading supplier of credit data, these scores include things like the number of times you've paid bills sixty days late, the size of your credit line (particularly the part that isn't being used), the number of recent inquiries into your credit history (an indication that you're looking for more spending power), and of course any bankruptcies, liens, and foreclosures.

4. Can I improve my score? It's not easy, but you can by improving your credit patterns. Your score is based on these patterns over time, but as negative information ages, it becomes less important. For example, the fact that you paid a few phone bills late four years ago will matter less than the fact that you've paid on time since then. Also, close accounts you're not using (lenders view them as a risk, imagining that you may go on a spending jag), don't hit all your credit limits (using 80 percent of the credit you have available is a sign to lenders that you're stretched), and keep applications for credit to a minimum in the six-month period before you'll be seeking a mortgage or other large loan.

5. Are agencies that promise to clean up my credit rating legit? No. These organizations often practice fraud—swapping your Social Security number or other identifying details with those of someone with cleaner credit, or no credit record at all, to allow you to start from scratch. They also rarely work. It's a harsh fact of life that bankruptcies and other blemishes on your credit report stay there for seven years or more before being erased. The only way to clean up your act is to do it yourself: Pay on time, don't borrow more than you can handle, and wait it out.

The Best Ways to Borrow

People concerned with paying off existing debts often forget that there's another side to the subject: making sure you don't overpay when you go to borrow in the future. That means learning how to find loans that sport the lowest available interest rates with the lowest possible fees. Consider this: Carrying a $2,000 balance on a credit card with an average interest rate of 18 percent will cost you $360 a year. If you had a card with a more reasonable 10 percent interest rate, carrying that balance would cost you much less—just $200 a year. On larger loans, the discrepancies can of course be much greater. On a $100,000 mortgage, an interest rate difference of even just one half a percentage point can cost you tens of thousands of dollars over the life of the loan.

That's why it's important to apply the same skeptical eye to shopping for a loan or line of credit that you would to shopping for a house or a car. In the pages that follow, we'll also talk tactics for getting the best in credit cards and home equity loans (you can find a lengthy discussion of mortgages in Chapter 8).

How to Pick a Credit Card

Here's some good news about credit card debt. More people are paying their cards off right away than ever before. Only 69 percent of charges were generating interest in 1999 compared to 74 percent in 1996 and 90 percent in 1990. That's a huge drop. And among baby boomers it's lower still—this group of consumers pays interest on less than 50 percent of its charges.

John, a Massachusetts teacher, unfortunately isn't among them. He has about $7,000 in credit card debt. For John, the most important card in his wallet at any time is the one with the lowest interest rate he can find; that's because he manages his debt by shuffling it from card to card, determined never to pay more than 9.9 percent in interest as he slowly but surely pays off his bills.

But what's the right card for *you?* There's no one right answer. You may be best off with a low-rate/no-annual-fee card, or a platinum card with frequent flyer miles that costs you $300 a year. Your best strategy is to pick a category that will work for you. Details on what you can expect from each of the major card groups follow. Then you can pick a card from within that category. For that, head to www.cardweb.com. In many cases, you can even apply online.

• **Low-rate cards.** The best low-interest-rate cards are also competitive when it comes to annual fees. Make sure your low-rate card has a grace period—typically a twenty-five-day window between the time when the billing cycle ends and the payment is due. Though most cards still have them, some issuers have been chipping away at them.

• **Frequent flyer cards.** Still the most popular perk, just about every airline now has its own frequent flyer card. The ones I prefer are called "travel cards," which allow you to fly on the airline of your choice. They typically work like this: You rack up one mile per dollar charged. Once you earn 25,000 or 30,000 miles, you qualify for a free domestic round-trip ticket with a value, typically, of $500 or less. You call your program's travel desk and they book the ticket for you. Because it's as if you're spending actual cash, there are no blackout dates or seat restrictions. And if the ticket costs more than $500 you can make up the difference. The Diners Club program is also a standout because it deals with more than two dozen airlines, but it has an $80 annual fee and you will have to suffer blackout dates.

• **Specialty cards:** Whether you're looking for money back toward the purchase of a car, rebates on gasoline, books or toys or dollars to spend on the Internet, there's a rebate card on the market for you. The thing to remember is that rebate points lapse at a rate of billions a year. Others just languish in their owners' accounts. Even if you're not getting the best dollar-for-dollar value, you win if you pick a perk you'll actually use. Some cards make that easier than others by automatically crediting your account or sending a check.

• **Cash-back cards:** This is the way to go if you earn rewards you never use. Discover is the granddaddy in this field, but heavy chargers will probably do better with a card like the Cash Back Card from American Express, which pays 1.5 percent back on total purchases over $5,000.

• **Platinum cards.** Platinum cards can be extremely pricey. But the benefits may be worth the high up-front cost. Take the American Express platinum card, for example. It's $300 a year, but its perks include buy-one-night, get-one-night-free hotel deals and free first- or business-class companion airline tickets. One ticket to Paris (or even California) could easily top that annual fee. On the other hand, there are some platinum cards on the market that offer very little more than you get on a gold card (purchase protection, travel accident insurance, and so forth) at a much higher fee. Not every platinum keeps up with AmEx, so make sure you know what you're getting.

• **Secured cards.** If you keep getting turned down for credit cards, a secured card is the way to go. Here's how they work: You make a deposit with the bank that issues the card. That money is held as collateral in case you don't pay your credit card bills (in the best cases you earn a respectable rate of interest on it). The amount you deposit is also, typically, your credit limit. In return, you get a secured Visa or MasterCard. It doesn't look any different from a regular credit card—you don't have to worry that some smug store clerk is going to give you a wink or a nod and that you'll be mortified. You just use the card and pay the bills at a slightly higher interest rate, generally, than standard counterparts. After eighteen or twenty-four months of on-time payment, the best programs will convert your card to a standard Visa or MasterCard and return your money.

Five Questions to Ask Your Credit Card Company

1. What will your card cost me? Sounds like a simple question, but in fact it has a number of moving parts. If you're carrying a balance, the most important cost is your card's interest rate, which can be anywhere from 7.9 percent to more than 30 percent annually. If you pay your balance in full every month, the interest rate doesn't matter. But you'll want a card with a low (or no) annual fee and a long grace period (the range is twenty to thirty days and getting shorter). Most annual fees are in the $50 range, but some—like the American Express platinum card—can be several hundred.

Red Flag! Be wary of low introductory rates—teasers—that are raised considerably after a short period of time.

2. Can you give me a better deal? Look around and find a card with a lower interest rate than yours. Call your issuer and ask them to beat or match that rate. Tell them you are going to transfer your balance to the other card if they won't. This was a relatively new game a few years ago, and credit card issuers, though somewhat taken aback, were largely willing to play. It's not as easy as it used to be but it's still possible at many banks. Department stores, however, are notably inflexible.

3. What happens if I pay late? Most card companies charge a late fee of about $20 to $25, in addition to the interest that begins to accrue on your charges. Some card issuers will also raise your interest rate if they don't get your payment on time, in some cases quite substantially. Remember: The date of your payment is not the date you postmark the envelope containing your check. It's the date the check arrives.

Red Flag! If your interest rate goes up after just one late payment, call to complain. If the card company insists, take your business elsewhere.

4. How is my balance calculated? Almost all card issuers use the "average daily balance including new purchases" method. It's a mouthful, but it's a number figured by adding the outstanding balance each day to new purchases, then deducting payments and credits. That figure is then divided by the number of days in the billing cycle—and over the course of the cycle the days are averaged. Purchases made during the cycle raise the balance and thus the finance charge. If your card issuer is using the "two cycle average daily balance method," it's averaging the daily balances over about sixty days, rather than thirty. This method isn't as good for consumers because it adds interest on the current month's balance together with interest on the previous month's balance.

5. Are you going to penalize me for not using my card? If you're one of those customers who insist on using a card "only for emergencies," chances are the credit card company is losing money on you, and they may charge you for it. Some will write you a letter insisting that if you don't start using your card, your interest rate will go up by a few points. Others may assess an inactivity fee. Either way, it's time to get a new card.

Finding the Best Deal on a Home Equity Loan

According to the Consumer Bankers Association, home equity loans now account for more than half of all consumer credit. While these loans were traditionally used for home improvements, they're now being used for all sorts of things from paying for college to consolidating other debts. The allure is that, depending on how much of the equity you've taken out of your home, these loans may be tax deductible, just like a mortgage. How do you sort out your options?

The first thing to understand is that there are two different ways to borrow. *Home equity loans* are fixed rate loans. They usually have a ten-year term (although five- and fifteen-year terms are also available). You get your money as soon as your loan closes. As with mortgages, there are likely to be a wide range of rates even within a community. The difference between a crummy deal and a great one can be 4 percentage points or more, according to HSH Associates, which surveys 1,000 home equity lenders four times a year. Not shopping carefully could cost you a great deal. *Home equity lines of credit* are variable rate loans that typically fluctuate with the prime interest rate and have a lifetime cap of around 18 percent. Unlike home equity loans where you get a chunk of cash up front, home equity lines of credit work like a checking account with a sizable balance. You draw on the money (and, of course, pay it back) as you need it, usually for a period of ten years.

In years past, you couldn't combine a first mortgage and a home equity loan or line of credit to borrow more than 80 percent of the equity in your home. No more. These days, many first-mortgage lenders will allow you to borrow 97 percent of the value of your home without even raising your interest rate. Home equity lenders, who are essentially issuing you a second mortgage, will let you take 100 percent of the equity out of your home—and more, up to 125 percent. You need to understand that the more you borrow and stretch your pocketbook, the greater the risk you represent to the lender, so the more your loan or line of credit is going to cost you.

How much you *can* borrow is a very different question from how much you *should* borrow. It's very important to remember that the valuable asset you have on the line is your home. Default, and you could lose it. So think carefully about why you need the extra cash in the first place. If you're renovating, this is a no-brainer. But if you're a compulsive spender—and have been all your life—paying off your high-rate credit cards with a home equity loan isn't going to solve your problem. You'll probably just charge your cards back up again. You need credit counseling instead. Still, for the many of you who go the home equity route, there are a number of key shopping issues. Let's walk through them.

• **Do you want a loan or a line of credit?** That depends on what you need the money for. If you're dealing with a one-time home improvement, like adding a second story, or a one-time debt consolidation, you'll be better off with a fixed rate home equity loan. That way you'll alleviate worries about rates rising in the future. But if you have ongoing needs for the money such as college tuition payments, a stream of medical bills, elderly parents who need financial support, or if you're planning a series of home improvements, you'll be better off drawing on the money only as you need it. Why pay interest on the whole chunk of change when you don't have to?

• **How do you get the best deal?** Start by canvassing the lenders in your area. If you've been listening to the radio or reading the paper, you know that your town's biggest lenders often advertise heavily. Sometimes they offer good deals. But because that advertising brings so much traffic to their institution, they don't have to cut their rates as far to meet their sales goals. But smaller lenders don't have big ad budgets; they need to offer even better deals to bring borrowers to their door. You also want to use your banking relationships to your advantage. Call the bank where you have your checking or savings accounts or credit cards and ask for a preferential rate.

• **What if my credit isn't up to par?** Don't worry. There are dozens of lenders who are now writing loans for people with so-called B or C credit. You won't get the lowest rates, of course. In fact, you'll pay rates 2 to 9 percentage points higher than customers with clean credit do.

• **Is it better to refinance my mortgage completely and take extra cash out of the deal?** Sometimes, but that's not an option available to everyone. On a "cash-out refinance," lenders are often reluctant to allow you to withdraw the first dollar if you don't have at least 25 percent equity in your home. But if you have paid down much of your loan, or if the value of your home has greatly appreciated, then you'll often be better off with a new mortgage. Rates typically run at least a point or two lower than home equity rates.

• **I'm really strapped for cash; should I go for one of those 125 percent loan-to-value deals?** In general, these aren't home equity loans. They're a complete refinancing of your first mortgage. They're also a terrible idea, for several reasons. Not only do the rates on these loans tend to be exorbitant, but you lose tax-deductibility on money borrowed above 100 percent of the equity in your home, which makes them an even more expensive proposition. Also, by borrowing more than your home is worth, you're digging yourself into a hole. It can be ten or even fifteen years before you've paid back enough money so that you only *owe* 100 percent of the value of your home. And then there's this unpleasant scenario: What if you have to move? Even if you sell for a little more than you paid, you may be scraping to come up with enough money to allow you to pay back your original loan. The *only* time to opt for a 125 is if you're using the money for home improvements that you know—without a doubt—will dramatically increase the value of your home. (For more on which renovations pay off and which don't, see Chapter 8.)

The Fed Watch: What Happens to Your Debt When Interest Rates Rise and Fall?

During the 1990s, watching Federal Reserve Board chairman Alan Greenspan became a major league sport. If his briefcase was thick, an interest rate hike was on the way. If it was thin, Wall Street could rest easy. The guy couldn't even go to Bloomingdale's with his wife without the papers reporting on it. To some degree, you couldn't blame the Greenspan-watchers. The stock market moved on his every word. His moves affected our wallets. But not every form of debt moves in lockstep when the Fed raises or cuts short-term rates. Here's what typically happens:

• **Credit cards:** About three quarters of all variable rate credit cards are tied to the prime rate. If the Fed hikes short-term interest rates, say a quarter of a point (which equals 25 "basis points"), the prime rate will move in lockstep and the interest rate you're paying on your credit card will go up by that amount. The same will happen if rates go down. Both of these changes usually take about three months to be reflected on your credit card statement. Fixed rate credit card holders will experience no rate change.

• **Home equity loans:** Since these are fixed rate products, if you've already taken out a home equity loan, you'll feel no rate change. If you're shopping for a loan while the Fed is maneuvering, however, you should be aware that prices on these loans move with prime. When the Fed changes interest rates, the prime rate at major banks around the country usually follows in lockstep if not that very day, then the next. In the case of a rate hike, you'll see home equity loan prices rise within a week or two. On the other hand, if rates fall, it often takes longer.

• **Auto loans:** When interest rates go up, car loans that are tied to the prime rate reflect the full jump almost immediately, say the folks at HSH Associates. When rates go down, however, you'll only see about two thirds of the rate decline show up in car loan prices quickly. Only if we're experiencing a series of rate cuts will you feel most of the change. (The best deals often aren't tied to the prime rate at all; they're made with dealer financing priced to move cars quickly.)

• **Fixed rate mortgages:** As with a home equity loan, if you already have your mortgage, an interest rate hike is nothing to worry about. A drop in rates, however, may be a clue that it's time to refinance. As for new loan prices, in past years they would move when the Fed announced a change. Now, there are so many expectations of what the Fed will do built into the marketplace that they move in anticipation. If you're out shopping for a loan and rates fall to a level that you can afford, it's best to lock in your rate rather than betting on the Fed.

THE BIG THREE: THINGS TO TAKE AWAY FROM TALKING DEBT

1. Credit card debt is a savings killer. It's impossible to think about saving for college or investing for retirement when the Visa bill is hanging over your shoulder. So make a commitment to start digging out from under.

2. You only need two credit cards—one that has a lower-than-low interest rate for purchases you need to pay off over time, and another that you pay off every month but use frequently and that gives you something (rebate points or miles) in return. If you have a walletful of cards, now's the time to eliminate them.

3. Your credit rating affects you in more ways than you think. It can hinder your ability to get a job, an apartment, even a decent rate on auto insurance. Those are three good reasons (and there are many more) to try to keep your credit nose squeaky clean.

CHAPTER 3

Talking Saving

W here did that money go?

How many times have you taken $100 out of the ATM on a Monday only to reach into your wallet on a Wednesday to find you have not even enough to buy a sandwich—and that you have absolutely no idea where the rest of the cash went? Have you ever noticed that your bank balance seemed to be shrinking? You have your bimonthly paycheck directly deposited to your checking account, but by the middle of week two, you're living on vapors. And again, you have not a clue how your hard-earned money slipped through your fingers.

Well, the truth is, if you sat down and really thought about it— even if only for five or ten minutes—you'd remember that you wrote a check for $25 to the dry cleaners, and paid $10 for your daughter's nursery school Halloween party in cash. You'd recall that you bought this week's groceries by sliding your ATM card through the reader on the counter, authorizing an immediate debit for $129.83. And—oh, yeah—there was the oil change, and the shoemaker, and the $15 you gave your husband because he was out of cash. And you had take-out sushi for lunch. Twice.

Seattle residents Michelle and Adam (whom we met in Chapter 1) have been there. Their problems began a few years ago, as newlyweds. Michelle was in her first job after completing her master's degree. Adam, a computer programmer, was working a series of freelance gigs. They were living—uncomfortably—paycheck to paycheck, which turned each month into a waiting game. They spent what they needed on rent, the credit cards, groceries, and gas, and sat around watching their bank balance, waiting to see when the money would run out. Only rarely—if by some miracle, they had a few bucks left in their account at the end of the month—did they treat themselves to an overdue date, which consisted of dinner or a movie, but rarely both.

As a result, their nerves were frazzled. Adam was feeling guilty because he wasn't a "good provider." Michelle was stressed about their $60,000 in combined student loans. And neither liked the fact that they had absolutely no money put away for emergencies. But they had no clue what to do about it.

Then one day Michelle saw a lecture by a financial counselor who talked about controlling your money by planning your spending. Even for people on tight budgets, the counselor said, this sort of system could work. The scenario sounded so familiar that Michelle made an appointment. Adam wasn't thrilled (he didn't think they could afford the $100-an-hour fee, for one thing), but he agreed to a session or two. "I figured she'd just tell us we were hopeless," he recalls.

The reality was just the opposite. The counselor saw their situation as a relatively easy fix. They were just approaching their money backward: letting it manage them, rather than the other way around. What they needed to do was to assert themselves, to take control.

So the counselor gave them the tools to do just that. First, she instructed them to spend a month following their money. For thirty days, they kept track of how much they earned, and they held on to every receipt (even the ones for less than $1). Then they sat in bed each night and categorized their expenditures: food, clothing, newspapers and magazines, every item had a place.

They went back to the counselor's office with their ledger in hand. Great, she said, now that they knew how much income they had to work with, they could come up with a spending plan, a road map for how they wanted to spend their income for the next thirty days. There would be no more haphazard spending. They decided how much they wanted to spend on groceries, on gas for the car, on dry cleaning. Every video rental, every Dunkin' Donut had to be planned out in advance. After the $15 they budgeted for books was gone, they had to wait until next month.

It sounds constraining—but they found it was liberating. They built in cushions for the incidentals they couldn't live without (comic books for him, lattes for her), which saved them from guilt every time they splurged on one. But they agreed up front to avoid those that really didn't matter. And what shocked them was that after planning for their debt service, their nonnegotiable living expenses, and their little luxuries, they had enough left over to designate money for dinners out twice a month.

The difference it made was incredible. The couple's stress level dropped. "It took the panic out of the situation," Adam said. As the couple got better at sticking to their spending plan, they freed up cash to pay off their $2,000 in credit card debt and to start a fund for small emergencies. Four months into the process, the clutch went on Michelle's car. They were amazed to find they actually had cash to install a new one.

Here's the problem with the word "budget." Like the word "diet," it has far too many negative connotations. (Try to think of the number of times you've heard either of them in a sentence that didn't also contain the word "blown.") But tracking your spending like a detective on a case, in order to come up with a spending plan, is something else entirely. It's a strong, positive, forward-thinking tool to use as you begin dealing with your money. It also happens to be key to accomplishing the rest of your financial goals. If you track your spending, you'll make sure you have enough to pay the credit card bill, to save, to invest, and to buy the things you know you can't live without.

Surprisingly, it's not just people without a lot of money who can be helped by this exercise. According to research by Harvard economist Juliet Schor, 27 percent of all households making more than $100,000 a year say they can't afford to buy everything they really need. Why? Because they're spending so much of their time and energy keeping up with their high-earning neighbors, they don't know where all that money is going in the first place. A 1997 survey from Fidelity Investments showed that the better off people are financially, the less likely they are to cut back on nonessentials. Three quarters of people earning less than $75,000 a year were willing to cut back on vacation expenses in order to save more; fewer than half of those earning more than $75,000 were willing to make the same commitment. And travel wasn't the only area where people felt the need to indulge themselves. High earners were similarly stubborn when it came to eating out, grocery shopping with a careful eye, and spoiling their kids.

The explanation for this behavior? Mind games. You're likely to think long and hard about whether you really truly need to make the biggest purchases—like a new television, a new suit, or anything else that seems large relative to how much money you actually have on hand—and whether you're getting the best possible price. But when it comes to little purchases—which, depending on your income, may run the gamut from a $7 car wash to a $65 massage—many of us don't think about what they mean to our bottom line. We just go ahead and spend the money. Unfortunately, if you make enough little expenditures, you'll soon find yourself short of money to pay off the Visa. That's why even though most people don't see themselves as reckless or frivolous spenders, they just can't seem to save enough.

That's a problem. But, as Michelle and Adam discovered, it's one you can solve. In this chapter, we'll talk about tracking your spending the old-fashioned way, using pencil and paper, and the allure of doing it on your home computer. Once you know what you've got, we'll talk about coming up with and reaching reasonable saving goals (by using the one very best way to save and eight good alternatives). And, of course, you'll need a place to put that money. We'll talk about investing it in the chapters to come, but here we'll focus on the institution that's likely to be your money's temporary home: a bank, and how to get the best possible deal from one. You'll need it. You're going to be amazed at how fast your money adds up.

Follow the Money

Think back to the last time you received a raise at work. You probably thought to yourself: "Great, now I can save $50 more a month." Or: "Now I can up my contribution to my 401(k)." And then you thought: "But first, I have to celebrate. I owe myself that." So you went out to dinner with your significant other or had drinks with your colleagues—and of course you picked up the check. Then you saw a sweater at the Limited that you had to have. And after several weeks, it seemed like you'd never even gotten that raise. Suddenly, everything in your life was costing a little bit more. You began to wonder how you ever got by on less.

But of course you did. If you've been in the workforce for a while, there was a time in your life when you got by on significantly less. But if you're like most people, you can't remember it because you've never taken the time to figure out how much life actually costs. Most of us have absolutely no idea how much money we spend. We may pride ourselves on the fact that the lease payment on our new SUV is exactly the same $369 a month we were paying for our old sedan, but we forget to adjust for the fact that we'll be paying $15 more a week ($780 a year) for gas. Our new apartment costs just $10 a month more than the old one, but it doesn't include utilities. Our package deal to Disney World includes airfare, hotel, and passes to the parks. But how about meals? How about Mouse ears?

More interesting is how the nonluxury items we spend money on each and every day add up. Here are a few calculations based on my own life: A large coffee and a toasted bagel (lightly buttered) each day at the deli run $1.70; that's $442 a year. Each Saturday we take our kids to a local restaurant for breakfast or lunch: $25 a week, or $1,300 a year. When I know I'm going to be bored on my commute home (about once a week) I'll buy a $3 magazine in Grand Central Terminal, where I catch my train; that's another $156. And when I need a pick-me-up every couple of weeks, my splurge (now you know everything) is a professional blowdry, which runs $25.80 including tip—for a total of $670 a year.

Could I do without some or all of these things? Probably. And then I could save the money. But until we know how much we're spending—and on what—it's very difficult to make the decision to set those assets aside. Or even to decide that we'd rather spend that money on something else (add all my extraneous expenditures together and you'd have a week at the beach). So before we come up with saving and spending goals, we need to start following our money. There are a few ways to do this:

• **Pencil and paper.** Get a receipt for everything, shove them all in an envelope or into your wallet (whenever you receive one of those nondescript, flimsy paper receipts, jot a note on the back to remind you what you bought). Then sit down once a week and record them by category (you'll find a list of categories below). Use a calculator to figure out how much you've spent on, say, food or entertaining. Don't underestimate the shock value of this exercise. Seeing that you spent $160 last month on substandard take-out Chinese is enough to send a lot of people back into the kitchen.

• **Credit card.** If you charge every possible item (even those $3 light bulbs you bought at the hardware store), your bill automatically becomes a tool to help you track your spending. The key to making this work is spending as little in actual cash as possible and, when you do, making sure you save receipts. The bonus is the frequent flyer miles (or bonus points) that anyone on this system ought to be racking up. The risk is interest. Only people who are completely sure they'll pay off their credit card bills every month without fail should go this route. (If you like the idea but your confidence isn't high, give it a test drive with the American Express card, which forces you to pay it off, or a debit card that pulls money out of your checking account each time you make a purchase, rather than sending you a bill at the end of the month.)

• **Computer.** Just as you can enter your expenses into a log you keep by hand, you can enter them into a computer program like Quicken or Microsoft Money. The benefit of going electronic is the ease of running "what-if" scenarios (like "What if I switched from Starbucks to the local deli?" or "What if I spent less on shoes?") and of charting proportionately how much of your take-home pay you're spending on clothes, entertainment, housing, and so on. Plus, you can keep tabs on your investment portfolio, downloading the most up-to-date stock prices with just a few keystrokes. (The downside: These programs can get addictive. I once wrote a piece called "The Cult of Quicken," about folks who were compulsive about tracking every single penny. Obsession, obviously, has its merits though. One of the people I profiled—David Gardner—has become a superstar in the world of personal finance. You know him as half of the Motley Fool.)

A List to Get You Started

To get to the list of categories below, I started with my own expenses; then I threw in everything else I could think of. Use it as is, if it fits your life, or tweak it to make it more appropriate for your needs. You don't necessarily need to be as detailed as I've been. But try to resist the temptation to put all of your cash expenditures into a huge "miscellaneous" category. Do that and you won't come up with enough accurate information to change your spending habits.

Income:
- Salaries and wages (after-tax)
- Moonlighting/freelance income
- Rental income (money you earn subletting your apartment to someone else, for instance)
- Pension/Social Security
- Dividends/interest income
- Maintenance/child support
- Other (regular gifts, inheritances, etc.)

Expenses:
- Housing (mortgage payments, apartment rent, etc.)
- Property insurance
- Property taxes
- Utilities (gas, electric, oil)
- Water
- Home repairs
- Lawn care
- House cleaning
- Garbage pickup
- Pest control
- Child care
- Baby-sitter
- Other (pet-related expenses, house sitter, etc.)

Transportation:
- Car/lease payments
- Car repair and maintenance
- Car insurance
- Gasoline
- Commuting costs (train tickets, bus passes, etc.)
- Tolls
- Other transportation (buses, taxis, subways, etc.)
- Parking

Food/Sundries:
- Groceries
- Drugstore expenses
- Take-out meals
- Restaurant meals
- Habits (alcohol, cigarettes, etc.)

Clothing:
- Clothes (break these down by family member so that you can see what you're spending on yourself, your spouse, and your kids)

- Shoes
- Dry cleaning/laundry expenses
- Tailoring

Education:
- Tuition
- Room and board
- Books
- School-related expenses (class dues, parties, fund-raisers, fraternity and sorority fees, etc.)

Health:
- Nonreimbursed visits (break these down by category: doctors, dentists, eye care, psychiatrists, physical therapists, nutritionists, massage therapists, etc.)
- Health insurance
- Nonreimbursed pharmaceuticals
- Health club dues/at-home equipment

Recreation:
- Vacations
- Entertainment (cost of going out to movies, theater, etc.)
- Entertaining (cost of parties in your home)
- Books, newspapers, magazine subscriptions
- Country club/social club dues

Gifts:
- Charitable contributions
- Gifts to friends/family/etc. (you may want to break this down to get holiday and nonholiday expenses, particularly if you feel you're overspending in December)

Other regular monthly/quarterly payments:
- Insurance (life, disability, liability, etc.)
- Dues for your house of worship
- Maintenance/child support

- Child care
- Credit card/loan payments
- Retirement contributions
- Savings account contributions
- Investments

Using Your Data to Spend Less, Save More

What you have when you've completed this exercise is a personal cash flow statement—a quick look at what you have coming in and where it's going. It's incredibly useful. You may discover you're spending a bigger portion of your income than you thought possible on restaurants or entertaining. Or that you're not investing a piece of your income that's big enough.

Once you see the hard numbers, you can use them to help you set goals. Maybe you'll decide that you want to put another $100 a month toward paying off your credit card. By looking at your cash flow statement, you can figure out where that $100 will come from. Perhaps you'll decide to eat out once each week instead of twice. Or that you can come up with some of the money by washing your own car each week instead of having it done professionally.

The primary reason to go through this exercise is to help you save (and then invest) more by spending less on items that really aren't so important. That brings us to a very important question: What should your savings goal be? What's a reasonable number to shoot for? The answer is (you knew this was coming): That depends. Most financial planners would tell you you're doing well if you save 10 percent of your take-home pay for those far-off goals. But realistically, the only way to know what you need to save is to figure out what you need—for retirement, for the down payment on a new house, for whatever, and then work backward. If you want to have a globetrotting sort of retirement you may need to save more than 10 percent. You may need to put away 15 percent or even 20 percent. But if you expect to stay in a home you'll soon have paid off and to work part-time after you retire, then maybe saving 5 percent or 7 percent of your take-home pay will do. There's no way to know until you run the numbers.

What I can tell you is this: For many people, saving anything is going to feel impossible at the beginning. That's because saving is a habit that, like all habits (at least all of the ones that are good for you), requires some practice. It's okay not to be able to put away 10 percent (or whatever you're reaching for) right out of the box. But you can put away something. Just start. Take small steps. Save $25 a month to show yourself you can do it. Then $50. Then $75. Then $100. Keep increasing until you feel that you've gone as far as you can go.

Or you might just find that 10 percent is easy. If that's the case, save more while you have the chance. You'll reap the payoff eventually. Perhaps you'll even find that your savings get you out of a bind. Money is a moving target, after all, and for most of us there are lean years as well as healthy ones. Your savings may provide you with freedom you couldn't have otherwise afforded.

In the end, it helps to remember that the only thing that ever really happens to money is that it gets spent—if not by you, then by your kids, or by the charity to which you give it. That's why you have to keep saving in perspective. Try to remember at all times what saving really is. It's reducing your standard of living today so you'll have a better standard of living tomorrow.

The One Very Best Way to Save (and Eight Second-Place Alternatives)

Spending and saving are so tightly interwoven, I struggled with which one to put first in this chapter. If you spend too much, it's impossible to save. If you save too little, you have more free cash. What do you do with it? Spend it, naturally. I've come to the conclusion that the best solution is to work on both parts simultaneously, which brings me to this point: There is one way to save money that is vastly superior to all others. It's called Paying Yourself First (also known as The Oldest Trick In The Book, and most certainly in this one). The idea is that you pull funds out of your primary spending account (typically your checking account) before you have the chance to blow them, and stash them somewhere out of your reach.

Technology has made this even simpler. We can have money withdrawn from our paychecks by our employers and deposited directly in our 401(k)s or used to purchase savings bonds. Once our money reaches our checking accounts, we can empower our mutual fund companies or brokerage firms to electronically withdraw a fixed amount (typically $50 or $100 and up) and invest it. (You'll catch me using the word "invest," occasionally, instead of "save." That's because sometime in the 1990s, the two words became synonymous. We no longer "save" for retirement or college; we "invest" for it. We'll talk about how those savings should be invested in the next three chapters. In this one, we're focusing on setting it aside.)

Marissa in Massachusetts has been paying herself first for years. Every time she gets a paycheck she has it automatically deposited—half in her savings account, the other half in checking. The half in checking goes to pay her monthly bills. The half in savings is strictly hands-off. In fact, it's worked so well that she's recently started having another $50 siphoned from her checking account each month and put into a third account: a money market fund.

My colleague Marion Asnes, a senior editor at *Money,* is the queen of automatic investing. For as long as she's been eligible, she's had a sum large enough to take advantage of any employer match zapped from her paycheck and deposited into her 401(k) account; but that isn't all. Even as she worked her way up the ranks in publishing (which doesn't exactly pay Wall Street–sized salaries) she has funded an IRA every year with freelance or bonus money, and she had the discipline to open an account with a large mutual funds family. First, she gave that company permission to deduct $25 from her checking account each month. Then $50. Then $100. Over the last year, she's added another automatic withdrawal to her program—and convinced her husband to do likewise. In fact, they jump-started a joint account with wedding gifts. "It's the system that works best for me," she said. "It's the easiest, the most time-efficient, and it's a no-brainer. I have too many responsibilities to juggle as it is."

Of course, despite its considerable merits, automatic investing has its naysayers. They say it prevents people from having available cash to invest when a truly spectacular opportunity comes along. If you're reluctant for that reason—or simply because you're worried that you'll need the money—you have to find another method of saving that does appeal. If you don't make saving habitual, you'll find it impossible to reach your goals. Perhaps one of these eight alternatives will work for you:

• **Bonus saver:** When you get a bonus, you take a substantial portion of it, sock it away, and forget you ever saw it. Scott, an insurance executive, started banking his bonuses the year after he graduated from college, in 1985. "I would save half—at least," he explains. "As my bonuses have gotten bigger, relative to the first (which was only $500), I now find that spending half is sometimes too much for me. I find myself saving—or trying to save—all of my bonus." The fact that this is a once-a-year transaction takes the pressure off trying to save daily. But don't try this without giving yourself at least a small reward; that's a sure road to resentment.

• **Raise saver:** The next time you receive a pay increase, calculate exactly how much more you're taking home each paycheck, then start saving that amount. You'd think this would work just like the bonus saver. But it's much harder. When most people get a raise, they spend the increase as fast as they see it in their paycheck. It's that pair of black loafers they've been eyeing. That trip to Hilton Head they can't do without. That's why the key here is making your new saving automatic. Either boost your contribution to your retirement account or have the money automatically deducted from your paycheck.

• **"I-spend-you-save" saver:** They say two can live as cheaply as one. Couples who adhere to this plan, where you live on one income and bank the other, can prove it. It has a couple of advantages. Not only do you know that you're putting beaucoup bucks away, but if you're thinking about having one parent stay home once your kids are born, you'll find out early whether you'll be able to swing it financially.

• **Second-income saver:** John, an art director in New York City, lives on the income from his day job. He banks all of his moonlighting money—income he receives from the book jackets he designs on the side or the design classes he teaches at a local college. The added benefit to this system is that if he ever loses his job, he'll still have a small stream of income and plenty of contacts to help him find a new one.

• **Tax refund saver:** There are two schools of thought on banking tax refunds. The first is that you shouldn't be getting a refund in the first place. If Uncle Sam is writing you a check each and every year, that means the government has had use of your money during the previous twelve-month period. It's been earning interest you should have been earning. Sit down and adjust your withholding so that you're paying less in taxes with every paycheck. Unfortunately, once those dollars start to show up in your paycheck, you're only going to save them if you make an effort to do so. And again—sorry to sound a bit like a broken record here but it's true—the best way to do this is with electronic transfers.

But if you're one of those people who simply won't get on an automatic investment plan, and you're also one of those people who have, in the past, banked your refunds (or to whom it sounds appealing), then I say: Go for it! Losing twelve months' worth of interest to the government is a drop in the bucket compared to losing those returns over a lifetime.

• **Group saver:** I first heard of group savings from one of my children's baby-sitters. She and a group of seven girlfriends had formed what they called a "sys," short for system. Each week, each of them put $25 in the pot. Every four weeks, one of them took the whole pie—which by then was a whopping $800 (a chunk so large that saving it seemed the only sane thing to do). The system had its ups and downs (one of her girlfriends had to be nagged for her contributions) but by and large it worked well. They kept it going for years.

Marissa in Massachusetts (who saves primarily by paying herself first) supplements her savings with a group plan. Each month she and her sister contribute $50 to a joint mutual fund account. Because her sister is also chipping in, Marissa feels compelled to set her money aside. Investment clubs work on this principle as well.

• **Free money saver:** The Employee Benefits Research Institute has studied the ways employees use their 401(k)s and 403(b) accounts and here's what they've found: There are two different types of contributors to these retirement accounts. Some people contribute as much as they're allowed in a particular year. But many more kick in just enough to take full advantage of any matching dollars their employer is kicking in.

Why? Because matching dollars are, literally, free money. And for many people, that's enough of a psychological nudge. (I've seen parents who are trying to teach their kids to be savers use a similar system. Your son wants a $50 Pokémon card or a new add-on for his PlayStation? Don't buy it for him. Tell him you'll match every dollar he saves. Making a game out of it ups the chances that he'll actually reach his goal. We'll talk more about teaching your kids about money in Chapter 11.)

• **Piggy bank saver:** At the end of every day, Barry Katz, a Florida-based financial planner, takes the change out of his pocket and puts it into a five-gallon water jug. By the time he's finished filling the jug, he has about $120, a decent amount of money, which he puts directly in the bank. This probably shouldn't be your only savings plan (if you save an average of 75 cents a day, that's only $274 in a year). But it can be a start. Just make sure you commit to leaving the house every day change-free, and returning with a substantial jingle. And get ready to roll those coins yourself. Using one of those grocery store change counters will cost you 7 percent of your savings.

Ten Ways to Add to Your Savings

When I was fresh out of college, working as an editorial assistant for practically no money, the only way I was able to save was by moonlighting. I'd write a freelance assignment for *Cosmo* or *Bride's* and stick that money in the bank. Or I'd teach an SAT preparation course for Princeton Review and bank the proceeds. My friend Susan did the same by writing speeches.

In fact, particularly for people for whom money is tight (whether it's because you're making too little, trying to put your kids through college, or caring for an older relative), the biggest challenge can be coming up with new and creative ways to save. Studies have shown we're willing to sacrifice in order to do it. According to data from Lincoln Financial, nearly half of Gen X'ers say they're willing to eat out less frequently in order to put away money for the future. One third say they're willing to purchase less expensive housing and cut back on vacations in order to shore up their retirement. And one quarter say they're willing to take second jobs. Older generations—who are closer to and therefore more frightened of retirement—say they're willing to take even more dramatic steps. Here are a few other suggestions to boost your savings:

1. Refinance your mortgage. Anytime rates fall a half percentage point or more below your existing loan, it pays to look at going back to the table to see if you can save money by refinancing. For more on this see Chapter 8.

2. Get some fresh air. Put your gym membership on hold for the summer and exercise outside.

3. Use pay-per-view. I can't be the only one who forgets to return videos and has to pony up for an extra day (or three). Using pay-per-view has proved far cheaper in my house.

4. Stop paying ATM fees. If you're paying ATM surcharges every time you use a machine, and you do so three times a week for a year, it'll cost you $234 on average. That's insane. Instead, make sure you're banking with the institution that has the most machines that are convenient to you.

5. Make your annual IRA contribution in January. Far too many people wait until the April tax filing deadline to make their IRA contributions for the previous year. Big mistake. If you make it as soon as you're eligible—in January of the filing year—your money will have an extra fifteen months to grow.

6. Pay for a year's worth of cable, satellite TV, or Internet access in advance. You can often save a month's charges (or more) by prepaying for the year.

7. Be early with birthday and other gifts. What happens when you're just on time with birthday gifts—or worse, a day or two late? If you're like me, you pay $20 or more to have an overnight carrier whisk them across the country. Two-day Priority Mail from the post office is a bargain at just over $3.

8. Moonlighting. Do you have time to take on another job? I'm a big fan of moonlighting—not only can it be profitable, it can be social. And it gives you an out anytime you decide you can no longer stomach your regular job by giving you experience in another area.

9. Skimp a little. There are hundreds of variations on this theme. I know, you're probably sick of the latte example, but there are so many others. Think about the trip to the deli you make each day for lunch. At $5 a pop, it's costing you $1,300 a year. Bag your lunch twice a week and you save $520. You can do the same by switching from bottled water to the stuff from the tap, pumping your own gas (if you're prone to full serve), or by eating one or two fewer restaurant meals each week. (According to the Zagat guides, these run—on average—about $30 apiece. One fewer each week for the year is $1,560.) You can even get off cheaper at holiday time without feeling like a Scrooge. Talk to your siblings about a gift exchange rather than purchasing individual gifts for each person.

10. Turn old debts into new savings. One of these days, your car loan will be paid off, and so will your student loan, and even (believe it or not) your mortgage. You're used to writing a check for that amount each month to the lender, so instead of using the money to live a little larger, save or invest it. If you think you'll be tempted to spend it instead, have your bank or brokerage firm withdraw it automatically.

Where Does All This Saving Get You?

By the time Bob, a sixty-year-old retiree in Florida, was twenty-five, he was married and supporting not only himself, but his wife and her three children from a prior marriage. It was a responsibility he took very seriously. His own father had been killed in a railroad accident, leaving his mother strapped for cash. Bob was determined not to do that to his own family, but on his small salary it wasn't easy to make ends meet. "I began reading budget books," he recalls. "But a lot of them didn't make any sense to me. They all showed how to set up a monthly budget or a weekly budget, but I felt I needed something that would give me a sense of what I was doing for the entire year."

So Bob abandoned the books in favor of pencil and paper. He added up all the money he needed for the family's house, car, and food and discovered he wasn't making enough to cover it. So he broke out all the household expenses and tried to figure out where cutbacks could be made. He trimmed the grocery outlay, and the money spent on baby-sitters and nights out. His wife said she'd cut down on trips to the beauty parlor. And then they tried to stick to their guns. At first, they stumbled, plowing through the year's grocery money in just eight months. And just as it seemed they were getting the hang of it, unexpected bills popped up; the worst was when the car died and had to be replaced. But after a year or so, their system started to work. "I never really worried about money again, which is what I wanted," Bob said. "I also found that friends who were making more than I was just didn't seem to know what they were doing with their money . . . they never seemed to have any."

No matter who you are, there's no arguing that saving has a substantial payoff. In fact, it has three:

Payoff No. 1: Security

You need savings for the same reason you need insurance policies: in case. In case you lose your job and it's two months before you can land another one. In case your child is ill and you want him to see a specialist not affiliated with your HMO. In case you have a fender-bender that you decide isn't worth reporting to your auto insurer. For all these reasons, and many more, it's crucial to have some money you can access simply: with a check, a withdrawal slip, a wire transfer, or even an ATM card. (We'll talk more about your emergency fund in the next section.)

Payoff No. 2: Freedom

Financial planner Dee Lee has always badgered her kids to save. From allowances to holiday money to birthday money to money earned around the house—a portion always went into the bank. And when her kids reached their teens, if they managed to scrape together some money from a summer job, she'd match it so that they could make a deposit to an IRA. The result: By the time Lee's son Brian was in his mid-twenties he had a substantial chunk of "go to hell" money. The purpose of this money was that if he ever decided he hated his job he could tell his employer to "go to hell" and walk out (deeply satisfied) in a huff. That never happened, but a few years ago Brian did find himself aching for a bit of a break. He planned to go to graduate school in a few years and had always wanted to live in Colorado. He didn't know when he'd have the chance again, so he quit his job, took some of this mad money, and rented a house out in Denver with a friend.

Having substantial savings allows you to take an extra week off without pay, to not kill yourself racking up overtime, even to quit a job that's making you miserable. It affords you the freedom to live your life on your terms, rather than on your employer's. Even if you never use that money to tell your boss to take a walk, there's a huge psychological benefit in knowing that you can.

Payoff No. 3: The Pleasure of Watching It All Add Up

Saving, to revisit our exercise metaphor again, is a little like doing sit-ups. When you first add them to your exercise regimen, you wonder why you're putting yourself to the trouble. You don't see a difference for days—maybe even weeks. And then all of a sudden, your pants are a little looser, and you can't wait to hit the gym for more crunches. That's how it works with saving. When you're putting those first few dollars away, you wonder: Why? You couldn't buy anything substantial with this small a sum, anyway. But you'll glance at your balance a month or two later and be surprised at how much money you have. If you picked a good home for that, you may be even more surprised at how much interest you've accrued. And nice surprises like these will encourage you to do more.

In a larger sense, when we're talking about watching your assets add up, we're talking about your personal balance sheet. A balance sheet is a financial statement, and whether it's for a person or for a company, it's a snapshot of where you stand financially at a single moment in time. In very rough terms it shows your assets minus your liabilities. The difference between those two numbers is your net worth. If you're using your personal cash flow statement to your best advantage, to trim your spending, cut your debt, and increase your saving and investing, you'll soon start to see the results on your balance sheet. Your net worth will be heading up.

A Bank: The Best Holding Pen for Your Dollars

All this talk about saving raises a very important question—how much of your money really belongs in the bank? For most people the answer is just a few months' salary. Here's why: Even though the money in a bank account is insured by the federal government for up to $100,000 (unlike a brokerage account), savings accounts can still be risky. In fact, bank savings accounts recently earned interest, on average, in the 2 to 3 percent range. Any money sitting in those accounts was actually losing value after taxes and inflation. In other words, it probably cost you money to leave your savings in the bank!

Which is not to say that some money doesn't belong there. Despite the grab for your checking account business by brokerage firms, most people still want and need a bank for checking purposes. Your paycheck goes in twice a month (preferably by direct deposit). You write checks against it to pay your bills and withdraw small chunks of change at the ATMs for walking-around money. Any surplus sits in your account until you decide to transfer those funds into a savings, money market, or investment account.

The first need that surplus must fulfill, as we said above, is building a decent emergency fund. An emergency fund is a cash cushion that exists solely to bail you out should you lose a job, become unable to work, or need to do something to keep your life going—such as replacing your dishwasher when it dies. For two-paycheck couples, it should consist of three months' worth of living expenses. For singles dependent on themselves for support, and particularly single parents, the measure should be six months' worth. For the sake of convenience, that money needs to be in the most liquid form possible, and quickly accessible; put it in a money market account at your bank. That account won't cost you money over time like most savings accounts will, though it's not going to earn you much either. That's okay. This time, we're more concerned with access than growth.

You don't even need a savings account. Instead, beginning savers should open checking and money market accounts (MMAs) with the same bank. Every couple of weeks, have your paycheck directly deposited into your checking account. Then, once a month, arrange to have a predetermined amount transferred to your money market account. Pay your bills out of checking and keep your hands off the funds in your MMA. Once you've accumulated a sufficient safety cushion in your MMA, stop funding that account—just let it sit and grow—and instead make automatic transfers each month into your 401(k) at work or into a brokerage account.

An added bonus of keeping those accounts at the same bank is that if and when you bounce a check, you'll have the funds to cover it. You can authorize your bank to dip into your money market account should this happen by linking your accounts. And to be doubly safe, sign up for overdraft protection—but be sure that if you ever use this protection, you pay it back immediately. Otherwise, it'll cost you dearly in interest.

Picking the Right Bank (and Bank Account) for You

Opening a bank account used to be simple. Whichever bank was closest to home won. Not anymore. Opt for the wrong bank, or even the wrong account in the right bank, and you could be spending hundreds of unnecessary dollars each year. The usual culprit: ATM surcharges.

On average across the country, if you use an ATM machine that isn't owned by your bank, you'll pay $1.50 a pop. Do that twice a week for a year and you're looking at a $156 tab. That's why frequent users (including the many people who use small withdrawals as a budgeting tool) are best off banking with the institution that has the most machines convenient to them. It's the main reason I have my accounts at Chase Manhattan Bank. There are two Chase machines in the Manhattan office tower where I work, half a dozen in Grand Central Terminal (which I pass through every morning on my way to work), another on the way to my grocery store, and another near my dry cleaner. Unless I'm desperate (stranded on a dark corner without taxi fare) or in another city, I refuse to pay surcharges; it's a matter of honor with me. But because Chase has machines practically everywhere I turn, I don't have to.

Still, that's not the only piece of information you want to factor into your decision. The first thing to decide is whether you're better off at a large bank, a small bank, a credit union, or an online bank.

• **Large bank:** Heavy ATM users will generally find large banks are the answer for them. (If some or all of the small banks or credit unions in your town have agreed not to surcharge each other's customers in order to compete, this is a viable alternative.)
• **Small bank:** If you're a small-business owner and might be applying for a loan, a small bank (where the owner or manager knows your name) is probably a better bet.
• **Credit union:** If you're counting every penny and have access to a credit union, you'll probably find that it not only charges the

lowest fees for checking as well as for nuisances (like bounced checks), but also lower interest on loans—an average of 1.5 percent less than banks. Credit unions also pay 1 percent more on interest-bearing accounts, on average, according to studies by the Consumer Federation of America.

• **Online bank:** These are another animal entirely because they have no branches. You deposit your paychecks either by mail or by direct deposit. Then, as with a brick-and-mortar bank, you draw on your money by writing checks, paying your bills electronically, or visiting an ATM. Because online banks have no ATM machines of their own, they typically offer to reimburse you for at least a handful of the ATM charges you incur each month for using other banks' machines. (USAA Federal Savings Bank was rebating the most—ten transactions per month—at the time this book went to press.) Online banks are also very competitive on fees. And it's not unusual for checking to be free and for money market and CD rates to be at the top of the rankings.

Five Questions to Ask your Bank

1. How well do you know me? Thanks to sophisticated customer monitoring systems, even the tellers on the front lines may have a slew of information about precisely how much business you do with the bank—and how valuable a customer that makes you. A teller's computer screen might tell her, for example, that you have not only checking and savings accounts with the bank, but that you also have a mortgage, an auto loan, and a credit card. It's this kind of information that tells her how far she ought to go in making you happy when you come in to complain that you were assessed a $25 fee for depositing someone else's check that bounced. The existence of systems like these argues for giving at least a substantial chunk of your business to one institution. That way, chances are good that there's one place in town you can count on for service that's above par.

2. Can I have my money, please? Believe it or not, the answer is often maybe. After you deposit a check, a bank is allowed to hold on to that money for two business days, ostensibly so that the check can clear. ATM deposits and out-of-state checks can be held, in some cases, up to five days. There are also exceptions to those rules during which the bank can hold your money even longer—if you have a history of overdrafts, if you're redepositing a check, if you're depositing more than $5,000 in the same day, or (and this is the one that gets most people in trouble) if your account is less than thirty days old. Banks are supposed to warn you in these cases, but if you know you're going to need the money make sure you ask precisely how long it'll be tied up. *Red Flag!* Don't make a large deposit at an ATM and expect immediate access to your money. Also remember, most banks limit the amount that can be withdrawn from each account via machine each day.

3. How much will overdraft protection cost me? The fact that we're able to withdraw money from our checking accounts in so many different ways—via check, ATM withdrawal, by using a debit card—may be convenient. But it's also costing us. The number of bounced checks is up to 125 million a year, according to bankrate.com, the Web site of the *Bank Rate Monitor,* and each of those infractions is likely costing consumers $25 or more, according to the latest research from the Consumer Federation of America. The need to avoid these charges makes overdraft protection a very attractive option; just make sure you know what it's costing you. Ask not only about the interest rate (most overdraft protection comes in the form of a credit line) but whether there are fees or transaction charges involved.

4. Is it possible to have my paycheck direct-deposited? There are some distinct advantages to banking with an institution where your pay can be wired directly from your employer to your account. First, most banks will give you a $1 to $2 monthly break on checking account fees if you go the direct deposit route. You'll also have quicker access to your money because there's no check to clear. And, particularly if you work for a large employer, if there's ever a mistake, a bank is more likely to bend over backward to fix it for you. They know that if they're unhelpful, you'll report their behavior back to your employer, possibly costing the bank future business.

5. Is this the best place for my money? If you're looking for good borrowing rates, you should definitely consider it. Credit unions not only tend to offer low rates on their credit cards (not every member gets one, of course; you still have to apply) but on auto loans, mortgages, and unsecured personal loans. About one third of American adults belong to a credit union, according to bankrate.com, and they're pleased with that relationship. One recent Gallup poll showed that 77 percent of credit union customers are very happy with the service they receive, compared to 59 percent of bank and savings-and-loan customers. If you're interested in finding a credit union, check with your benefits department at work to determine if your employer is affiliated with one. Also, ask your relatives. If they're members, some credit unions will extend you privileges as well. *Red Flag!* The one big negative to many credit unions is the lack of a substantial ATM network. You may want to keep some money in a credit union specifically to qualify for loan deals— and the remainder in your town's biggest bank.

Don't Hesitate: Automate

Willie, a retired fireman living in Florida, has the closest thing I've seen to a totally automated financial life. It's not just that he spends his days monitoring his portfolio and trading his stocks over the Internet; he gets his financial news on the Web, uses a software package to track his spending, even banks and pays his bills on the Web. In fact, when I caught up with him he was debating whether a new checking account deal from one online bank was better than the deal he was already getting from another.

Willie is definitely ahead of the pack. But by 2003, analysts from investment bank Piper Jaffray expect that 25 million households will be banking online. They'll go paperless, experts say, because of a technology that's expected to grow much more common early in the new century: electronic bill presentment. What that means, exactly, is that not only will you be able to pay your bills online, but you'll start receiving them online. Talk about eliminating clutter.

The good news is: You can already automate much of your bill-paying process. Here's a look at what's currently on the menu and the advantages of each.

• **Direct deposit.** Not only is it easy, but most banks will knock $1 to $2 off your monthly account maintenance fees if you have your paychecks direct-deposited. You can also direct-deposit expense and travel reimbursements, Social Security and Veteran's payments, retirement and mutual fund distributions, and tax refunds. In all of these cases, direct-depositing saves you a trip to the bank. In the case of your taxes, if you file electronically and elect to have your refund directly deposited, you'll shave weeks off the time it takes to get your money back.

• **Electronic bill payment.** According to the American Bankers Association, every checking account customer in the country now has the ability to pay bills electronically. Many banks have their own Web-based bill payment sites; you can also get similar service through independent providers like CheckFree. Monthly fees range from around $3 to $10, though some Internet banks charge nothing. You'll get some of the money back in savings on the stamps you no longer have to buy.

• **Preapproved bill payment.** Even simpler than electronic bill payment, you can authorize the creditors you pay a fixed amount each month (for your mortgage, car loan, insurance, health club, and so forth) to automatically debit your account on the same day each month. A system like this can save you much more than paperwork. Student loan lender Sallie Mae, for example, will reduce your interest rate by a quarter point if you elect to have your payments automatically debited. Just don't forget to cancel the transaction when your debt is paid off.

• **Electronic bill presentment.** The future is starting to trickle in as some utility companies, phone companies, and a few credit card companies are testing the waters of electronic bill presentment. Surveys show customers want to be able to receive four or more bills each month before this is a worthwhile venture for them. That day is just around the corner. According to a study from *American Banker*, by 2002 almost every major biller will offer this option and 13 percent of consumers will have switched. Will it save you money? Not necessarily. But if you're a bit of an administrative mess, having your bills consolidated into one electronic file (and receiving e-mail reminders to pay up) may keep you from incurring nasty late fees.

THE BIG THREE: THINGS TO TAKE AWAY FROM TALKING SAVING

1. It's impossible to save if you don't know where your money is going. So start tracking it and making decisions proactively about how much you want to spend on which items. It's time you started running your money—rather than the other way around.
2. The very best way to save is to do it automatically. Whether you're moving money from your paycheck into your 401(k) or from a checking account into a brokerage account, simply arrange for the transaction to happen each and every month. Then sit back and count your money as it adds up.
3. Don't make a random decision on a bank. Choose the one that offers the things you need most—whether that's a huge array of ATM locations (using another bank's machine can cost big-time) or a branch manager who's willing to provide the services you need for your at-home business.

CHAPTER 4

Talking Investing for Safety

Kip, the manager of a car dealership in Wisconsin, doesn't think of himself as much of a risk-taker. As an investor he lives and breathes dollar-cost averaging, plowing money into the same batch of mutual funds each month without fail. He contributes as much as he can into his 401(k). And if he's one to stay the course, his wife, Juliann, he says, is even more so.

And yet, when he and Juliann were ready to build their dream house—a four-bedroom saltbox on a nice plot of land—back in 1998, Kip put their future on the line. The couple had been putting house money away every month for years. They were compulsive about making their deposits. And they'd picked a home for that money that gave them a good shot at allowing it to grow—a growth mutual fund. It was aggressive, with a good record, and it had done well for them. "It was fun every Sunday to look in the paper and see that it had picked up a point, or a point and a half," he recalls.

Kip felt comfortable. Too comfortable. By early that year, even though the couple's investment time horizon had dwindled to practically nothing as the day they needed to break ground approached,

Kip still had his money in the fund. Why bother moving it, he figured, when it was doing so well? But in hindsight, he admits, that wasn't a particularly prudent move.

The Asian financial crisis hit, and Kip began to worry that he'd missed his opportunity to pull his nest egg out of the market. Even a small loss had the potential to shelve the house project. "I'm not a rich man," he said. "If I'm down even $1,000 it makes a difference. Around here, $1,000 is half your landscaping." At one point, he was down 20 percent. He could hardly remember a day when his heart wasn't in his throat. Worse, Juliann didn't know: He couldn't bring himself to tell her.

But still, he didn't get out. In fact, at that point, he felt that all he could do was cross his fingers and hold on tight. Thankfully, that turned out to be the right move. The markets rebounded and he got out with no losses. But it could have been a disaster—and in retrospect, he says, the weeks of trepidation weren't worth it. "Had I been thinking," he said, "I probably would have pulled the money out earlier and moved it into savings."

Here's the all too common scenario: In any extended bull market, investors become overconfident. We start thinking that we can't lose and as a result we start taking risks with our money that we wouldn't take in a flat market—or certainly in a down one. Then, inevitably, markets correct. The Dow drifts down a few hundred points over the course of a week—or worse, plunges down a few hundred points within a single day—and investors become petrified. Often, when that happens—as it did in April 2000, for example—I get a call to go on television the next morning and help investors figure out what move to make next.

My advice is always basically the same. If we're talking about your long-term funds, the money that you don't need for at least the next five years, then it's fine—in fact, advisable—to leave your money where it is. As long as you still believe in the fundamental soundness of your particular investments, then it's perfectly reasonable to stick with them. Why? Because stocks—up an average 10.6 percent annually since the crash of 1929—have historically outperformed bonds and other asset classes over the long term. Doing anything but staying the course means that you're trying to time the markets—to pull your money out of stocks in order to avoid the decline, and to reinvest in time to experience the next run-up—which is a fool's game. It's nearly impossible to get it right.

But if what we're talking about are your short-term funds—money you know you're going to need within the next three to five years, like Kip and Juliann's house money—it didn't belong in the stock market in the first place. Kip hoped and prayed that the markets would rebound and leave him with his shirt, and he got lucky. But not everyone does. The potential gains the market has to offer have made so many of us forget that the market can also wipe out a lifetime worth of savings as quickly as you can say "1929."

The key is remembering that the money you need to send your eighteen-year-old daughter off to college next year, and the cash you've been stockpiling to pay for your second honeymoon in Italy next February, *simply don't belong there*. But that doesn't mean they belong in your mattress either—or in a bank savings account where, over the last decade at least, they were likely to lose spending power after taxes and inflation.

So, where do your short-term funds belong? There is an entire menu of conservative short-term investment alternatives, places you can invest for safety. Some involve no risk whatsoever. Others involve a small to moderate amount. None, though, represents the sort of risk you take when you invest aggressively. Which ones suit your needs depend on whether you need the money in six months or three years, how fast you could earn back these dollars if you faced a setback, and also on your tolerance for risk. Are you willing to take a small extra risk for a little extra return, or does the thought of losing even one dollar of your down payment make you sick to your stomach?

In Chapter 5, we focus on the sorts of long-term investing to which you'll devote most of your attention (to fund retirement, for example, or college for your kids). But before we do, this brief chapter is devoted to your short-term choices. Don't let the fact that it's shorter than most of the other sections of this book deceive you. I can't think of a more important subject than knowing what to do with your money over the next year or two. Fortunately, there's not too much to learn if you understand a few basic concepts.

What Is the Short Term?

When we talk about long-term investing, we talk about putting your money into the stock market for more than five years. The idea is that if you commit to leaving those assets in stocks, you'll have time to ride out bumps in the road: to let your money sit while the market stabilizes and then makes up lost ground. Sometimes this takes several years, and though we often forget them, these rocky patches hit more often than you may think. Of course, everyone remembers the crash of 1987 when the Dow Jones Industrial Average took a year to recover, but there was the period in 1990 when the Dow dropped more than 21 percent in less than three months. And there have been many other downturns—including the tumble in early 2000. For people with a lot of time left on their investment clocks, setbacks such as these haven't been a problem.

But what if you needed that money sooner? What if you couldn't afford to wait? If you were depending on assets you had in stocks to make a college tuition payment, or to pay the bill for sleepaway camp for your kids, or to write a check to your contractor for the final third of a kitchen renovation—if for whatever reason you needed to get at that money *fast,* then you could have been in trouble. You may no longer have had enough to make those payments. Even if you'd had a year or two until that money became due, you might not have had enough time to make up any lost ground.

In numerical terms, the short term is anywhere up to three to five years. That's a sizable range, and as you might expect, the savings vehicles appropriate for someone with a three-month time horizon differ greatly from the short-term investments appropriate for someone who has three years. So I've divided the short term into three groups: first, the money you need in under six months, on which you can afford to take no risk whatsoever—the short-short term. Next are the funds you're planning on using in six months to two years. While you still can't afford to take *much* of a risk with this money, you may feel comfortable tying it up for that period of time in exchange for a little extra return. Finally, there's the money you know you won't be using for three to five years. You may want to take a small to moderate amount of risk in order to boost your returns.

Two additional notes before we turn to those options: First, when you're looking for a specific short-term investment, you should consider not only how much time you have on your hands, but how much *money* you're starting with. Doing your homework and stretching for a little extra return is a terrific idea, but you have to consider what the actual payoff is going to be, in dollar terms. Say you shop the Web and get a 6.5 percent return on a $10,000 investment, which sounds exceptional because the bank next door is only offering 6 percent. In terms of actual money, however, the difference amounts to only $50. That means you also need to take into account how much time it will take you to capture that additional return. You may decide it's just not worth the stretch.

The other thing to keep in mind is your "gut." Investors turn to short-term investments not only when they've made a conscious decision that they need safe havens, but when the markets feel unstable. Nowhere in this book will you find a suggestion that you time the markets, that you try to guess when they're heading up and heading down and pull your money in and out accordingly. But there may be a time or two in your life when you find that you can't sleep at night because you're convinced your stocks are going to take a major tumble. That certainly won't do. So the solution is to pull out enough of the funds to make yourself feel comfortable. Start with 20 percent of your portfolio and see if that does the trick. If it doesn't, pull out some more—and park that money in one of the places described below.

The Short-Short Term: Up to Six Months

If you know you're going to need a certain pot of money in up to six months, you shouldn't be subjecting it to any risk whatsoever. It also needs to be completely liquid, that is, accessible at any time. Period. The end. Here are your options:

Money Market Accounts

What are they? Money market accounts are bank and credit union accounts that typically provide a higher rate of return than you'll get on a regular savings account. They carry Federal Deposit Insurance Corporation insurance at banks for balances (per institution, not per account) of up to $100,000 ($200,000 for joint accounts). (Most but not all savings-and-loans offer similar insurance; you'll want to be certain yours does before opening an account.) And they carry no risk.

How do they work? In exchange for the higher rate of interest, you have slightly more limited access to your money. Usually withdrawals are limited to six per month, and you're only allowed to write up to three checks without running up against additional withdrawal charges. Minimum balance requirements also run higher than those for savings accounts; they're usually in the $500 to $2,500 range. Some banks will link your MMA with your checking account and automatically transfer money if you write a check so big that you don't have enough to cover it.

How do you find the best rates? The list of the banks offering the best interest rates changes all the time, and not because of shifts in short-term interest rates by the Federal Reserve. Some banks make a conscious effort to stay at the top of the MMA rankings as a way to lure deposits, and they set their rates accordingly. The difference between the highest rates and rates on average can be substantial. As I write this the best MMA in the country is returning 5.24 percent while the average account is returning 3.18. I don't want to think about what the *worst* account is paying. You can find the most up-to-date list of the top MMA rates in every issue of *Money* magazine (it's in the "By the Numbers" section), or on the Web at bankrate.com.

Money Market Mutual Funds

What are they? Unlike MMAs, which are bank *savings* accounts, money market funds are mutual funds that invest in the lowest-risk, shortest-term (sometimes as short as overnight), most highly rated debt securities available, including Treasury bills, certificates of deposit, and municipal bonds. The Securities and Exchange Commission (SEC), the government agency that oversees investments, doesn't like to see a lot of fluctuation in these safe havens, so it requires money funds to keep the average maturity of their portfolios under ninety days; that keeps them safe from the risks a change in short-term interest rates might pose. Additionally, because these are pools of securities, investors get the safety that comes with diversification. Your shares will always be worth the same: $1 per share. As your money grows, you'll see the gains in terms of additional shares, not in terms of a fatter price for each share. These funds aren't insured like the ones in money market accounts, but don't let that worry you; these are extremely safe.

How do they work? You open the account by making a deposit, typically with a brokerage firm, though some banks offer money funds. Each day, dividends will be credited to your account in the form of additional shares (or pieces of shares). If you ever want to take your money out, you can access it immediately by mail, by phone, or by check—with no penalties for early withdrawal. Most money funds keep their minimum investment requirements low. Some set them at zero, others require an initial deposit in the $500 to $1,000 range but will then let you buy additional shares in small amounts. These days, most funds have check-writing privileges. If you're planning on drawing on this money occasionally (perhaps you're using it to fund the progress payments on the renovation of your home, or to write monthly checks for college tuition), you'll want to make sure those check-writing privileges don't have too many strings attached. While money funds, unlike MMAs, don't limit the number of checks you can write each month, some won't allow you to write one for an amount smaller than a few hundred dollars. Others charge a fee per check if you don't keep a substantial balance in your account.

There are two basic types of money funds: *taxable* and *tax free*. Any income you earn in a taxable money fund is subject to federal, state, and local income taxes. Income you earn in a tax free fund may not be subject to any of those (or may just be subject to state and local taxes). Compare the returns from taxable and tax free money market funds and you'll see that the latter return less. That doesn't mean they're less valuable for you, however. The fact that you pay no federal taxes on these funds (and sometimes no state taxes as well) ups your take. But by how much? In order to answer that question you need to do some quick division. To get to the comparative yield (called the "taxable equivalent yield"), take the tax free yield of the investment and divide it by 100 minus your tax bracket (if you're in the 28 percent bracket, the divisor would be 72, if you're in the 36 percent bracket it would be 64, and so on).

The higher your tax bracket, the more of your return you're going to end up paying to Uncle Sam, and the better off you're going to be going tax free. In general, taxable securities are going to be the better option for most people. However, if you're in the 36 percent tax bracket or higher, you'll likely be better off with the tax free alternative. If you're not confident in your ability to make the decision, any fund company or brokerage firm that offers tax free funds should be able to run these calculations for you. Let's take a look at the more specific types of money funds you can choose from:

• **General purpose.** These funds invest in the broad spectrum of short-term options from highly rated commercial paper to bank certificates of deposit. They're usually affiliated with the institution where you open the account. For example, Vanguard has its own money funds, as do many banks.

• **Government.** The one hesitation investors sometimes have with money market funds is that—unlike deposits in bank money market accounts—they're not FDIC insured. If you're concerned about risk, you'll be better off sticking with money funds that invest only in government securities that have the backing of the U.S. government. Some invest only in U.S. Treasuries (you'll know them because they have names that include the words "U.S. Treasury"). Others invest not only in Treasuries but in other government-backed securities, like Ginnie Maes and Freddie Macs, and these tend to have the words "Government" or "U.S. Government" in their names. The yields on these funds are typically lower than those on general-purpose funds, because the investments in the funds aren't as risky; but you can't beat them for safety. They may also have tax advantages; in many states the income from these funds isn't subject to state income taxes.

• **Federal tax free funds.** These funds invest in short-term municipal bonds from across the country. Because of this, their income isn't subject to federal income taxes, but is to state and local income taxes.

• **State tax free funds** (also called double- or triple-tax-free funds). These funds invest in the municipal bonds not from across the country, like federal tax free funds, but in the bonds of a single state. If you're a resident (or taxpayer) in a high-tax state, you may find that funds specifically marketed to Arizonans, Californians, or New Yorkers make sense for your needs. But again, it pays to run the numbers. Because the managers of these funds have a smaller menu of securities to choose from, you may find the taxable equivalent yield on a federal tax free fund is higher than the one you can get from your state's fund. "Double-tax-frees" are free from federal and state taxes, "triples" are free from federal, state, and *local.* The prospectus (or your sales rep) will tell you which you're looking at.

How do you find the best rates? During the late 1980s, as investors became smarter about their short-term investing strategies, money market funds were the biggest beneficiaries. And why not? They were routinely trouncing the returns for certificates of deposit (which we'll talk about momentarily) and money market accounts. The problem with money funds, as with just about every item on this list, is that the majority of them perform far less well than the best of them.

The best boast returns that are easily 50 percent greater than those of the worst funds, and substantially better than the *average,* according to data from IBC (you can find rankings of the best money funds on their Web site, www.ibcdata.com), which tracks the country's universe of 1,400 money market funds (and counting). It's not what's in the portfolios that accounts for the differences. The SEC rule requiring the average maturity of these portfolios to stay under ninety days ties the hands of the portfolio managers, who, by and large, all end up owning pretty much the same stuff. As a result, the differences in returns boil down to one thing: expense ratios. The lower the expenses associated with buying into the fund, the better the money fund will perform over time.

At Morningstar, the mutual fund rating company and Web site, analyst Eric Jacobson ran a graph comparing the five-year returns of money funds to their expense ratios, and he found a direct correlation: The cheaper funds outperformed the others. In order to get cheap and assure themselves a seat at the top of the money fund rankings, some money funds waive expenses. Others, like Vanguard's funds, just keep their expenses to a minimum. Your concern needs to be whether a fund is waiving fees for the long term or the short term. (You don't want a fee waiver to evaporate after you've opened your account.) Call the fund issuer's 800 number before you make your deposit and ask how long the fund has been waiving fees (six months to a year is a good sign) and whether it's scheduled to stop anytime soon. And don't be overly greedy. Don't try to grab for extra return by dealing with a fund that's unknown or too small ($10 billion is a good starting point).

Six Months to Two Years

It's fairly easy to predict the expenses you'll face in the next twenty-four months. If you're already house hunting, your down payment is undoubtedly on your list. If your car is on its last legs, you know you'll need the up-front money for a new one. You want to keep the risks you're taking on this money low; but since you're also certain that you won't need the money any sooner than, say, six months, it's okay to consider tying these funds up in a short-term certificate of deposit or Treasury bill. You may find, however, that you can get an equal—or even better—rate on a carefully selected money market account or fund. The rates banks offer often have more to do with how aggressive they're being about pushing certain products than it does with interest rates.

If you find yourself looking at T-bills, certificates of deposit, and money market funds that all have similar returns, you should focus on two points: your own liquidity needs and where you think interest rates are headed. If a great deal on a CD suddenly becomes available, and if your time horizon permits, you can always pull the money out of the money market and change course, but you won't be able to pull the money out of that CD if money market rates shoot up without facing penalties. Get the picture? As far as interest rates go, if you think they're headed down, it's best to lock in the better deal with a CD or T-bill, rather than going with a money market where the rate floats. Remember how envious you were of people with long-term 18 percent CDs when rates fell to the low single digits? I do.

U.S. Treasury Securities

What are they? Treasury securities is an umbrella term for three groups of securities with differing maturities. *Treasury bills* (or T-bills) mature in three to twelve months, *Treasury notes* mature in two to ten years, and *Treasury bonds* mature in up to thirty years. You can't get any safer than Treasury securities. Interest on Treasuries is deductible from state and local, although not from federal, taxes.

How do they work? Treasury bills are sold at what's called a discount from face value, and then redeemed at that face value upon maturity. For example, as I write this, to buy a $1,000 T-bill at a 6 percent yield, you'll pay $943 today. As long as you hold Treasuries until they reach maturity, you're guaranteed to get your principal back as well as the promised return. You can sell them before they reach maturity, but that gets risky. If interest rates have fallen since you purchased your Treasuries, you're in luck. Treasuries are bonds—and when interest rates fall, bond prices rise. In this scenario, you'll get more in return than you paid for them. However, if interest rates rise, bond prices fall. If you decide to sell your Treasuries after that has happened, you're going to lose principal.

How do you get the best deal? You can buy Treasury securities from your broker, but you'll pay a commission. Some brokers charge more than others—so if you go that route, shop around. But if instead you open an account with Treasury Direct—and buy directly from the U.S. Treasury Department—you can invest as little as $1,000 in bills, bonds, or notes, commission free. In fact, the entire program is free unless your account is over $100,000, and then you'll pay a yearly fee of just $25. You can open a Treasury Direct account on the Internet at www.publicdebt.treas.gov or by requesting a form from the Bureau of the Public Debt, at 800-943-6864. Once your account is open, you can buy Treasury securities by submitting what are called "noncompetitive bids." Essentially, this means you agree to take the rate of return on the Treasury security that is set by an upcoming auction, and you're guaranteed a security in return. Transactions, from buying and selling to checking your balance, can be conducted over the Internet, by phone, or through the mail. About forty-five days before your Treasuries mature, you'll receive a form asking if you'd like to reinvest. You can reply by phone or over the Internet as well as through the mail. Or if you know you'd like to reinvest your money in advance, you can sign up to have this done automatically.

The Treasury Department says this program was set up for investors who want to hold their securities until maturity. However, if you need to sell before your security reaches maturity, Treasury Direct will help by soliciting quotes from different brokers and executing the transaction for a flat fee of $34. Understand, if you're only dealing with a $1,000 T-bill, that's going to eat up a huge portion of your return. That's why, if you know going in that you'll want to sell before maturity, you should use a broker to *buy* your Treasuries. As with stocks, commissions vary greatly from discounters to full-service brokers, so shop around.

Certificates of Deposit

What are they? *Certificates of deposit,* or CDs, are deposit accounts with strings attached. You agree to put your money away for a set period of time (ranging from three months to ten years). In return, for that loss of liquidity you can—if you choose wisely—earn a rate of return that's higher than the one you'd get from most money market accounts. CDs sold by banks have FDIC insurance for deposits of up to $100,000 per institution; CDs from brokerage firms do not. The catch is that you sacrifice liquidity. If you need to pull your money out before the CD has matured, you'll pay a penalty of three to six months' interest. The size of the penalty depends on the terms of the CD.

How do they work? Practically every bank sells CDs, most with minimums of $1,000. To open one, find a bank with attractive rates and fill out the forms. When the CD comes due, you can either "roll it over" into a new one tying up the money further, or you can withdraw it. (Many banks will notify you a few weeks before this is going to happen, but some will not, so you should make sure to keep your own records.) There are two important numbers to know when you're evaluating CD deals: the rate and the yield. In order to earn the yield (which is always the higher number) you need to leave your CD at the bank for a full year at the same rate. That means if you have a three- or six-month CD, you're not going to earn the full yield unless you roll it over enough times to get to that year.

Bank CDs are by far the most prevalent, but you may also see attractive broker-sold CD deals. Brokered CDs usually come from small banks that can't afford their own marketing teams, so they hire outsiders—brokers—to be their sales force. These brokers don't get paid on commission, however, and as a result you don't pay a commission if you buy them. Instead, your broker earns the difference between what he or she paid for the CD and the selling price to you, which is higher. A good broker will have shopped the country for the best possible deals, and you may be able to eke out a slightly better return as a result. The other advantages: If you're looking to park more than $100,000, you can buy two or more different CDs from your broker in one transaction. Plus, working with a broker means someone is monitoring your accounts when it comes time for a rollover.

How do you find the best rates? By shopping around. If you want the best CD rates in the country, you'll have to chase them. It's not complicated in any way to open an account. You just have to consider what your time is worth. Bankrate.com keeps an up-to-date tally of the best rates in the country on its Web site, and many magazines (like *Money*) and local newspapers print a similar list once or twice a month. You'll also want to check with your broker to see what deals he or she is offering. You may also find that the larger the deposit you're able to make to a CD the higher the rate of return. If that's the case at your bank, try to time your rollovers so that you can eventually consolidate several smaller CDs into a larger one to capture the higher rate. (Note: If you're trying to choose between CDs or T-bills, you'll need a special calculator to put them on a level field. You can find them on the Web.)

Ultrashort and Short-Term Bond Funds

What are they? Both *Ultrashort* and *Short-term bond funds* are mutual funds that invest in the short-term debt of corporations, governments, and municipalities.

How do they work? In order to understand how bond funds work, you need a basic understanding of bonds. Bonds are essentially IOUs. When you (or your bond fund) buy bonds, you are lending money to a corporation (corporate bonds), a government (Treasury bonds), or a municipality (muni bonds). In return for making that loan you are paid interest, also called a *coupon* payment. If you hold the bond until its *maturity*—the end of its life, which is typically anywhere from thirty days to thirty years—you'll get back your *principal,* or your original investment.

Different types of bond funds invest in different types of bonds. There are muni bond funds, government bond funds, and bond funds that aren't categorized as either, which invest in a variety of bonds. Bond funds and bond investors make money on the interest payments, but they also make money trading bonds from their portfolio before they mature. Bonds are typically sold in $1,000 increments, but their prices vary from that original $1,000 mark with changes in interest rates. If rates go down, bond prices go up and vice versa. So if interest rates drop, you may decide to sell your bond for more than you paid for it.

The *duration* of a bond is often confused with its *maturity*. The shorter the life of the loan, the more these numbers tend to mimic each other. The duration of a bond is a complex calculation that bond analysts use to try to assess the interest rate sensitivity of a portfolio. It's far less important to understand how to get to the number than to know how to apply it. The basic rule is if interest rates move a full percentage point, then what's called the "modified duration" of a fund is how much you'd expect the fund to gain or lose, expressed as a percentage. If you held a fund with a five-year duration, for example, and interest rates fell a full percentage point, you'd expect that fund to gain 5 percent; likewise if interest rates rose by that full percentage point, you'd expect the fund to lose 5 percent.

Funds holding bonds with an average modified duration of less than a year are categorized as ultrashort. Those that hold securities with an average modified duration of between one year and three are called short-term funds.

Buying securities that are at the long end of acceptable duration (one year for ultrashort-term bond funds, three years for short-term funds) is one way that bond fund managers stretch for extra return. Essentially, they're taking on additional interest rate risk. This is a move that doesn't always meet with approval from bond fund watchers; they say it's akin to trying to time the market in stocks, and on occasion funds have gotten burned. The other move managers use to increase their return is to take additional credit risk. They may take on lower-quality corporate bonds, for example, figuring that the portfolio's diversification will protect them. Again, this may be more risk than you're willing to take, or you may—based on the fund's record—decide that you're willing to put yourself in the manager's capable hands. It's simply important that you know what's going on behind the numbers.

How do you find the best ones? Start with the databases at Morningstar.com. When you're looking at ultrashort funds, what you'll find are very conservatively managed bond funds where the goal is to protect principal but pick up a little more yield than a money market fund will produce. It's a low-risk gambit. Not too long ago, the folks at Vanguard compared the performance of short-term bond funds with those of money market funds over various rolling periods from 1987 to 1996. What they found was that the bond funds outperformed the money market funds in 98 percent of twenty-four-month periods and in 100 percent of thirty-six-month periods—and that study included 1994, which was one of the worst years ever for the bond market. What you give up most often by opting for ultrashort or short-term bond funds over money market funds are some of the conveniences, like check-writing privileges.

That said, the amount of credit and interest rate risk a fund manager is taking varies considerably. If you want a fund that's taking very few risks with your money, be sure the literature about the fund (the fund's prospectus, the Morningstar report) talks about things like risk control and predictability. You'll know that a fund has a conservative approach to risk if it states in its literature that it matches its duration to a benchmark index; that way you'll know the manager isn't actively managing the duration of the portfolio to stretch performance. At the Morningstar.com Web site, you'll also get a good look at the credit quality of the portfolio. Morningstar breaks out the portion of each fund that's invested in triple A rated securities, double A, all the way down to B as well as the portion that's in nonrated securities. Funds that include securities rated B and below aren't safe enough for your short-term purposes. Why? Because if the market hiccups just as you need to get at your money, you may not find the account as flush as you'd like it to be.

In all cases, you should look for a fund with a very low expense ratio. As this chapter went to press, for example, the vast majority of the 200-odd short-term bond funds rated by Morningstar were returning between 5 and 5.5 percent. The ones that rated best kept a tight lid on their expenses. Note: Be careful when you see a bond fund outperforming others in its category by leaps and bounds. One fund out of the 200 was returning not 5.5 percent like the other solid performers, but an extraordinary 7 percent. It turned out not to be a short-term bond fund at all, but a prime rate fund—a fund comprised of loans made by banks—which is a much different animal. It just happened that Morningstar had lumped the fund into this category. So watch out!

Three to Five Years

These are the rest of your short-term investments. They're often assets that were at one time invested for the long term, but now must be guarded against losses. For example, as retirement starts to approach, it's smart to begin moving at least some of your money out of the stock market and into the safer fixed income havens you'll find in this section. The same is true for college tuition money. It is fine to be very aggressive when your child is under ten years old. It's not so fine when he's fifteen. Because you have a longer time horizon, you can stomach moderate risk here, as well as a loss of liquidity. Once you get into this category, however, it's important to make sure that your short-term holdings are every bit as diversified as your long-term ones. You want to be certain that you're guarded against economic changes. If interest rates rise, bond prices will be hurt, but your money market funds will perform better. And vice versa, if interest rates start to fall, you'd see less of a return from your money market funds, but your bond funds will probably make up the difference. As before, the even shorter-term options presented earlier should still be on your shopping list, particularly if the current interest rate environment makes them look attractive. Here's another type of fund you may want to consider:

Balanced Mutual Funds

What are they? According to their charters, most mutual funds are formed to invest in one type of security, such as small capitalization stocks, or U.S. Treasury securities. Balanced mutual funds were designed to invest in several kinds: not only stocks and corporate bonds, but cash and government securities as well. This built-in diversification should provide some degree of safety, under the notion that, for example, if the stock market were to take a tumble, the bonds and cash in the portfolio would provide some stability and buoy the entire portfolio.

How do they work? Balanced funds differ widely in performance. If you check out the returns in Morningstar or in the mutual fund charts in many personal finance magazines, you'll see they're all over the map. The difference in returns is attributable to the portion of the portfolio that's in equities versus the piece that's in fixed income. Some funds keep 40 percent or more of their assets in bonds at all times, but others give themselves more flexibility. When the stock market is on a roll, they let their bond allocation fall to 20 percent or even lower, favoring stocks. That may mean added returns, but it also may mean they're taking more risk with your money than you feel comfortable with.

How do you find a good one? Again, Morningstar, either on the Web or in your local library, will be your best source of information on these funds. Make sure, however, that when you pick a balanced fund, you're truly getting a balanced fund and not some other hybrid. Growth-and-income funds, which invest in companies that pay dividends, and equity-income funds, for example, typically don't provide the same safety or stability.

THE BIG THREE: THINGS TO TAKE AWAY FROM TALKING INVESTING FOR SAFETY

1. Money you need in the short term—which means anywhere from a few months to the next three to five years—doesn't belong in the stock market. Instead, look to park the money in one of a large handful of safer places.
2. Shopping around for the best rates on money market accounts and CDs can be hugely profitable. The best boast returns that are often 50 percent greater than the worst offerings, and substantially better than the *average*.

3. When you're operating in the short-term arena, investment expenses can be a killer. Look for investment houses that perennially waive expenses on their money market funds. And if you're in the market for Treasury securities buy them directly from the U.S. Treasury and eliminate the costly middleman (i.e., your broker).

CHAPTER 5

Talking Investing for Retirement and College

So you want your kids to go to college. And you'd like to stop working one day. In the meantime, you'd probably like to buy a couple of big-ticket items that you and your family can enjoy right now, and maybe even stop worrying enough to get a good night's sleep once in a while as well. The key to making all of these things happen is learning to invest. It doesn't have to be complicated; some very successful investors hold a few basic mutual funds, period. Others really get into the details. They find picking individual stocks a fun and interesting challenge, and watching those stocks (on good days at least) a pleasure.

The difference between the simple approach and the more complicated one boils down to one thing: time. How much of it are you willing to devote? Buying and holding individual stocks the right way requires considerable energy—you have to do your homework on each company you're considering, and then monitor your holdings vigilantly. Go with mutual funds and you can take a slightly more laissez-faire approach (which, by the way, is not the same thing as paying no attention at all). But one thing's for sure: the sooner you start the better. That's because of something miraculous called compounding, which we'll get to in a few pages.

In this chapter, you'll learn everything you need to know to get going. We'll talk about figuring out your life goals and how much money you need to accomplish them. That'll dictate not only how much you ought to be investing, but how aggressive you need to be in order to hit your targets. We'll talk about what you need to know about stocks, mutual funds, and bonds before you buy them (and just as importantly, how to know when to sell). Finally, we'll focus a bit on the stock market. In the 1990s, the market became as big a spectator sport as any of the major leagues. (Don't believe me? Turn on CNBC's *Squawk Box* in the morning and listen to the lingo.) There's a ton of information out there; we'll boil it down to the few pieces you really need to absorb. Although it may seem like there are many new terms to learn and lots of figures to assemble, investing really isn't all that complicated if you learn the basics. After all, there's a reason you've been working so hard: to make your life more comfortable, now and later on. That's the real goal of investing.

Your Goals: How Much Should You Be Investing?

In Chapter 4, we focused on your short-term goals. When it comes to things you want to purchase in the next few years, it often doesn't make sense to put your money at risk by investing in stocks. But when your goals are long-term, like retirement and college, investing in stocks makes perfect sense. Over the long term, stocks have a better return than any other type of investment: 10.6 percent annually, on average, since the crash of 1929.

The big question for most people is how much to invest to meet those long-term goals. Here's my no-numbers answer: as much as you possibly can. The more you can put away now, the better off you'll be down the road. That doesn't mean you should skimp so much you don't enjoy your life; it just means you need to put some effort into it. Every dollar you put to work today is many times more valuable than every dollar you may invest a decade or two from now—simply because it has more time to grow.

Want proof? Say you put $100 into the stock market every month for the next ten years, and that these dollars grow at a rate of 8 percent. After that decade, you stop making contributions, but you don't take the money out of the stock market; you just let it sit there, continuing to grow at 8 percent. Your alter ego, who we'll call P-You (for the *procrastinating* you) doesn't think he can squeeze $100 out of his monthly paycheck right now. Instead, he waits for a little more financial leeway—so long, in fact, that in ten years, just as you stop making your contributions, P-You is just starting to make his. He also earns 8 percent. P-You may be a late starter, but he's got stick-to-it-iveness. He continues putting money into the market for forty years.

Who do you think comes out ahead? Let's say you make the investment in a tax-deferred account. Here's what your respective balances will look like:

Year	You	P-You
5	$7,495	$0 (because he hasn't started investing yet)
10	$18,510	$0
15	$27,197	$7,495
20	$39,962	$18,510
25	$58,717	$34,921
30	$86,274	$59,368
35	$126,765	$95,787
40	$186,260	$150,042
45	$273,677	$230,867
50	$402,121	$351,273

P-You can't win. In fact, at an 8 percent rate of return, the gap between your balance and P-You's widens every year—in your favor. That's the miracle of compounding—of time. Now let's take a look at someone who's seriously diligent. Call her S-You (for the *super* you, of course). She started making her $100 contributions just as you did; but unlike you, she never stopped adding $100 each month. Here's what her IRA balance looks like:

Year	S-You
5	$7,495
10	$18,510
15	$34,921
20	$59,368
25	$95,787
30	$150,042
35	$230,867
40	$351,273
45	$530,464
50	$797,863

The Ballpark Estimate

Putting away as much money as you can is a way to start, but often I find looking at how much it'll *cost* to retire is the best motivator. You can get to those numbers by sitting down with a financial planner or with a software program. Or you can just turn the page.

A few years back, Don Blandin, president of the American Savings Education Council, gathered a handful of actuaries and locked them in a room for three days. Here's the problem, he told them: People aren't saving for retirement because they have absolutely no idea how much they need to save to get there. Because they don't have a goal, they feel like it's futile to save anything; so many people spend every dollar they make. Then Blandin put these financial people to the test. He asked them to come up with a simple, easy formula Americans could use to ballpark their retirement needs. The killer: He insisted it fit on not more than a single sheet of paper. "They knew they weren't coming out until they hit on something that was truly simple," he explains.

The fill-in-the-blank document you see here is the result. You can use it before you start saving to get a good idea of how much you need to put away, or—if you've already charted a course—to see how you're doing. A few caveats: It assumes a life expectancy of eighty-seven, and you could live longer, and that you'll begin receiving Social Security income at age sixty-five.

Is it as sophisticated and precise as some of the retirement calculators you'll find on the World Wide Web? Absolutely not. If you're willing to spend the time, I'm all for your sitting down in front of your PC and pointing your browser at www.financialengines.com. That'll not only tell you how much you need for retirement, but the chances (in percentage terms) that your current saving and investing strategy will get you there. Meeting with a financial planner would still be a worthwhile use of your time; but if you're not ready or willing to go that far (and many people aren't), this is as good an approach, for starters, as any I've seen (and I thank Blandin and the rest of the folks at ASEC for allowing me to reproduce it here). Finally, if you are married, you and your spouse should each fill out your own worksheet, taking your marital status into account when entering your Social Security benefit in number 2 below.

1. How much annual income will you want in retirement? (Figure 70 percent of your current annual income just to maintain your current standard of living. Are you planning to play golf every day and eat out every night? Figure 100 percent. If you're dead-set on a jet-setting retirement—not the kind where you stay with your kids and longtime pals, but the kind where you stay at nice hotels—figure 120 percent. Really.): $____

2. Subtract the income you expect to receive annually from: Social Security (Since the Social Security Administration now must send everyone an up-to-date estimate of their benefits each year, you may know this number exactly.* If you don't, go by these estimates: If you make under $25,000, enter $8,000; between $25,000 and $40,000, enter $12,000; over $40,000, enter $14,500. For married couples, the lower-earning spouse should enter either their own benefit based on their income or 50 percent of the higher-earning spouse's benefit, whichever is higher.): –$_____

Traditional employer pension (a plan that pays a set dollar amount for life, where the dollar amount depends on salary and years of service—in today's dollars): –$_____

Part-time income (Don't just blow off this answer! According to recent research, more than half of all retirees believe they'll work at least part-time in retirement; the difference that income makes to your bottom line can be significant): –$_____

Other income (real estate rentals, annuities, etc.): –$_____

3. This is how much you need to make up (your income gap) for each retirement year: =$_____

Now you want a ballpark estimate of how much money you'll need in the bank the day you retire. For the record, ballpark assumes you will realize a constant real rate of return of 3 percent after inflation.

4. To determine the amount you'll need to save, multiply the amount you need to make up (your answer from No. 3) by the factor below: $_____

---

*If you didn't receive an estimate of your Social Security benefits, you can request one by going to the Social Security Administration Web site at www.ssa.gov, or by calling 800-772-1213. The statement will tell you what your benefits will be if you retire at age sixty-two (the earliest anyone can start receiving payments), and if you wait until you're seventy.

Age you expect to retire:	Your factor is:
55	21.0
60	18.9
65	16.4
70	13.6

5. If you expect to retire before age sixty-five, multiply
your Social Security benefit from No. 2 by the factor below.   +$____

Age you expect to retire:	Your factor is:
55	8.8
60	4.7

6. Multiply your savings to date by the factor below (include money you've racked up in 401(k)s, IRAs, and other
retirement plans):   −$____

If you want to retire in:	Your factor is:
10 years	1.3
15 years	1.6
20 years	1.8
25 years	2.1
30 years	2.4
35 years	2.8
40 years	3.3

7. The total additional savings you will need at retirement is: $____

Okay. Now to the really crucial answer. How much do you
need to save each year in order to reach that total savings
amount? Blandin's actuaries devised another formula to figure
this out; it factors in compounding (earning interest on your interest to create a snowball effect).

8. To determine the annual amount you'll need to save, multiply the total additional savings you'll need (your answer from No. 7) by the factor below: $____

If you want to retire in:	Your factor is:
10 years	.085
15 years	.052
20 years	.036
25 years	.027
30 years	.020
35 years	.016
40 years	.013

This worksheet simplifies several retirement planning issues such as projected Social Security benefits and earnings assumptions on savings. It also reflects today's dollars; therefore, you will need to recalculate your retirement needs annually and as your salary and circumstances change. You may want to consider doing further analysis, either yourself, using a more detailed worksheet or computer software, or with the assistance of a financial professional.

And Away We Go . . .

What did that worksheet tell you? Probably that you need to start saving more and investing *pronto* to meet the needs of the retirement you envision for yourself. Okay, now I'm convinced that you're convinced: You're ready to dive into the world of investing. But before we get going, let me clue you in on a few facts that can insure your success (you might as well have a leg up . . .):

The Four Keys to Making Your Money Grow

As we discuss your investments throughout the next few pages, here's a thought I want you to keep in mind at all times. It doesn't take a genius to be an excellent investor. It doesn't even take a lot of time. All it takes is resolve, the ability to stick to your guns. Decide this is a game you're going to start playing—today—and that you're not going to stop for decades. And don't let all these new terms frighten you into *not* investing. Now that you know about the types of investments open to you, here are the most important secrets I can share with you:

Key No. 1: Buy and Hold

Forget day trading. If you really want your investments to serve you well, buy your stocks or mutual funds and hold on to them.

It's an approach that works. Just ask Terrance Odean, a finance professor at the University of California, Davis. His research shows that the more you stir the pot, the more damage you do to your financial stew, that Americans simply do too much trading in equity markets, and that overactive investors tend to make trading choices that lead to below-market returns. In other words, they hold on to losers for too long and sell winners too soon. Odean's findings hold true for discount brokerage customers as well as active money managers.

Key No. 2: Don't Try to Time the Market!

It's tempting to try to "buy the market low and sell it high." But it's also complicated, and in fact rarely works. That's because bear markets are notoriously unpredictable. Stocks don't head down all at once. They slip a little, then head up for a day or two, then slip some more—giving back all they'd recouped and more. The pattern repeats itself again and again and again, dragging investors along for a rocky ride. And when the market is finally (finally!) ready to head back up again, the confidence of most investors is shot. They miss the bottom of the market because they don't believe it really *is* a bottom.

That's why many experts don't believe in even trying to time the market. What they do believe in is a tactic called *dollar cost averaging*. That means putting money into the market regularly. For most people that's every month, for some it's every other week (with the deposit of each paycheck) or every quarter. The idea is that if you're putting money into the market consistently, you'll catch it when it's high *and* when it's low. You won't win the risk of dumping a huge nest egg into stocks just before they take a sizable dive; likewise, you're apt to make some of your purchases at bargain basement prices. And—and this is a big plus—you don't have to pull out your hair wondering if you entered the market at the right time. Dollar cost averaging has been proven to work in both good and bad times, and even through the Great Depression of 1929 to 1938.

Key No. 3: Don't Hesitate: Automate

Successful investors make their jobs as easy as possible. In fact, they make it automatic, by signing up for electronic transfers. Money is swept out of their paychecks and deposited in their 401(k)s, or out of checking and into brokerage accounts, where it's used to buy shares of stocks or mutual funds that they've preselected. You make one decision, sign one form, and your employer or brokerage firm does the work. Just about every brokerage firm, mutual fund company, or bank on the planet will do this for you. Monthly minimums range from $25 to $50 and up. It's a great way to simplify your life as an investor and make the whole process more pleasant.

Key No. 4: Keep Your Expenses Down

When you combine broker's commissions, mutual fund management fees, the money you pay to your accountant, and taxes, average investors lose 5 to 10 percent of the total value of their investments year in and year out, according to my colleague Jason Zweig at *Money* magazine. One great way to trim those expenses: Buy an index fund. These have lower expense ratios than actively managed mutual funds, because they're not compensating a manager to make choices trying to outperform the market. And since they buy and sell shares less frequently, there's less of a tax impact on you.

The Investment Triumvirate

If you've ever turned on CNBC or read an article about how to build an investment portfolio, you've probably run across the word "diversification." That's Wall Street's word for not putting all your eggs into one basket. What it means in tactical terms is that there are three basic classes of assets you'll want to own: *Stocks* are shares of ownership in publicly traded companies. *Bonds* are IOUs from those companies (or from federal, state, and local governments); you lend them money and in return they pay you an agreed-upon rate of interest for a set number of years. And *cash,* which in this context isn't the green stuff, but your short-term investments: money in a money market fund or CD. (Mutual funds aren't a separate asset class—they are groups of stocks, bonds, cash investments, or some mix of the three picked by a professional manager to jibe with an investment strategy. Owning a mutual fund gives you built-in diversification. More on these momentarily.)

When you're properly diversified, you won't own just one stock, bond, or cash investment but a mix of several or more of each. Stocks are generally riskier than bonds, which are riskier than cash. But they also come with a potentially greater payoff. As we've seen, over the past seven decades, even with a flat market from 1966 to 1983, stocks have returned nearly 11 percent a year on average, whereas bonds have returned just 5.5 percent. And cash you put into a savings account all those years ago would have earned less than 4 percent. When you make an educated decision about how much money you want to keep in each of these three pots, you are *managing your risk.*

That's the idea behind *asset allocation,* a concept that dates back to the work of two Nobel Prize–winning economists, Harry Markowitz in the early 1950s and William Sharpe a decade or so later. They showed how risk and return were related and how investors could better control both. These ideas finally seeped out to investors in the late 1980s and early 1990s. There are years where diversification works against you (in the late 1990s, with small stocks stalled, it didn't help much, for example). But in down markets particularly—

and there have been six over the last thirty years, including the long 1973 decline and the 1987 crash—asset allocation can help tremendously.

Asset Allocation 101: Two Approaches

The percentage of your money you want to allocate to each type of investment depends upon how far away you are from actually needing to use that money. The longer your time horizon, the more years you have to weather the ups and downs of the stock market and the more you can put in stocks. The other factor that weighs on how much risk you want to take is your tolerance for it. A simple gut check will tell you if you can take it. How will you feel if the market takes a tumble? Could you shrug it off, believing that it'll come back eventually? Or does it make your stomach hurt, keep you up at night, fill you with a sense of overwhelming dread? If you fall into the first category, use formula A to get a general idea of how to allocate your assets. If you're in the second crowd, use formula B. Note, these percentages are meant to apply to your investments overall. If you have some of your money in a 401(k) at work, some more in an IRA, and other funds in a discretionary account, remember that the answers you get below take all three kinds of investment into account.

Formula A: For Risk-Takers
Subtract your age from 115 _____
The answer is the percentage of your total investments you put in stocks.
Subtract that number from 100 _____
Divide the remaining amount (up to 100) by 2 _____
The answer is the amount you put in bonds and cash.

Formula B: For the Risk-Averse
Subtract your age from 100 _____
The answer is the amount you put in stocks.
Divide the remainder by 2 _____
The answer is the amount you put in bonds and cash.

Investing Your Money: The Simple Route

Once you determine your asset allocations, you can divvy up your money by going the simple route or you can make the job tougher on yourself. The difference between the two is how much home-work—how much research into individual stocks and mutual funds—you're willing to do.

You can take care of all your portfolio needs by putting your money in three mutual funds: an *index fund* that invests in the total U.S. stock market, a *bond index fund* (also broadly diversified), and a well-diversified international fund.

Investing Your Money: The More Complicated Route

If you want to do more than buying the indexes, then you have some homework to do. This is just as true if you're picking an ac-tively managed mutual fund (one where a manager makes decisions about stocks he or she likes rather than just trying to stick to an index) as if you're buying individual stocks. Here's what you need to know to make decisions about each.

Five Questions to Ask Before Buying a Stock

1. What is the price/earnings ratio? The *price-to-earnings ratio,* better known as a stock's P/E, measures the ratio of a stock's current price to its earnings. P/Es are mostly used to compare simi-lar stocks: one health care stock to another, for example. That gives you a sense of how expensive or cheap one stock is compared to others like it. You can also compare a single stock's P/E to the av-erage P/E of its group, or use the Standard & Poor's 500 average P/E as a gauge. You can also take a predicted five-year earnings growth rate and hold it up against the P/E ratio to judge the stock's value; if the P/E is greater than the projected growth, the stock is pricey.

Or you can estimate what is called the *PEG* ratio by dividing the P/E by the earnings growth rate. A typical growth stock has a PEG ratio of 1.5. A stock with a PEG much higher is expensive.

2. Where does this fit into my portfolio? You buy different stocks for different purposes. First, you'll want to own not just large-company blue-chip stocks, but stocks in small companies (which have the potential to grow faster because they're starting from a smaller base) and those in between. (For simplicity's sake, we'll say large cap stocks have a market capitalization—the number of shares outstanding multiplied by the stock price—of $5 billion and up; small caps $1.5 billion and below, mid caps are in between.) History has shown that stocks of companies with different market capitalizations behave differently in terms of return and risk. Larger companies tend to be more established, smaller stocks more risky, mid caps in between.

You also need to be aware of the difference between stocks you buy for growth and others you buy for income. Solid growth stocks are recognizable because they usually hold a strong position in a growing industry, where they're either gaining or maintaining their share of the market. You buy them in the hope that they'll appreciate greatly before you sell them. Income stocks are less flashy. Many companies, particularly large blue-chip companies and utilities, make quarterly payments to investors called *dividends*. You can automatically reinvest your dividends, which you may want to do as you're building your portfolio—or you can take the dividend payments as a form of income.

3. Who's running this company? How long has the management team been there? What are their backgrounds and experience? What sort of confidence does Wall Street have in their abilities? You can get this information from a number of sources: a company's annual report, its own Web site, research reports from stock analysts, and the daily papers. Ideally, a company should not only have a stellar leader, but strong bench strength, clear succession strategies, and a solid record of training people (or at least recruiting them).

Red Flag! Overdependence on any one individual, no matter

how brilliant, is dangerous. Some years back Disney stock suffered for months when CEO Michael Eisner had emergency heart surgery and it became clear he had no designated heir.

4. How's business? What position does the company occupy within its industry—and how does the future look for that industry overall? In order to truly understand a company, you need to understand what it does, the scope of the market it serves, whether it's the dominant player, and the threat of surrounding competition. Knowing all that, you can be confident investing in a company with a winning product, particularly if it's a leader in its industry and there are barriers preventing competitors from challenging it. That could mean it has long-term contracts with large customers, a lock on distribution channels, or expertise or knowledge that is hard to duplicate.

TWO PROS ON WHEN TO SELL

For my earlier book, *The Rich and Famous Money Book,* I got to talk to some of the best minds in top-rung investment circles. It's hard to imagine getting better advice on when to unload a loser stock than what I got from Alan "Ace" Greenberg, the chairman of Bear, Stearns & Company, and from Lou Dobbs, then the anchor of CNN's *Moneyline,* and now the founder of a new Web site called Space.com. Both had strict sell strategies. Greenberg recalls his father telling him: "If you own something bad, sell, because tomorrow it's going to be worse." He limits his losses by selling anything that goes down 10 to 15 percent. That means that even though this trading pro has made plenty of bad buys, he never takes a really terrible hit. Dobbs attributes the health of his portfolio to a similar selling strategy. When a stock takes a 10 percent dive, he says goodbye. His feeling is that it's safer to get out and then get back in at an even lower price if the stock drops further. Otherwise, he thinks it's too long a climb back.

5. Is the company getting a lot of attention (good or bad) at the moment? You don't necessarily have to back away from a firm that's having a bad PR moment. In fact, if you know something about the company's business and feel it's fundamentally sound, then buying when it's a bit depressed could be an opportunity. In other words, if you feel that you're looking at a company with a strong franchise, brand recognition, and a quality product with a nice market share, don't let a momentary dip in popularity turn you away. Likewise, a media darling is not necessarily a winner.

Five Questions to Ask Before Buying a Mutual Fund

1. Who's running this show? Think of buying an actively managed mutual fund as hiring someone to run a piece of your portfolio. You want a manager with a solid track record (performance in at least the top 50 percent of their fund category in most years, preferably in the top 25 percent). If you're buying a fund because you've heard it's been performing well, you should also make sure the manager responsible for that track record is still in the hot seat. Longevity is also an appealing quality—not necessarily with one fund, but in the business. Because stocks have been on a tear for so long, many managers haven't had the experience of running money during bad times. The best thing about managers who have been in the business for decades is that you can see how they held up in a bear market.

2. How has this fund held up over time? Whenever you hear an ad on the radio for a mutual fund, you're likely to hear these words: "Past performance isn't indicative of future results." That's true. But past performance is also the best indicator we have. When you're evaluating a mutual fund, it's imperative to check out its returns over as many time periods as possible (the last one, three, and five years are good for starters) and then compare them to the other funds in the same category (growth funds vs. growth funds, for example).

Red Flag! When a fund company spotlights a specific result in an advertisement, make sure you know what you're looking at. A number may look phenomenal standing on its own, but pale when you look at how competitors did over the same period.

3. How much is it going to cost me? One very important fact to dig out of any mutual fund prospectus is the *expense ratio.* That's the percentage of your investment being spent to run the fund, and these expenses are all over the map. In general, look for large-company stock funds whose expenses are below 1 percent. Small-company funds should get a little more leeway: about 1.5 percent is reasonable. And while newer funds might have higher ratios, the prospectus should call for lower management fees when the assets grow.

The other cost to keep an eye on is a sales charge, known in the industry as a *load.* It's fine to limit yourself to *no-load* funds, which don't have sales charges, as long as you're not compromising on performance. But it's often worth buying a load fund if you can't get access to a great fund any other way—and if you know you'll stick with it for a while, to give these costs a chance to amortize.

Red Flag! If you're buying no-load funds through a financial planner to whom you're paying a commission based on a percentage of assets, your costs are probably no lower than they'd be if you bought load funds. Remember to consider your overall costs.

4. Does this fund fit in my portfolio? These days, the names funds choose can be very misleading. That's because fund managers have a great deal of flexibility in choosing the stocks in their portfolios. Small cap funds venture into mid cap stocks, and mid cap funds can hold large-company stocks. Stock fund managers can hold fixed income securities and vice versa. They can hold a substantial amount of the fund's assets in cash instead of in stocks and bonds, or very little at all. And depending on the number of funds you own, you may find to your surprise that much of your portfolio overlaps. If every mutual fund you buy holds Microsoft stock, for example, you may not be getting the diversification you'd wanted. Check out the top ten holdings of any fund before you buy. You can get that information in Morningstar, from the fund's toll-free number, and often on the fund's own Web site.

5. Is an index fund a better bet? If you still don't feel you know enough to make a decision on a managed mutual fund or group of funds, you can buy index funds, which invest in all the stocks of popular measures such as the S&P 500. You may even do better this way. Index funds beat the returns of managed equity funds in seven out of the ten years ending in 1998. In 1998 alone, only 20 percent of managed funds outperformed the S&P 500 index. Over the past decade the numbers were even more dismal: Only 11 percent of managed funds were able to accomplish that.

Red Flag! If you want to own one of the best five or ten performing funds for a particular year, an index fund isn't going to get you there.

A Quick Bond Primer

You need bonds in your portfolio as well as stocks. Why? Because they hedge your stock portfolio. In years when the stock market isn't doing especially well, a bond portfolio can usually temper your overall losses. Though economists only consider short-term U.S. Treasury bonds to be completely risk free, there's a wide array of bonds that are relatively safe places to park your money. That includes corporate bonds: If a company goes belly-up, for instance, stockholders can lose their entire investment, while bondholders are among the first people to be repaid. (For an explanation of bonds and how they work, see Chapter 4.)

One decision you will need to make is whether you're better off with a bond or bond fund. Buy an individual bond and you get two things: an income stream over the period of the loan and your principal back at the end. Buy a bond fund and you're buying a portfolio full of bonds. Unlike a bond itself, there is no maturity date, no point at which you can in theory get all of your money back; it's more of a rolling proposition. You earn dividends along the way and sell your shares when you decide the time is right to get out. The trade-off: You can lose principal in a bond fund—which won't happen if you hold a bond to maturity. For most people with less than $50,000 to invest, a bond fund is a good investment, and they come in all the varieties described above. Unless you have more than $50,000 to play with, it'll be hard to build a diversified bond portfolio anyway. Here's a look at the types of bonds (and bond funds) you'll likely be considering and the investors they're good for:

Treasuries. These are issued with the full faith and credit of the U.S. government. They have no credit risk at all—and because they're so safe, don't return a great deal. You park the money you need to keep safe in Treasuries.

Tax-free municipals. These are issued by millions of local authorities around the country. The federal government doesn't tax income from municipal bonds. If you buy a state-issued muni in your own state, you won't have to pay state taxes on the bond, either. In some cases, local taxes are also exempt. One thing to bear in mind about munis is that they're not all of similar quality. You have to look carefully at the quality of the underlying debtor.

Corporates. Companies issue bonds to foot the bill for all sorts of activities, from expansions to acquisitions. The risk in corporates is higher than that from Treasuries—but so is the payoff, typically 1 to 4 percent higher than a comparable Treasury bond, depending on the credit risk of the company. Though the interest you earn is taxable, you can try to hold corporates in an IRA, so that the income they generate is not taxed as income, but rather at the lower capital gains rate.

GNMAs. Ginnie Maes. These bonds consist of the repackaged debt from government-funded home mortgages. Again, the interest you earn is taxable, so the rate of return is slightly higher than that of Treasuries.

Invest for Retirement Now; Pay the Taxes Later

Now that you know what you want to own, you need to know *how* best to own it—i.e., what sort of account to put your investments in. One of the smartest money moves you can make is to stockpile your investments in tax-deferred accounts. These are your retirement and college-savings accounts, and they go by several names you may already be familiar with, including 401(k) accounts, IRAs, SEPs, Keoghs, Education IRAs, and state-sponsored college savings plans. They allow you to put money in now, let it grow without paying taxes on it for decades, and generally pay the taxes when you take the money out. This works to your advantage because if you don't have to pay taxes year after year, you'll have a larger asset base to grow from.

Where do you begin? If you work for a company—particularly one that will match your contributions—put your first investment dollars in a 401(k) account. If that's not an option, or if you can do more, contribute to an individual retirement account (IRA), or a Roth IRA. And if you're self-employed (or if you moonlight), check out SEPs, Keoghs, and SIMPLEs. Exhaust these possibilities first. Then move on to any tax-advantaged college options: Education IRAs, trusts, state-sponsored college savings plans. Any money you manage to scrape together above and beyond those contributions gets invested in taxable accounts.

401(k)s. A huge 25 percent of eligible employees don't participate in their companies' 401(k)s. Big mistake! You should actually max out your contributions if possible, or at least kick in enough to take advantage of any matching dollars your company offers. Why? This is a huge benefit. Money is taken out of your paycheck *before* it's taxed (the way most of your wages will be), and then grows on a tax-deferred basis until you retire. If you withdraw money before age fifty-nine and a half, you'll have to pay the taxes immediately and face a 10 percent penalty. But you can often borrow from your account; the rules are fairly lenient.

Who can contribute?	
Traditional deductible IRAs	People without 401(k)s or similar plans, who make less than $32,000 a year (singles), or $52,000 a year (married filing jointly), can contribute $2,000 tax deductible dollars each year. If you make up to $42,000 (single) or $62,000 (married), you can still deduct a portion—the deduction is reduced by about $200 for every additional $1,000 worth of income.
Roth IRAs	Singles earning up to $95,000 annually and marrieds earning up to $150,000 jointly a year can make contributions of up to $2,000 annually on which income taxes have already been paid. Singles earning between $95,000 and $110,000, and marrieds earning between $150,000 and $160,000 can make partial contributions.
Traditional nondeductible IRAs	Anyone. Even folks who have a 401(k) at work or who are over the income limits for deductible or Roth IRAs can make a nondeductible contribution of $2,000 each year.

HOW DOES IT WORK?	WHAT IF I PULL MY MONEY OUT BEFORE AGE FIFTY-NINE AND A HALF?
You put in pretax dollars. Your contributions grow tax-deferred until retirement. When you begin withdrawing the money (allowable at age fifty-nine and a half without penalty), it is taxed at your then current rate.	Money can be withdrawn for educational purposes without penalty—though it will be taxed like your normal income. Other withdrawals will face a 10 percent penalty.
You put in money that's already been taxed. Then it grows tax free. When you pull it out starting at age fifty-nine and a half, you owe no additional taxes.	Since your contributions have already been taxed, they can be withdrawn at any time without penalty. Withdrawing the income earned by those contributions is subject to the same 10 percent penalty as a traditional IRA, however. You can also withdraw money at any time without penalty to pay for college costs (though you will be taxed on the income you've earned when you make the withdrawal). After you've had the account for five years, you can also withdraw up to $10,000 in income to pay for the purchase of a first home.
You make contributions with income on which you've already paid taxes. It grows tax-deferred. When you pull it out at retirement you pay taxes on the income the account has generated over all this time, at your then current rate.	Again, you'll pay taxes and penalties on most withdrawals—educational withdrawals being the exception, since they're only taxed and not penalized.

WHEN DO I HAVE TO START MAKING WITHDRAWALS?	
Traditional deductible IRAs	You can start making them without penalty when you turn fifty-nine and a half. You must start making them by April of the year after you turn seventy and a half. When the money comes out, you pay income taxes at your then current rate.
Roth IRAs	You don't. Unlike a traditional IRA, which forces you to start taking the money out at age seventy and a half, a Roth is a good estate-planning vehicle. You can leave the money in forever if you like and pass the entire sum on to your heirs.
Traditional nondeductible IRAs	As with a deductible IRA, you can start withdrawing without penalty at age fifty-nine and a half; and you must start withdrawing by April of the year after you turn seventy and a half.

Once you're in your plan, make sure you get the most possible out of it. DO NOT (did I say that loudly enough?) be one of the nearly 60 percent of individuals who take their money out of their plans when they change jobs. Do that and you'll have next to no nest egg when you reach retirement. Instead, when you change jobs, you should simply roll the money into an IRA, into your new employer's 401(k) plan, or—if you have a balance of $5,000 or more and like your current investment choices—leave it with your former employer's plan.

Individual Retirement Accounts (IRAs). There are, essentially, three different kinds of IRAs: traditional deductible IRAs; traditional nondeductible IRAs; and Roth IRAs. You can open these accounts at just

WHO SHOULD CONTRIBUTE?

If you expect your tax bracket in retirement to be lower than your tax bracket during your working years, there's a benefit to a traditional IRA. Also, if you're getting into the game late—and you don't have a lot of time to allow your earnings to accumulate, paying the taxes when you take the money out is the right way to go, because you're front-loading. You're getting more money into the account sooner where it can compound and grow.

Most people who are eligible for Roths should go this route. You should especially do this if you're in a low tax bracket now, but expect to be in a higher one at retirement. Also, if you have many years to allow your account to rack up earnings, and if there's a possibility you'll have enough assets at retirement to leave your IRA untouched, a Roth is the better way to go.

Everyone who's not doing one of the other two. If you have extra money that you'd like to sock away, this can be a very smart thing to do simply because it can grow tax free for a decade or two.

about any bank, mutual fund company, or brokerage firm. But be choosy: Annual fees vary widely.

To: CEOs of the Home
Re: Spousal IRAs

Just because you don't earn a paycheck, that doesn't mean you can't contribute to an IRA. If you're a stay-at-home parent or spouse, you can—and should—put $2,000 into an IRA every year. The deductibility guidelines work the same as those for traditional and Roth IRAs. Want evidence that this is a smart move? Say a mother who had a baby when she was thirty plans to return to the workforce in seven years, when the child goes to school. If she puts $2,000 into a spousal Roth IRA that earns an annual tax free return of 9 percent, by the time she retires at age sixty-five, she will have more than $225,000 in that account. No matter what happens to the cost of living, that's a significant chunk of change!

Retirement Accounts for the Self-Employed (Moonlighters: Listen Up!)

If you're one of America's 10 million self-employed individuals—or one of the many more who make extra money by freelancing—you have the ability to sock away much more than your basic IRA contribution on a tax-deferred basis, but you have to do it in a different account. You can even take advantage of some of these plans if you have a 401(k) plan at work. Again, you can open these accounts at just about any brokerage firm, bank, or mutual fund company. Contributions are tax deductible. You'll be taxed when you withdraw the money, which you may do without penalty after you turn fifty-nine and a half and must start to do by April of the year you turn seventy and a half. Withdraw early and you'll face a 10 percent penalty and be taxed immediately. Your options:

• **Keoghs.** These accounts allow you to sock away up to $30,000 a year. If you have employees, a Keogh is a better option than the SEP plan, which comes next. Both require you to kick in the same percentage of earnings for your employees that you do for yourself. But with an SEP your contributions become the employees' immediately, while Keoghs give you the option of having them vest over time.

• **Simplified Employee Pension (SEP).** SEPs are lighter on the paperwork than Keoghs (opening one took me fifteen minutes) and work similarly. Each year, you can contribute up to 13.045 percent of your business's net income (currently capping out at $20,870), and then you can invest the money however you like.

• **Savings Incentive Match for Employers (SIMPLE).** The newest option on this list. Companies with anywhere from one to 100

RETIRING WHEN YOU'RE A STEP BEHIND

Maybe you're fifty or fifty-five. Maybe you're sixty. Suddenly retirement is no longer something you're thinking about for the distant future. If your retirement planning is a little late, how do you play catch-up?

Get amnesia. Forget the mistakes you've made in the past and just dive in. You may not have *as much* money ten years from now as you would have if you'd started saving at age thirty, but at least you'll have something. And it might be substantial. Say you, at age fifty, refinance your mortgage, freeing up about $2,000 in extra cash each year. If you put that money into a Roth IRA (or another tax-deferred retirement account) and invest it in stocks—and we'll assume that it earns 11 percent annually—in ten years, $39,123; in twenty years, $144,530; and in thirty years, when you're eighty and really need it, $443,826.

Get a grip on your goals. Too many retirement stories today are out to scare you. Instead of thinking in numbers, focus on how you'll really want to live and how much that will cost. Thinking: "I want to move to Scottsdale and build my own house; how much will that cost me?" is better than thinking: "I need to have $1.3 million by age sixty-five." Even the rule of thumb that says you need 70 percent of your preretirement income to live comfortably after you slow down is up for debate. Some people can retire comfortably on 50 percent. Those who plan on summering on the Riviera and wintering in Telluride obviously need more.

Give up some nonessentials. Run through your monthly expenses to see what you can live without. Start with your last Visa bill. Can you swap your weekly manicure for a biweekly one? How about eating out one or two fewer times each month? And then there are the big-ticket items. Do you really need a new car right now? Would a used one do? Come April, make sure you're taking all the deductions you can; and, if you end up with a refund, be sure to invest it instead of spending it.

employees are eligible. SIMPLEs work like 401(k)s with a forced employer match. Employees can put in up to $6,000 a year pretax; employers must match (dollar for dollar) up to 3 percent of employee compensation or put in voluntarily 2 percent of compensation for each employee. Employees are vested from day one and can't borrow from these plans. But withdrawal penalties are greater: 25 percent in the first two years, 10 percent thereafter.

Investing for College as You Invest for Yourself

There's no way around it. College costs big bucks. Paying for a public four-year college ate up 13 percent of a middle-class family's total income during the early 1970s; today, it's 17 percent. As if that wasn't hard enough, as costs rose, Americans started having kids later in life. The chances that your tuition-paying years butt up against your retirement ones are suddenly better than ever.

How are you ever going to pay for both? By socking away as much as you can—for both—and then holding fast to the following thought: *There is financial aid for college. More than half of all students receive it. But there's no similar aid for retirement.* That means your retirement savings must come first. *First,* you max out all of your tax-deferred retirement options; *then* you can start looking at similar ways to put away money for your kids' education. In the best of all possible worlds, you can do at least a bit of both.

One general rule: College savings shouldn't typically be in a custodial account in your child's name. Under federal rules, cash, non-retirement savings, and real estate equity (other than the primary home) are tapped at about 6 percent for college contributions. Any assets in your kids' names will be tapped at a whopping 35 percent, the expectation being that paying for college should be a child's top priority. (Some private colleges have reduced that chunk to 25 percent in recent years.) That means unless you're certain you won't be eligible for financial aid, steer clear. And consider these options:

Financial Aid: The Lowdown on Student Loans

Odds are, if you have kids entering college anytime soon, they'll receive some sort of financial aid. And, odds are, at least some of that aid will come in the form of a student loan. Two decades ago, grants (which don't have to be repaid) made up three quarters of all financial aid, compared with one quarter for loans (which do). Now the equation has reversed itself, with loans accounting for 75 percent.

That makes knowing how to get the best deal on a student loan all the more important. Unfortunately, it's a concept that's widely misunderstood by both parents and kids. Why? Rates on student loans are set by the government. That means they don't vary from lender to lender. What does vary are the repayment options—and those can make a big difference in the amount of money that you pay over time. You need to shop the lenders available to you—typically in the state where you live or where you're attending school—with an eye toward your future situation. Look for:

• **Discounts for electronic transfers.** When you start repaying the money, some lenders will give you a break on the interest rate of about a quarter point if you have the funds automatically withdrawn from your bank account.

• **Reduction in origination fees.** If you pay on time for the first twenty-four monthly payments, some lenders will forgive origination fees on your loan in excess of $250. If you have a large amount of debt, that can be very attractive (on a $70,000 loan, for example, you could save nearly $2,000).

• **Possible rate cuts.** If you pay on time for the first forty-eight months, some lenders will knock 2 percentage points off your interest rate for the remaining term of the loan.

• **Capitalization of interest.** If you're taking out an unsubsidized Stafford loan (one you have to begin paying back while the student is still in school), you can elect to have the interest capitalized. It's important to look at how—and when—the lender is doing so. The preferred method is to have it done *once* when you start paying the principal. If it's done more than once you start paying interest on your interest.

Where to Put Those College Dollars

How THEY WORK

State-sponsored college savings plans	You open an account with your state (or another state, if yours doesn't have a program you like), make a deposit, and your state's chosen plan manager takes over, putting the money in a combination of stocks, bonds, and mutual funds. In these 529 plans (named for the section of the tax code that covers them), the money is invested more aggressively while your child is very young, more conservatively as the child ages, so that you don't have to worry about a huge loss just before Henry heads off to Haverford. Money in the plan grows tax-deferred, and when it's withdrawn it's taxed at your child's lower tax rate, rather than your own; typically, this will be 15 percent. Some states offer residents other bonuses: deductions on their state tax returns, or even matching dollars. Money accumulated in these plans can be used for any college expense at any school in any state, and may be shifted to siblings. But it must be used by the time your child turns thirty or the funds will be taxed and penalized.
Prepaid tuition plans	The money you put in is guaranteed to cover tuition for a certain number of years at a certain school (or group of schools) by the time your child is ready to attend. If your child opts not to attend that institution or attend college at all, what you get in return varies. Some programs only give back your contributions—with little to no return on your investment.

THE UPSIDE	THE DOWNSIDE
These plans let you sock away far more than an Education IRA (see next page). Also, although the account is for a specific child, the money in these accounts is considered an asset of the parent when it goes into the financial aid equation. Finally, they're handy estate-planning tools. Grandparents can put up to $50,000 apiece into a child's account in a lump sum (it counts as five successive $10,000 annual gifts), which moves a significant sum of money out of any estate *and* gives that money more time to grow.	You have no control over how the money is invested, and some of these plans are very conservative. If you're disappointed and decide to pull the money out early, you'll face taxes and penalties.
These plans are attractive when college costs are rising 8 or 9 percent a year (as they were in the early 1990s) because they lock in your return. Lately, tuition inflation has been around 4 or 5 percent at private schools (lower at public schools), so they're not as alluring. But if inflation takes off again, you're sitting pretty.	Trying to determine where a two-year-old will want to attend college (or *if* she'll want to attend college) seems like a crap shoot. The more restrictive these programs are, the more I'd steer clear.

Where to Put Those College Dollars (continued)

HOW THEY WORK

Education IRAs	Up to $500 each year can be put away (by the parents or anyone else) for any child under age eighteen. That money isn't deductible from your taxes, but the interest earned in the account can be pulled out tax free as long as it's spent on college. There are income limitations: Only singles with incomes of less than $95,000 or couples with incomes of less than $150,000 can make full $500 contributions. But the fact that *anyone* can make a contribution for your child means that you could gift $500 to a lower-earning relative and ask him or her to open an account. Any money that hasn't been used by the time the child hits age thirty must be withdrawn. It's taxed as income and the child is assessed a 10 percent penalty.
Custodial accounts, also called UGMA accounts (for Uniform Gifts to Minors Act)	*Each* parent can put up to $10,000 (including $10,000 worth of appreciated stock) into these accounts annually without paying gift tax. Until the child is fourteen, the first $700 the account generates in income is tax free, the next $700 is taxed at the child's lower tax rate (typically 15 percent), but everything else is taxed at the parent's rate. Until the child reaches the age of majority (eighteen or twenty-one depending on the state) the custodian controls how the money is invested and used (there's some flexibility here; the money can typically be used for the benefit of the child).

THE UPSIDE	THE DOWNSIDE
If your child doesn't go to college, the account can be transferred to a sibling tax free. Also, unlike 529 plans, you control the investments. If you're not contributing to a 529 plan and you're fairly certain that at least one of your children will go on to college, this can be a great deal.	You won't make much of a dent in college costs with this money. If you feel you can do more, then you're better off combining the Education IRA with savings in your own name, or opting for a state-sponsored college savings plan. Note: You can't typically contribute to 529 plans and Education IRAs in the same year without being penalized (the amount in the IRA is considered an overcontribution and assessed a 6 percent annual penalty).
If you're certain you're not going to qualify for financial aid, the eventual savings on estate taxes can be meaningful.	Putting money in your child's name will significantly reduce the amount of financial aid he or she qualifies for when applying to college. Plus, the giving is irrevocable. Once the child reaches majority, she could decide to spend it on anything and everything *except* college.

What About the Rest of Your Money? Taxable Accounts

If you find you have additional money to invest after planning for long-term needs like retirement or your kids' educations, you can do so in a taxable account that you open at a brokerage firm (discount, online, or full-service), bank, or mutual fund company. But unlike the tax advantages you get from the kinds of accounts described on the preceding page, when you trade stocks and make money, you'll have to pay taxes on that money in the year in which you take the *capital gain,* generally the amount your investment earned, taxable in the year when you finally cash out your investment. To simplify your life, make sure this account is housed at a place where you feel commissions are reasonable for the amount of service you're getting, and that the institution offers you the ability to buy all of the different instruments (stocks, bonds, mutual funds) you're interested in.

Watching the Stock Market

Once you're a player in the market, watching its movements becomes a lot more interesting. But you'll need a basic education in order to understand what you're seeing. Inflation, interest rates, and corporate profits are the holy trinity of stock performance. When inflation is low, interest rates low, and corporate profits growing—as we saw during the bull market of the 1990s—the market chugs along nicely. Throw any one of those out of whack and you'll see volatility in the market; more than one, and you'll have market turmoil.

The Five Indexes You Need to Understand

In order to get an accurate reading on the market at any particular point in time, there are five market indexes you can follow. You can keep tabs on their varying performances in your daily paper, on the Web, and on financial channels like CNBC, and get at least an inkling of what's going on in the market—and in your own portfolio.

- The **Dow Jones Industrial Average** is the oldest index, and the one that most people think of when they consider the market. But it's surprisingly arbitrary and subjective, only following thirty stocks. Critics also say that the Dow's results are skewed because each stock's weight is based on its stock price rather than the company's market value. Nevertheless, the Dow remains the sentimental favorite. So many people follow the Dow that even if its readings aren't accurate, they still affect how people behave, and thus how they invest.
- The **Standard & Poor's 500** is an index of 500 large cap stocks accounting for about 80 percent of the total value of the market. That means it's a bit more telling than the Dow, but it still has its shortcomings. The index's forty largest stocks constitute more than half of the S&P's market value.
- The **NASDAQ Composite Index,** which measures the market value of all stocks listed on the NASDAQ exchange, was the darling of the last few years. As the home of super-hot tech stocks and IPOs (initial public offerings—when a company's stock becomes available to the public), the NASDAQ's performance is the best way to quickly gauge how the tech sector is faring.
- You won't hear the **Russell 2000** mentioned on radio updates, but it's the best available benchmark for how small cap stocks (those of companies with market capitalizations of $1.5 billion or less) are faring. If you look at the Russell in conjunction with the S&P, you've got a set of pretty good benchmarks on the entire market.
- Finally, there's the **Wilshire 5000,** which reflects the lion's share of publicly traded stocks in the U.S. and provides almost a wide-angle shot of the market landscape. As a broader index than the S&P, the Wilshire can be a better tool.

Monthly Data It Pays to Follow

Investors and traders also watch a group of key monthly economic reports. In the last few years, especially, these reports have had the ability to move the markets, because they're seen as predictors of whether the Federal Reserve's Open Market Committee will find it necessary to raise or lower interest rates. Here's a thumbnail sketch of each:

• **Gross Domestic Product** (GDP): Released four times a year, during the final week of January, April, July, and October, the GDP measures the nation's total output of goods and services. It's a measure of how the economy is growing—or not.

• **Consumer Confidence Index** (CCI): Released the last Tuesday of each month, this report takes the pulse of the shopping public. If we don't buy products, the companies that make them won't be profitable. Simple as that. When the index is over 100, people are feeling good; when it dips below 80 for a couple of months, it usually signals a slowdown.

• **Employment Situation Report** (ESR): On the first Friday of every month, this reports the number of jobs our economy created, along with changes in wages and hours worked, and the unemployment rate. It's best to look at the current three-month average against the prior three-month average to get a sense of the trend. The Federal Reserve likes to see the number at around 150,000 to 200,000.

• **National Association of Purchasing Management Index** (NAPMI): This number is released during the first week of every month. The Fed looks at this snapshot of new orders, prices, and deliveries of products to get a sense of the economy's growth rate. Using a baseline of 50, a 55 to 60 reading shows that the economy is moving along at a healthy pace. Below 44, and things may be grinding to a halt.

• **Consumer Price Index** (CPI): Released the fourth week of each month, the CPI prices a "shopping cart" of goods and services purchased by a typical urban consumer. An annualized uptick of about 8 percent is a warning that the economy will slow, because prices for these essential goods are rising.

• **Leading Economic Indicators** (LEI): The Conference Board, a nonprofit research organization in New York, releases this report during the first week of every month. It's an index of ten components including manufacturing orders, interest rates, and new construction. The LEI has successfully predicted the last six recessions.

The Soft Signals

Of course, it's not just these fundamental economic indicators that move markets. They move on management changes, news affecting a particular industry, and other factors. Sometimes, a simple mention of a stock or an interview on the right news show (think CNBC's *Squawk Box*) is all it takes to make the market respond. Or word that Warren Buffett is buying a significant block of shares. Should you buy on these sorts of soft signals? That depends. Let's take a look one by one.

• **Share buyback:** A company announces it is buying back shares of its own stock, literally pulling some out of circulation. Unlike some of the items discussed here, a buyback actually does increase the value of one share on a fundamental basis. The next time the company computes earnings per share, it'll be dividing its earnings by a smaller number of total shares—so each share of stock will represent a greater piece of ownership in the company. Managers institute buybacks as a way to trumpet their belief in the value of their company—often when the market isn't paying them enough attention. And it works: One study, published in *Financial Management* in 1996, noted that a company's stock rises an average 3 percent the day a buyback is announced. Even more significant, the study found that over the next four years those stocks rose an average of 12 percent more than the stock market as a whole.

• **Stock splits:** People tend to get very excited when these are announced—but that very excitement is what accounts for any increase in the stock's price. In other words, there's no tangible reason for a stock to rise in value simply because a company slices its stock in half. It's like eating two small pieces of chocolate cake instead of one large wedge—you're still consuming the same calories. If you hold one share of Disney at $200, and the stock splits, you simply have two shares valued at $100 each. One shred of positive evidence that a company will do well in the wake of a split: Often a management team that makes such a move is confident about their prospects. But that confidence might or might not be well placed, so a split is not a strong indicator of future performance.

• **Insider selling:** It's true that if a wave of senior executives are selling large blocks of stock in their own company it could mean that a big change is brewing. But it could also mean that several of them went to lunch and agreed that their portfolios weren't diversified enough. Or that several of them have kids about to go off to college, and they are cashing in some shares to pay the tuition. Or that one is buying a boat, another a house, and a third is buying his parents a condo. In other words, knowing that insiders are selling is not reason enough to act. You need to do some research to determine what's really happening.

• **Investment bank instituting coverage:** Large investment banks like Morgan Stanley or Goldman Sachs rate stocks regularly, showing how they expect the stock to perform. If one of them institutes coverage or changes its rating of a particular stock, should you react? If you hold GE stock, and Morgan downgrades the stock from a "buy" to a "hold," then you should start paying close attention. Look at other firms to see what their analysts are recommending and decide if you want to sell, buy more, or stay the course. Then you have to consider why you own the stock.

THE BIG THREE: THINGS TO TAKE AWAY FROM TALKING INVESTING FOR RETIREMENT AND COLLEGE

1. Most people have no idea how much money they'll need for retirement—and the usual rules of thumb (70 percent of your income during your working years) may fail you. Take the time to run some actual projections based on how you envision living. (The worksheet on pages 92–95 can help.)

2. The key to any investment strategy is diversification. You need a mix of stocks, bonds, and cash that you choose based on your own tolerance of risk and how many years you have until you need the money you're investing (the longer your time horizon, the more you should have in stocks).

3. When you invest your money, do it in a way that minimizes your tax rate. Max out your opportunities in 401(k)s, IRAs (all types), Keoghs, SEPs, SIMPLEs, and state-sponsored college savings plans before putting money in taxable accounts.

CHAPTER 6

Talking Insurance

When it comes to life insurance, Michael, a filmmaker, is probably typical of many young fathers. He and his wife, Grace, a caterer, didn't even think about life insurance until their daughter Lauren was born several years ago. But thinking about it and buying it were two different things. Life with an infant proved so hectic that, despite his best intentions, Michael never even made it to the library to *begin* to try to make sense of the array of plans on the market. "The reality hit us that we had to be responsible for this new life," he says, "but finding the time to do the research, get the blood test and the physical—all of it—turned out to be too complex an undertaking at the time. We were totally overwhelmed."

Two years later, the couple's second daughter, Ella, was born—and again they thought about insurance. But of course, time was even tighter. Then in 1998, Grace gave birth to twins and the issue took on a whole new level of urgency. "That tipped the scales," Michael says. "Since Grace wasn't working, we realized that if something were to happen to me, the demands on her would have been huge. And we felt we couldn't tempt fate. There were now five lives besides mine that were at stake."

Michael got on the phone and shopped around with a couple of different companies, finally settling on a $500,000 term life policy whose premium was $39.95 a month. The one big question that remains for him: Is it enough? Michael and Grace would have liked to take out a $2 million policy, enabling Grace not to work if something happened to Michael, but they couldn't afford it. "This amount, we felt, would at least alleviate any burden she might face," he says. For budgetary reasons, they also decided to insure just Michael and not both of them. Nonetheless, the relief they felt was immediate.

Michael and Grace did the right thing, and not just for their peace of mind. Too many people discover their insurance needs in hindsight. One fifth of Americans have been in a situation where they wished they had more insurance, according to a 1999 survey by the Lutheran Brotherhood, a financial concern. Still others are paying for insurance they don't really need. Currently, seven out of ten adult Americans have a life insurance policy—many through their employers. Are you willing to bet that they're the same Americans for whom life insurance is appropriate? I'm not.

From disability to long-term care to flood and earthquake insurance—even the collision coverage on your car—the decision is always the same: You may or may not need a policy, depending on the way you live your life. The only type of insurance that just about every person on the planet ought to have is health insurance—and in that case getting the right type for you isn't simple.

This chapter will walk you through the decision-making process for *all* the different coverages you may be considering. How do you figure out how much you need—and what's the best way to buy it? The evolution of insurers on the Internet has already made shopping for term life and auto policies much easier. I recently cut my auto insurance premiums in half with the help of the Web (and I didn't think I was paying too much to begin with). Let's go.

Life Insurance

When it comes to life insurance, the first question you need to answer is *Do you need it at all?* If you're a single person with no one depending on your income except yourself, the answer, 99 percent of the time, is going to be: No. No, thank you. No way. Unless you're buying a minuscule amount so that you don't have to burden your family with your funeral expenses, that's what you should tell any salesperson who tries to convince you otherwise. But if you have a spouse, a partner, or a family who is depending on your earnings—or if you're the stay-at-home parent and your partner would have to pay someone to care for the kids if you weren't around—then the answer is: Absolutely. Which brings us to the next question:

How much do you need? Life insurance agents (and some financial planners) have rules of thumb to answer this question. Some say four times your salary. Others say ten times. To me, such a wide variety of numbers says that rules of thumb like these don't work. What you really need to do is sit down with a calculator and add up your family's expense needs. You should consider questions like: If one of you were to die, would the other continue (or return) to work or want to be home with the kids? And if that person was working, how much could they realistically earn? Do you want enough life insurance to pay off the mortgage or pay for college for the kids? Would you want your family to be able to live off the interest from a policy's proceeds alone? The answers to these questions will lead you to good estimates. If you expect college for your four kids to cost $130,000 a pop, for example (because they're all brilliant and going to Penn), that's another $600,000 in insurance you need to buy.

Here's a simple worksheet that'll help you figure out your needs. It was developed by the folks at Equity Analytics, a consulting firm in Long Island, New York. If you're married or have merged your finances with a significant other, you'll need to go through these exercises twice—to figure out how much insurance to purchase on each of your lives.

Worksheet: How Much Life Insurance Do You Need?

Annual Living Expenses

1. What are your family's annual living expenses? (Include everything: mortgage—unless you're planning on using insurance to pay it off—car payments, food, vacations, etc.): _____

2. Now multiply the number in line 1 by .75, if you're a family with kids, by .5 if it's just you and your spouse because you're down one person: _____

3. Add annual cost of child care if you would need it if one spouse dies: _____

4. Total of lines 2 and 3: _____

Annual Expected Income (in the case of a death)

5. Social Security benefits (for an estimate of your benefits, call 1-800-772-1213): _____

6. Survivor's pension benefits: _____

7. Survivor's earned income: _____

8. Other income: _____

9. Add lines 5, 6, 7, and 8: _____

Living Expense Shortage (or Surplus)

10. Subtract line 9 from line 4: _____

11. How much money will you need to invest to produce your living expense shortage (divide line 10 by .06, which assumes a very conservative 6 percent rate of return to help compensate for inflation): _____

Lump Sum Expenses

12. Estimated funeral and estate (legal) costs: _____

13. Amount needed to pay off mortgage and/or other debts (if you're planning to do so with insurance proceeds): _____

14. College costs: _____

15. Emergency fund: _____

16. Other: _____

17. Add lines 12, 13, 14, 15, and 16: _____

How Much Money Do You Need?

    18. Add lines 11 and 17: _____

How Much Do You Already Have?

    19. Income-producing assets you currently have (include money, if any, already set away for college): _____

    20. Present life insurance: _____

    21. Add lines 19 and 20: _____

How Much Life Insurance Do You Need?

    22. Subtract line 21 from line 18. This is the amount of life insurance you need to purchase: _____

Okay, now that you've worked your way to a number, how do you feel about the result? Does it seem like too much? Not enough? Make adjustments until you're comfortable. Then you'll be ready to shop. And note: This isn't the sort of exercise you do once. Every three years or so (or if you go through a life-changing event—a birth, divorce, receipt of a large inheritance) you'll want to revisit your numbers.

What Kind of Life Insurance Is Right for You?

There are two basic types of life insurance, *term life* and *permanent*. Term life, as its name suggests, terminates when its term is up. You buy it solely for the death benefit, and when it expires and you stop paying your premiums, you'll have nothing to show for it. Term life works for people who are either on a budget or believe that they'll get to a point in their life where they won't need insurance anymore, because they'll have enough in savings, investments, and other assets to support their family if something happened to them. Because most people drop their term coverage as they age and it gets pricey, the percentage of term policies that pay out is extremely low. As a result, term is cheap. If you need to buy a lot of insurance (or want to spend as little on whatever you do buy as absolutely possible), you'll want to look no further than term.

FOUR DIFFERENT TYPES OF TERM INSURANCE

• **Nonguaranteed term life** is typically a one-year policy that pays out if you die during that year. You'll need a medical exam each time you purchase one of these policies, so if your health declines you may need to pay significantly more the next time around—or you may not be able to get coverage at all.

• **Annual renewable term** is a one-year policy that permits you to renew each year with no new medical exam. The catch is that policies are cheap when you're young, but prices rise with age, often a great deal. That's why most people are better off with . . .

• **Level-premium term policies,** whose premiums remain the same for typically five, ten, or twenty years (Note: Be sure that the premium remains level for the entire term, not just part of it). If somewhere during the course of the policy you decide you don't need the coverage, you can drop it. But when the policy finally expires, if you want to renew, you'll again have to go through a medical exam—and obviously, it'll be more difficult to qualify and much more expensive if you make the cut. That's why you should always buy a level-premium term policy that is also . . .

• **Convertible term,** which will allow you to pay more money to change your term policy into a permanent one. Most people convert either when the cost of the policy escalates or when they suffer a health-related setback. But if you know that this is something you'd like to do, the earlier you make the conversion, the better. It doesn't have to be done all at once. As your salary grows, you can convert your policy in pieces.

Permanent Insurance

More people own "permanent" insurance—which doesn't have an expiration date—than own term insurance. But that's largely because it's *sold* to them, not because they set out to *buy* it. Many of those people would be much better off with the cheaper term coverage. But before you can know if you're one of them, you have to understand what permanent insurance is, and how it works.

There are several specific types of permanent insurance, and in a way they're all like term insurance, except with investment accounts attached. When you buy permanent insurance, your premium dollars do three things: First, they pay the commission of the agent who sells you the policy (in the early years, this component is higher than you'd ever imagine it to be). Second, they pay the cost of insuring your life (funding your death benefit), which is low when you're young and not likely to die and higher later on. And third, they are invested in an account that builds up a cash value, which you can borrow against or draw on during your life.

It's this third component that complicates permanent life insurance policies. When you sit down with an insurance agent to talk about policies, you'll be shown charts and graphs called illustrations that show you how the cash value in your policy will accumulate over the years based on certain performance assumptions. The trouble is that these projections don't always play out as the insurer predicts. When a policy performs as well as expected, your premiums will decrease down the road, because the cash value in the account will help cover those costs. But when a policy underperforms, you'll be asked to pay more.

Three Different Types of Permanent Insurance

• **Whole life** is so named because it's designed to stay in force throughout your life. In the first few years, when you're young, its cost will be low, so the bulk of the money goes to pay the agent and into the investment account. As you get older, the cost of insuring you increases, so less of your premium goes into the investment account; the money that went into that account in the early years is able to grow. The cash value of your policy is the amount you'd get if you decided to surrender it.

Compared to the other types of permanent insurance, whole life is closer to a sure thing: Premiums are guaranteed throughout the life of the policy and so is your death benefit, though the cash value the policy is projected to earn will vary with the insurance company's investment performance. In most cases, insurers invest the money that's building your cash value fairly conservatively—that enables them to try to keep up with the numbers you saw in a policy illustration, but it also typically means that returns underperform other investments, such as stocks or equity mutual funds. That's why many financial advisers (especially those who don't sell insurance) recommend that instead of buying whole life as an investment, you buy term insurance and invest the difference. That's good advice in theory, but in practice you have to be motivated enough to actually do it and then monitor your investments. And many people—despite their good intentions—don't follow through.

In order to accrue any real cash value in a whole life policy, you need to stick with it for about ten years; it will be closer to twenty years before the gain begins to look impressive. So beware of any insurance agent who tries to convince you to swap one whole life policy for another "better" policy just a few years after you made your original purchase. Not only will you rarely have earned any cash value to speak of, but you may face high surrender charges for dropping the first policy. What that agent is really trying to do is keep his or her hefty commission checks rolling in.

• **Universal life** was designed for people who didn't want to pay for life insurance on an ongoing basis. It allows for flexible premiums. After you make the first payment, you can vary your premium payments in both the amount you send in and how often you send it. Pay little and your cash value and death benefit won't grow as projected, but write a bigger check and the investment account may grow so large it'll be enough to actually pay your premiums later on. Used wisely, this flexibility can be helpful. As your net worth grows and you don't need as large a death benefit, you can control it by lowering your premiums. The problem is, the illustrations you see when you purchase a universal policy count on the investment component to pay at least some of your death benefit when you get older and the policy becomes expensive. If you skimp on your premium payments, you may have to kick in big bucks just to keep the policy alive later on.

• **Variable life** is actually a subcategory of both universal and whole life. "Variable whole life" has fixed premiums like whole life; "variable universal life" has flexible premiums like universal. In both cases, you—not the insurer—control how the money in the policy is invested by choosing from the insurer's menu of mutual funds. The better your investments perform, the higher your death benefit and the more cash value you'll accumulate. If your investments don't perform well, you'll receive less (though sometimes a minimum death benefit is guaranteed). This makes variable life the most risky of the three types of cash value insurance—you could pay years of premiums and end up not having enough money to sustain your family in a catastrophe. Isn't that what you wanted life insurance for in the first place?

So Which Is Better? Term or Permanent? Or Both?

Working your way through the following set of scenarios should help you come up with an answer.

If you're on a budget ... then you should buy term. It's the cheapest way to get a lot of coverage for the least amount of money.

If you believe you'll be wealthy enough to self-insure twenty or thirty years down the road ... then again, you want term. It's cheaper, and a whole life policy wouldn't have a high cash value at that point.

If your assets greatly exceed $675,000 ($1.35 million for a married couple) and are thus subject to estate taxes ... you may want a whole life policy simply to pay for the taxes.

If you have a child with a disability or an elderly parent or grandparent who will always need care ... a whole life policy is probably the best way to guarantee that there will be enough money for the long-term care.

If you want your kids to have your money after you pass away ... whole life is a way to be certain you'll leave them a large inheritance.

If you prefer not to leave a lot of money to your children ... then you should buy term, understanding that you'll probably let it lapse after your kids are out of college and out of the house.

If you have short-term debt from something such as a business loan . . . then annual renewable term might be a good bet. It's the lowest cost in the first year, but always the most expensive in the long run.

If you have no debt, enough money to take care of your family should you die, and don't have an estate tax problem . . . you may want to purchase no insurance at all. The same is true if you don't have a family to take care of.

If you have trouble saving money or lack the discipline or desire to invest your money . . . permanent life insurance (whole, universal, or variable) will be better for you than term. It may not get you the biggest return on your money, but it will give you something when you get older because it forces you to invest, albeit conservatively.

If you married or had kids late in life, or have a much younger spouse . . . consider whole life. In this situation, you can live off the principal during retirement and still have a death benefit to take care of your survivors.

If you have maxed out on your tax-deferred savings, such as 401(k)s and IRAs . . . you may want a whole life policy, because its earnings aren't taxed until they're withdrawn, and even then only to the extent that they exceed the amount paid as premiums.

If you have an uneven cash flow . . . you may want to purchase universal life, which allows you to adjust your payments.

If you're a business owner with limited cash flow or you plan on selling or liquidating the business within a particular time period . . . term insurance is your best option, as it will cover you up to the point when you liquidate the business and have enough money to self-insure.

If you have highly illiquid assets that are likely to be sold or liquidated within a given period of time and personal cash flow is a problem . . . term insurance, again, is a good idea. It gives you a layer of protection until those sales occur.

Getting a Good Deal

First and foremost, you'll need to get at least three quotes. It's fine for one to come from the insurance agent you know best—someone who lives in your neighborhood, attends your church, or has worked with your family in the past. But stopping there is a recipe for overpaying. Make sure you get at least one quote from an independent agent or broker, who can quote from a variety of policies. You'll also want to check the prices from low-load insurers (where there is little to no sales commission). Ameritas (800-552-3553) is the biggest name in this part of the business, but you can find others through the Wholesale Insurance Network (800-808-5810). And, in the case of term insurance, you should also check prices on the Web, at sites like Quicken.com and Quotesmith.com.

If you have special health problems (or if you're a smoker) make sure you price policies from companies that specialize in people like you. Because they have a greater understanding of the risks of taking you on as a customer, their prices are often lower. And if you're looking for a reason to stop smoking, here's a good one: It can cut your life insurance premiums in half.

If you're shopping for term . . . the important thing is to make apples-to-apples comparisons. If you're comparing ten-year, level-premium policies, for example, find out which insurer will charge you the least for the same amount of coverage. Since there are very few variables, the Web is a useful shopping tool. Insurance sites can't do a deal from top to bottom (no life insurer you want to deal with will write you a policy without a physical) and they'll end up referring you to an agent to formalize the deal, but using these sites is a terrific way to check a lot of prices at one time. Some sites pride themselves on speed. They'll boast that you can get a quote in minutes—and you can—but only because you're asked very few detailed health-related questions. You'll only receive the rate if the physical checks out afterward; if health problems are later discovered, you'll pay significantly more. Other sites take longer to get back to you because they require more detailed health information up front—but they're more likely to be on the mark.

If you're shopping for permanent insurance . . . there are many more variables to consider, including:

- Commissions and expenses.
- Cash value.
- Dividends vs. interest.
- The ability to adjust the death benefit.
- The ability to adjust the amount and timing of premiums.
- Interest rates.

Your policy's cash value is the amount you pay minus commission, administrative costs, investment management fees, and the cost of paying off other insurance policies the company has written, which is one of the jobs of life insurance (this last item is called "mortality expenses"). Again, your goal is to compare apples to apples, looking for the policy where the cash value grows fastest when all other things are held constant. Make sure you know what happens if the policy doesn't pay off as the agent is predicting and that you can afford the planned premiums. (What if you should suffer a small loss of income—would you still be able to afford them?) And make sure you can trust both your agent and the company.

In both cases . . . if you get to the end of the shopping road and aren't sure which policy to go with, you can hire a fee-only insurance consultant or fee-only financial planner to review the policies and tell you which way to go. A cheaper alternative: The Consumer Federation of America, a not-for-profit group, will review your policies for a fee of $45 for the first and $35 for each policy thereafter. You can find them on the Web at www.cfa.org or by calling 202-387-6121.

What Should You Do with Your Current Policy?

It generally pays to dump your current permanent insurance policy only if you become convinced that your insurance company cannot pay the death benefit. Before you do dump anything, however, make sure you know how much of your cash value you'll get when you cash in now and how much will be lost to surrender charges. And before you cancel, find out whether your insurance company is going to "demutualize," or become a stock company. If so, you could benefit from a windfall stock distribution—if you still have your policy. This happens more often than you think.

If you already have a policy, how do you know if it's in trouble? Compare the actual cash value of the policy as reflected on your last statement with what it's supposed to be according to the illustration you received when you bought the policy. If it's not keeping pace, call your agent and ask for a new set of "in-force illustrations"—a projection of your policy's value going forward. You need to know how much more it'll cost you to maintain your policy. Or if your insurance needs are less than they were when you purchased your policy, you may want to take a look at reducing your death benefit.

Five Questions to Ask Your Life Insurance Company

1. Which is better for me, whole life or term? If you're under fifty and in good health and your agent suggests a whole life policy, make him or her give you a good reason. One may be that you are wealthy and may need liquidity to pay estate taxes; another may be that you have asset protection problems (i.e., you're being sued by creditors).

2. How much of my premium is going into my agent's pocket? You may be surprised to learn that, typically, agents get half of what you pay the first year, and there are cases where they receive 100 percent or more. This is true for permanent insurance and also, in some cases, for term, which has a much broader range of commissions.

3. How much coverage do I need? There's no easy way to calculate this, but take a look at the worksheet earlier in this chapter; you'll also find helpful tools on the Internet, at sites like www.insure.com. There are two major financial components to the equation: how much money your heirs would need to replace your lost income and how much money you've already accumulated. Other factors include the type of life your heirs lead, whether to set aside funding for education (four years of private college can now run $130,000 plus), special needs (like an expensive roof repair), or money to pay off the mortgage and the car. *Red Flag!* Be wary of companies that give you a "simple formula" to determine how much coverage you'll need—or tell you it'll only take a minute. These assessments can't be done quickly without missing something.

4. How can I cut the costs of my life insurance? Shop around. Particularly when you're looking for term insurance, it's easier and quicker to compare companies and policies than ever before, thanks to the Web. Try www.quotesmith.com, www.quick-quote.com, or www.insweb.com. With a whole life policy, shopping is more cumbersome, but not impossible. Lifestyle factors can trim your costs, too: Exercise, don't smoke, and try to manage your stress.

5. How do I know you'll be a solvent company decades from now when my heirs need you? Insurance companies are rated obsessively just for this reason. The most reliable ratings are available for free from Standard & Poor's at www.standardpoor.com. Generally, S&P ratings of AAA, AA+, and AA are companies you want to do business with. But don't switch companies simply because the rating goes down. You'll suffer what might be a needless surrender charge, because the rating can very easily go back up.

Red Flag! Watch out for any company that won't readily tell you its S&P rating.

Health Insurance

If and when health care reform will actually happen is something I'm not even going to address in these pages. But I will bet on two things: One, the price of health insurance is going to continue to rise. Depending on the type of company you work for—and how your employer feels about passing these increases along—this may or may not affect the amount you're asked to chip in for your annual premiums. But you can be sure you'll see it in the form of pricier co-payments, more expensive prescription drugs (particularly if you insist on name brands over generics), and fewer services covered on your menu.

If You Have Health Insurance Through Your Company

Most corporate employees have the opportunity to change their health plan selection once a year, usually in the fall. If you're on Medicare, you can make changes more frequently than that. But how do you choose? The first thing you need to know is what *type* of health plan is best for you. There are four distinct choices, though the lines between them have started to blur.

• **Health Maintenance Organizations (HMOs).** These restrict you to using a certain network of physicians in order to qualify for reimbursement. When you use one of these doctors, you are charged a "co-payment," usually a small charge in the $10 to $20 range, for your appointment.

• **HMOs with Point-of-Service (POS) Options.** If you see a doctor in the HMO network, you'll pay only the co-payment. But these plans also give you the opportunity to see anyone you like. Do that, and you're typically charged as if this was a traditional health plan; you may pay 30 percent of the bill and your insurer 70 percent after you satisfy an annual deductible.

• **Preferred Provider Organizations (PPOs).** These offer you a large network of doctors at discounted rates; you don't need referrals to see specialists who are part of the network.

• **Traditional Indemnity (Fee-for-Service) Plans.** If you're in a fee-for-service plan, you can see any doctor you choose. You typically pay 20 percent of the bill and your insurer 80 percent after you satisfy an annual deductible.

Choosing among these plans is a matter of figuring out how sensitive you are to choice and price. If you only rarely go to the doctor, and saving money is more important to you than being able to choose a particular physician, then a straight HMO may be a good fit. It'll cost you the least over the course of a year. If you're willing to pay a little more for a bit more choice in doctors, then either a PPO or an HMO that has a point-of-service option is the better bet. And if you absolutely, positively are *not* giving up that wonderful physician who refuses to join the HMO bandwagon, then the traditional plan will suit you best, despite the higher cost. In the real world, you probably won't be offered all four types of plans, but you'll want to make your decision the same way. The more choice you're willing to pay for, the less you want a plain vanilla HMO.

Once you've figured out the *type* of plan that suits you best, you're going to want to select the *specific* plan that suits your needs. If you work for a big company, for example, you may be offered several HMOs (with or without a POS option) as well as a PPO to choose from. Picking the right one for you means pulling out the manuals and checking how the medical procedures those plans cover conform to your needs. The key is to look at your health, your lifestyle, and the things you used health insurance for over the past two years. Single men and women who are essentially healthy, for example, will want a plan that provides regular, comprehensive physicals, access to high-quality doctors, and—if they're physically active—rehabilitation services like physical therapy. Families with young kids, on the other hand, need well-baby care and convenient emergency room access. And older individuals will want high lifetime caps on coverage and short periods of exclusion for preexisting conditions.

Make sure any plan you're considering has been accredited by the National Commission on Quality Assurance. This is a Washington, D.C., watchdog group that runs HMOs through an intensive screening process to see if it has the systems in place to run efficiently. It also checks up on doctor credentials and surveys member satisfaction. You can look up the plans on your list at the NCQA Web site at www.ncqa.org, or call the group toll-free at 888-275-7585.

Finally, if you have a good relationship with your doctor already, discuss your options with him or her. You want to know whether your doctor is satisfied with the way the plan is run (you wouldn't like to think this would affect the way your doctor treats you, but it might).

If You Don't Have Insurance Through Your Company

If you leave a company where you've had health coverage, they must make coverage available to you under a continuation of benefits, or COBRA, policy, for eighteen months. It won't be cheap, but it may be as good as most deals you could find on your own. As with all insurance, the more risk you are willing to assume, the cheaper the policy will be. If cost is a major factor to you, you'll probably want to take on a sizable deductible. Or you may want to consider taking a part-time job that offers health benefits or join a plan offered to your spouse or partner through their place of work. At the very least, you'll want to buy major medical, or hospitalization coverage. Another option is to join a professional organization, alumni club, or other organization that offers a group policy for its members. And if you're self-employed, don't forget about the tax break. Deductibility of your health insurance premiums is scheduled to rise to 100 percent by the year 2003.

Homeowners Insurance

You'd think buying homeowners insurance would be a no-brainer. After all, you know how much you paid for your house—it should be simple to figure out how much coverage you need. Well, it's not. Not if you want to be certain that in the event of a disaster (or even a small accident) you'd be able to replace your house and belongings with stuff of similar quality. A typical homeowners policy will cover you for everything except earthquakes, floods, war, and nuclear incidents. (If you live in an area where you feel you need coverage for the first two, you'll have to buy it separately. Call the National Flood Insurance program at 800-427-4661 for a referral to a flood insurance agent in your area. Most earthquake insurance, which is quite expensive and tends to have high deductibles, has come in recent years from the California Earthquake Authority. But other insurers, such as Geo Vera Insurance (www.geovera.com) and Pacific Select Property Insurance (www.quakeinsurance.com) also offer policies.

Insuring the Structure

First, you need to cover the actual house itself, or the structure. Some insurance agents (some *bad* ones) will recommend you insure for the value of your mortgage. Wrong. Mortgages, because they often include the value of your land (which doesn't need to be insured) often exceed the amount of insurance you need to buy by tens of thousands of dollars. The real questions are: How much would it cost to replace this house? And, can I afford to insure for *that* amount? There are two (sometimes three) types of coverage to choose from.

• **Cash value.** The cheapest option, cash value coverage pays you only what the destroyed house was worth after depreciation. That means if you own a house built in the 1970s, with out-of-date fixtures, that's a little rough around the edges, you will be paid the amount needed to rebuild the house minus depreciation. You could save some money by purchasing 80 percent coverage, which might be enough if, say, a fire burned down the house but left the foundation. But if your house is totaled, you'll wish you'd had that other 20 percent.

• **Replacement cost.** In the event of a disaster, replacement cost coverage will pay the full cost of rebuilding your home. The key is understanding what that cost would be (at today's prices) and buying enough coverage. With this kind of coverage, you typically can't insure your home for more than 120 percent of what it's worth today, but if your house has special features (beautiful handpainted tile in the kitchen, old-fashioned dentil moldings in the living room), you'll appreciate having the extra leeway. Make sure you stay aware of the real cost of rebuilding; particularly if you're in a hot real estate market, that may mean buying a slightly larger policy every single year. And if you improve your house in any way, you'll have to add to your policy to cover the new additions. Some companies sell an inflation rider (an extra policy tacked atop yours) to protect you against cost of living increases; you may want to price that as well.

• **Guaranteed replacement cost.** In past years, insurance companies routinely sold guaranteed replacement cost coverage, which will cover the cost of rebuilding your home even if it exceeds that 120 percent cap. It's a good defense against price gouging, which sometimes happens in cases of widespread disaster. Typically it costs about 10 percent more than regular replacement cost coverage. It's not everywhere anymore but if you search carefully, you can still find it from some companies, including Chubb.

Insuring the Contents

The amount of coverage you have on the structure of your house determines how much insurance you can buy for what's inside; most insurers will cover your possessions for 50 to 75 percent of what the structure is covered for. That may be plenty. But if you buy the best of everything it may not be enough, and you can always get more coverage. To see how much you might need, walk through your house taking inventory and adding up prices as you go. (This is not a wasted effort. In fact, it's something you should do as a matter of course because if you ever need to file a claim you'll have to prove you owned what you say you owned. So don't just jot down items and values on a legal pad. Take Polaroids of everything—or even better, use a video camera to pan through each room. Save receipts for pricey acquisitions. And make sure you keep all this evidence in a safe deposit box or some other secure place outside your house.)

Even under a replacement cost policy, certain items will only be covered up to a very low limit; they include jewelry, art, antiques, and expensive electronic equipment. You'll need to buy *riders* to insure these separately. The good news is that these riders aren't all that expensive. If you work from home, you'll also need to insure your computer and other office equipment separately. Some companies may set dollar limits, for example, $2,000 for all jewelry. In that case, you'll want *floaters,* which are separate policies for individual items, like your engagement ring. Have each item appraised and be comfortable with the amount you have it insured for.

Renters Insurance

According to the Insurance Information Institute in New York, only about 30 percent of renters in the U.S. have this coverage. All of them should. It covers not the dwelling (your landlord gets to worry about that) but your personal belongings, protecting them from the same laundry list of perils as do homeowners policies—everything but earthquakes, floods, war, and nuclear incidents. As with a home-owners policy, the question is whether your stuff will be covered for what it was worth when it was damaged or stolen or what it would cost to replace it. Because these policies are so cheap to begin with ($90 to $350 per year, depending on what state you live in), there's absolutely no reason not to buy the best possible policy. But again, if you have pricey art, jewelry, antiques, and so on—or if you work from home and have invested in expensive computer equipment—you'll need to buy riders to cover those items separately.

How Do You Get the Best Rates?

As with all insurance coverage, your first step in purchasing home-owners or renters coverage should be shopping around. If you already have an auto insurance policy, start by calling that agent or insurer. Often you'll get a discount by purchasing both coverages through one company. Then make at least three more calls for quotes, including one to a *direct writer*—an insurance company that uses an 800-number-based sales force, like Amica (800-242-6422). Or, if you have a military connection, call USAA (800-531-8100). You should also call at least one insurer with its own sales force, like State Farm or Allstate, and one independent agent, who can quote you a variety of prices.

Discounts abound, but you have to know to ask for them. Here are some places where you can save significant money:

• **Boost your deductible.** Increasing your deductible from $250 to $500 or $1,000 can save you more than 20 percent of your annual premium.

- **Invest in safety.** Get a burglar alarm and you could save 10 to 20 percent on your annual premiums. Other safety devices, like smoke alarms and state-of-the-art deadbolts, can net you smaller discounts.
- **Stop smoking.** Smoking in bed is still the cause of too many fires each year for the insurance industry's comfort. If no one in your house smokes, you may be able to receive a 2 to 5 percent discount.
- **Membership pays.** Belonging to certain alumni or automobile associations may result in a discount.
- **Retire.** If you're home more, you ought to be able to save 5 to 10 percent on your homeowners policy. The logic: You're less likely to be burgled and more likely to notice small fires or other problems. Note: The same is true if someone else is typically home—if you have a live-in housekeeper, for example.
- **Buy smart in the first place.** New homes made of materials that aren't likely to burst into flames can net you a discount, as can brick homes in some parts of the country (because they're less likely to suffer damage from hurricanes), and frame houses in other parts (because they're less likely to succumb to earthquakes).

Auto Insurance

Here's some good news about auto insurance: Rates are headed down. They fell about 4.5 percent in 1999, after a 2.8 percent drop in 1998, according to the Insurance Information Institute. That's partly a result of competition among insurers, but it's also a result of the aging of the population (now that the boomers are more mature, they're having fewer traffic accidents). We can also credit safer cars, low inflation, and the fact that some antifraud precautions the industry put in place a few years ago worked as they were meant to. That said, getting a good deal on your coverage isn't necessarily simple, so let's talk about what you need, and then we'll discuss how to get it for the best price.

Four different components make up the typical auto insurance policy:

• **Collision/comprehensive.** Collision coverage pays to repair or replace your car after an accident while comprehensive pays for damage to your car that occurs in other ways. If your car is vandalized, in a fire, damaged by water from a major storm, or stolen, for example, comprehensive coverage kicks in. If your car is totaled, this coverage will only pay up to the amount that your car is actually worth according to the *Kelley Blue Book*. And it can be very expensive, usually encompassing about 40 percent of your premium. That's why as your car gets old and its value declines, you may want to consider dropping collision and comprehensive altogether. When should you make the move? According to the Insurance Information Institute, you want to start thinking about it when your car hits the five-year mark. Two caveats: You can't typically drop coverage if you're still paying off your car loan; since the bank owns part of your car, it wants to make sure it's insured. And remember, if you're in an accident and don't have coverage, you'll have to pay repair costs yourself.

• **Liability.** If you're in an accident and someone other than your passengers is injured, liability coverage will pay for medical expenses, lost wages, and any settlements (for pain and suffering) and legal expenses. It will also kick in to cover repairing or replacing property you may have damaged. Most states require that you have at least $50,000 of coverage per person and $100,000 per accident. But that isn't enough. The Insurance Information Institute recommends at least $100,000 worth of coverage per person, $300,000 per accident, and $50,000 for property damage liability. If you're worth more than $300,000 that's *still* not enough. You'll want an additional liability policy—called an *umbrella policy*—as well (see page 150).

• **Medical payments/personal injury protection.** If you're involved in an accident where you or others in a car you're driving are injured, medical payments coverage will pay for your medical expenses and for the funerals of anyone who is killed. It's pretty liberal in that you don't have to be driving your own car; you can be at the wheel of someone else's (as long as you didn't run off with the car without permission). This protection also covers you or your family members if you're injured while walking. It can also pay for missed wages if an accident keeps you out of work.

• **Uninsured/underinsured motorists.** If you're injured by a driver who doesn't have enough auto insurance or any at all, this component will pay medical and funeral expenses for you and your family. Like liability insurance, buying this component is required in some states. If it's not, buy it anyway. It's inexpensive—as little as $5 to $10 in some states for $100,000 of coverage—and it's crucial.

• **Other.** Some policies also offer other add-ons like reimbursement for a rental car if yours is in the shop or stolen, broken glass coverage, or coverage for towing and other emergency road service. I've used the rental car reimbursement feature myself and think it's worth having (at a typical cost of $20 to $30). You don't need towing coverage if you're a member of AAA. Some luxury auto manufacturers are also throwing in a towing package, gratis.

How Do You Get the Best Rates?

First, understand, being loyal to a single insurer can cost you. In 1999, *Consumer Reports* surveyed its readers and found that they had been loyal to their carriers for eleven years; 75 percent regularly renewed their coverage without shopping around. That's a mistake. Safer cars (with air bags and antilock brakes) with tougher theft protection devices, coupled with the aging of the population, have boosted profit margins for auto insurers. They're willing to pass those savings on to consumers in the form of cheaper rates—but you're not going to get a discount unless you ask for one and shop around. The Insurance Information Institute suggests you call at least three different insurers before making a decision. These should not only include a traditional insurance agent, but a direct writer like GEICO or Progressive that sells via an 800 number. Spending an hour or two on the phone can save you serious money.

Also, don't forget the Web. Two recent surveys, from Progressive, the country's fourth largest insurer, and InsWeb, a leading insurance site, found that electronic shoppers could save $400 to $500 a year over their current auto insurance rates. Typically, you fill out a brief online questionnaire providing details about your car and driving record and you receive quotes in return. You should also:

- **Buy the right car.** Say you're choosing between a Dodge Intrepid and a Mustang GT. Similar price tag. But the cost of insuring the Mustang is nearly double that of the Intrepid. Why? The Mustang is stolen more often and has a higher accident rate. Moral: Call your insurer for a quote before you buy a car.
- **Increase your deductible.** Raising your deductible on the collision/comprehensive component of your coverage from $250 to $500 will save you 15 to 30 percent annually. Increasing it from $250 to $1,000 should save you 30 percent or more. And if your car is worth less than $3,000 to $4,000, think about dropping this coverage altogether.
- **Stop commuting.** Retirees who stop driving to work (and cut their annual miles in half) can typically get a 20 percent discount on their policies, and so can you. If you put fewer than 7,500 miles on your car each year you may qualify for a similar discount. You can also usually lop 10 percent off your auto insurance premium by taking a defensive driving course. Just remember to ask for the discounts.
- **Stick with one carrier.** Insuring your house and your car (or, better yet, *cars*) with the same company can net you a 15 to 20 percent discount.
- **Watch your credit rating.** Auto insurers have discovered that your bill-paying patterns are even more indicative of the number of claims you'll file than your driving record: yet another reason to pay your bills on time.
- **Ask about other discounts.** You may be able to cut your rate by being a good driver (with no accidents in the past three years), the parent of a good student, or mature (over age fifty), and if your car has air bags, antilock brakes, or other safety devices, and an antitheft system. And if you're a nonsmoker, some insurers will slash up to 30 percent off the medical portion of your premium.
- **Don't file too many claims.** Insurance companies will penalize you for filing more than one claim in a two- to three-year period. In

some states, insurers aren't allowed to penalize you for accidents you didn't cause, but in other states you may be better off paying small claims out of your own pocket instead of reporting them.

Umbrella Liability Coverage

You already know that we live in a litigious society. That's why you need liability coverage on your home. It will write a nice check in case someone slips and falls on your wet bathroom floor and sues you. As with auto insurance, most homeowners policies come with $100,000 to $300,000 of coverage. But unless you're worth less than that (including all your assets), you should buy more in the form of an umbrella liability policy.

Umbrella liability insurance is a relatively inexpensive way to make sure you have complete liability protection on all of your turf as well as your car. It may also cover you in other liability cases, such as if someone sues you for libel. And basic umbrella coverage may include all owner-occupied residences, up to four rental units, drivers under twenty-five, and small boats.

Typically, umbrella policies start to pay only after the liability protection under your homeowners or auto policy exhausts itself. To make the purchase most cost-effective, you'll want to increase the liability coverage on both your home and auto insurance to $300,000 before you buy the umbrella. According to the Insurance Information Institute, you should then be able to buy $1 million of umbrella coverage for $150 to $300.

Disability Insurance

All employed adults need disability insurance, but only about 60 percent of them have it. Particularly for single people who don't have another income (or potential wage-earner) to fall back on, disability insurance is crucial. Even if you are receiving some disability coverage through your employer, chances are it's not enough.

Your disability policy should cover 60 to 70 percent of your gross income. Don't expect a policy to pay more than that. Insurers are willing to cover you but they also want to be certain that you have some incentive to return to work. It's also important to look for a policy that covers your ability to work in your own occupation, rather than to work at all—and not just for two years, as most policies do, but on an ongoing basis. There aren't as many ongoing, "own-occupation" policies in the marketplace as there used to be because of the high number of claims, but they do exist. It is usually higher-paid professionals who get own-occupation policies, including doctors, lawyers, architects, and so forth. If a surgeon hurts his hand, for example, he might be able to earn a living as a medical lecturer, but he may not want to. The difference in cost between an own-occupation plan and one that simply covers your ability to work at all should be about 20 percent.

To complicate matters further, that own-occupation coverage—which sometimes comes in the form of a rider—isn't the only add-on that disability insurers are pushing. From inflation protection to nursing home coverage, insurers have thought of lots of extras to sell you. We'll get to them momentarily. Your first goal is to make sure that you have enough basic disability to cover you, just in case.

The basics. Here's what you want in a basic policy. First, make sure your insurance company is financially strong and in the top three or four rating categories. You'll also want to make sure that the waiting period from the time of your disability to when the benefits kick in is reasonable considering your current financial situation. Benefits might pay for one year, two years, five years, or—best of all—until you're sixty-five. Of course, they also stop if and when you go back to work. If you don't require own-occupation coverage, the key thing to think about is income replacement. Try to make sure that full benefits are the equivalent to your current after-tax salary. If, due to a disability, you are limited to working part-time, then you may receive partial benefits to make up for the lost income. Some policies will provide total benefits for a specified period, say five years, but discontinue benefits if you are unwilling to work in another occupation. If you have preexisting medical conditions, you should also ask an insurance broker to help you find a policy—and once you get it, don't ever cancel it!

The extras. In addition to a basic liability policy, there can be many add-ons. You may save money on premiums, for example, by purchasing an accident-only policy, which only pays benefits if your disability is the result of an accident but excludes many illnesses. You may pay more for a guarantee to renew your policy without a medical exam, or for a cost of living adjustment rider. Another rider, which many upwardly mobile people choose, is an automatic increase option, which increases your benefits as your salary rises. Also popular is a Social Security rider, which will pay you in the event of a disability that Social Security doesn't recognize as such. Even if you get basic disability insurance through your employer, you may want to consider purchasing a supplemental policy with some of these features.

Long-Term Care Insurance

As the U.S. senior population grows, many people are asking whether they should buy long-term care insurance—to pay nursing or home health care costs—either for themselves or for their aging parents. The answer is: Perhaps. Think of long-term care insurance as insurance in the truest sense of the word—because the likelihood that you'll use it is slim. Forty-three percent of people sixty-five and older spend some time in a nursing home, but more than half of them spend less than a year, and only 9 percent spend more than five years. The waiting period before your policy kicks in can vary, typically from thirty days up to a year.

Realistically, long-term care policies make the most sense for people with a net worth of $200,000 to $1 million. Those with less will exhaust their assets and qualify for Medicaid; those with more can probably invest their assets and fund their own care.

More than 120 insurers offer long-term care policies, with average premiums from several hundred to several thousand dollars a year. And you ought to be dealing with only the most reputable. As with every other type of insurance we've talked about in this chapter, you need to get at least three quotes. Here are the other rules of the road:

- **Buy young.** Though the motivation is rarely there when you're young, you can purchase long-term care insurance at any time. And if you are young, your premiums—and chance of rejection—will be much lower. Start shopping around age sixty.
- **Shop for a policy with a three-year term.** Why? Most people who turn out to need long-term care need it for two and a half years. And, though it's controversial, going this route gives you the option—which some choose—to transfer your assets in order to qualify for Medicaid.
- **Buy flexible coverage.** Get a policy that covers not only a stay in a nursing home, but home health care, particularly if you think you'd like to stay at home (and who wouldn't) for as long as possible.
- **Keep an eye on costs.** Look for a daily benefit at least as large as the average daily nursing home cost in the states that you may want to reside in a nursing home (it does not necessarily have to be the state you currently live in; perhaps it will be where a friend or relative lives).
- **Inspect policy triggers.** The best policies kick in as soon as a physician says that care is necessary, but in other cases policyholders need to be unable to perform certain tasks like feeding themselves, dressing themselves, bathing, and so on, before a policy will pay out. You want as much wiggle room as possible here. A seasoned agent who knows the language is an invaluable resource.
- **Buffer your costs with a waiting period.** To keep costs down, make sure you get an elimination period (the amount of time before payment kicks in) of ninety days. Most people can afford to pay for their own care for three months. And the price difference between a policy that kicks in on Day 90 and one that kicks in on Day 1 can be 30 percent.

THE BIG THREE: THINGS TO TAKE AWAY FROM TALKING INSURANCE

1. Get a grip on your own needs first. Insurance, primarily life insurance but to some extent all types, is sold much more often than it's bought. The best way to make sure you don't waste money on coverage you don't need is to know what those needs are to begin with.

2. Most people don't have sufficient (sometimes any) of the following types of insurance: disability insurance, renters insurance, umbrella liability insurance. On the other side of the coin, there are many policies that most people don't need: credit life insurance, mortgage life insurance, travel accident insurance, and—if you're a single individual with no one relying on your income—*any* life insurance.

3. In the homeowners and auto insurance arenas, discounts abound. Ask for the right ones and you can cut your total bill by one third. Among them: discounts for driving fewer miles, for having state-of-the-art security equipment (in both your home and your car), and using one carrier for both coverages.

CHAPTER 7

Talking About the Things You Don't Want to Talk About (aka Talking Estate Planning)

W hen Lisa was thirty-three years old, her husband died suddenly, leaving her with three children—ages five months, two, and nine—to raise on her own. Thankfully, he'd thought ahead. He'd established a trust, worth $1.2 million, naming Lisa and his kids as the primary beneficiaries, and a sister, two brothers, and two of his friends as secondary beneficiaries. His intention was for Lisa and the kids to live on the money, while his friends and siblings only had the right to ask for a payout in an emergency: if they got sick or lost a job, for example. "He was the kind of guy who wanted to take care of everyone," Lisa recalls. Unfortunately, he went a little too far, naming the two friends trustees as well, essentially giving them control over the entire $1.2 million pie.

At first, Lisa didn't realize she had a problem. Every month she received payments from the trust, which, while they didn't allow her to live lavishly, covered her household expenses. When she remarried two years later, however, she and her new husband took a closer look at the trust's accounting—and they discovered that one of the trustees had been using the money to make unsecured loans to himself and his friends. Within four years, nearly 90 percent of the trust was comprised of these loans, most of which were being paid back sporadically, if at all. The terms were excessively generous: One borrower had thirty-six years to repay $7,000. They also discovered mountains of checks made out by the trustee to such inappropriate recipients as lawn care companies and tanning salons. To make matters worse, the other trustee either hadn't noticed—or had looked the other way.

Lisa tried to get the trustee to turn over the records and provide a full accounting. But by law he was forced to do so only once a year. Finally, she hired a lawyer and forensic accountant—think of an accounting detective—who confirmed her fears. "Several lawyers said it was the worst-written trust they'd ever seen," she recalls. "It gave the trustee almost unlimited power, with no oversight, no checks and balances. I was advised to do everything possible just to get rid of the trustee. It took a year, but he finally agreed to step down." Today the assets—which should have multiplied in the bull market—are worth just $300,000. "My CPA estimates that if it had been prudently invested for the last seven years or so in the stock market, even by conservative estimates, it would be worth between $2 and $3 million. It kills me to think about that," says Lisa. "That was my children's inheritance."

A terrible story, particularly because this was a set of parents who actually tried to take care of their estate planning responsibilities—and failed. Many people don't do nearly *that* much. One of them, knowing that I was working on this book, sent me this e-mail a few months back. "Please don't attach our names to this," she wrote. "Too ashamed." Her confession? "We don't have wills. We kept delaying ostensibly because we thought we were moving and different states have different rules. But really, it's one of those things that we talk about but never quite get around to doing. In the meantime, we are incredibly irresponsible, with a toddler and a baby on the way and no will. I hate to even admit this, it's so terrible," she continued. "Our families do have a general idea of what we would want, but not anywhere near the kind of detail they *should* have. In fact, as I write this, I'm thinking we *must* do this before the new baby arrives."

Behavior like this defies logic: We are willing to go to such great lengths to take care of our children, to make sure that they're *happy*. We get up before the crack of dawn and drive them to hockey practice or soccer practice so that they can make the team. We make sure they have music lessons, skating lessons, swimming lessons, French lessons, whatever it takes to turn them into well-rounded individuals. We shepherd them off to SAT tutoring services and college counselors, to give them the best shot at getting into a terrific school. We wait in line for hours so that they can see the Pokémon movie (or whatever the latest craze happens to be) on its first weekend. Where our children are concerned, we go to lengths that we wouldn't go to for ourselves. And yet . . .

Nearly three quarters of us don't have wills.

I hope that statistic, from a landmark *Consumer Reports* survey, landed with a nice round thud. It was meant to. Because the bottom line is this: Nobody is going to want to take care of *your own kids* as much as *you* do. So, if you're one of those many, many parents who haven't given the basics of an estate plan—including a will and guardians for your kids—much thought, it's time.

For many people, though, basic wills aren't enough. As soon as you've accumulated an estate worth more than $1.5 million—which isn't as much as it sounds when you consider that your estate includes your home, your pension, your retirement accounts, *and* your life insurance (assuming your spouse receives the payout)— then you need to start thinking about estate planning to save money. You need the strategies outlined in this chapter to make sure that it gets into the proper hands both before and after you die—and that the government gets as little of it as is legally possible.

Finally, we'll talk about giving money away (a major part of the estate planning job), and also about receiving it. With more than 650,000 *different* charitable organizations looking for a handout, choosing a charity is more complicated than ever before. We'll walk through how to do it.

The Musts: Estate Planning Basics You Shouldn't Be Without

Our son, Jake, was a baby when Peter and I had our wills drawn up for the first time. The impetus for us, as for many people, was an airplane. We were going somewhere—funny, I have no memory of where—without Jake. On an airplane. So *of course* we needed a will. I like to think that if I had it to do over again, I might have pushed to have our wills drawn up before he was born. Not doing so was a mistake. But, like many people, I was reluctant. I didn't want to think about anything happening to me, because that might imply that I wouldn't be around to raise this child. And what parent wants to entertain thoughts like that?

But we did sit down with an estate planning attorney named Ashley Steinhardt. And it wasn't as gut-wrenching an afternoon as I thought it was going to be. Steinhardt walked us through all the necessary decisions, from choosing guardians, to developing a plan to pass our assets along to a minor child, to taking other children—whom we weren't even thinking about at the time—into account. He found appropriate ways to ask us questions about the strength of our marriage: to determine if the answers we were giving him belonged to both of us or, in reality, just one. I left feeling clearer about our choices than when we arrived. I felt relaxed. And by the time we received the documents in the mail, a week or so later, I was emotionally prepared to sign them. We sat down at a friend's kitchen table (you'll need witnesses) and did it that weekend.

In addition to our wills, Steinhardt helped us make the following decisions and obtain the other documents we needed. I've called them "The Musts" because most of them are items you must have, while the others are processes you must go through. Here's the lowdown:

The Musts: A Will

Let's just talk for a minute about what a will is. It's a legal document that tells the world, the court system, and your heirs how and to whom you want your assets (and your liabilities, for that matter) handled after you die. It dictates what assets should be given to whom, what to do with your remaining property (sell it, give it to charity, use it to pay off any remaining debts you might have), who will care for your minor children as their legal guardians, and whose job it is to carry all these instructions out, as your executor. A will can be very simple (documents purchased in stationery stores for a couple of bucks have been known to stand up in court, and though I wouldn't recommend going that route, it's better than nothing). You can do it yourself with the help of a software program like Will-maker from Nolo Press (it runs around $60). Or you can have one drawn up by an attorney for about $500 and up.

Who needs a will? Anyone and everyone—married, single, divorced, or widowed—who cares what happens to his or her stuff. Why? Because if you die without leaving the court system a set of legal instructions, you die *intestate,* which means that some judge you've never met is going to make the decisions for you based on rules your particular state has established. Among them:

- Who your assets will go to. In most states if you die intestate, they'll go to your spouse, then your kids (or some combination of the two), then your parents, siblings, and on down the line. For people who aren't married that's often bad news, particularly if you have a significant other you'd like to take care of. Unless they're mentioned in your will, they'll get nothing.
- Should you and your spouse both die, your assets will go to your kids, as you'd probably desire. But if your kids are minors and you haven't chosen guardians and executors in your will, your assets will be managed (perhaps not well) by someone not of your own choosing. You were saving for four years at Duke? Tough luck. If the court-appointed financial custodian thinks that's too expensive, your kids may be going to state schools. The court will also go through the often harrowing process of picking guardians for your

kids—with little to no prior knowledge of the relationships in your family.

Is that what you want?

The Musts: Picking Guardians

If you're a parent, naming guardians for your kids is a struggle—no two ways about it. You don't want to have to decide, formally and on paper, whether you'd prefer to ask your brother or sister-in-law or your best friend from college to take on this responsibility. Your reluctance is perfectly understandable. But it's not excusable. So let's decide now that you're going to get over it. Try to think of choosing a guardian as if it were any other decision you had to make, except that you have to make this one right away. Think of it like buying a car or refinancing your mortgage and approach it methodically. (And I'll let you in on a little secret: Once you've selected a guardian, other than asking them if they're willing and filling in their names on the dotted line, *no one else needs to know.*)

So sit down at the kitchen table with your spouse, pencil and paper, and a pint of Ben & Jerry's if you need it for strength, and list everyone who could possibly fill this role. Then, using the following criteria, start evaluating:

• **Health.** You want someone who will live for many years and who is in good overall physical condition. Siblings, for this reason, are probably better choices than your parents.

• **Resources.** The person you choose should have the time and (if your child won't be financially self-sufficient) the money to handle the responsibility. Picking someone who already has parenting experience is a plus, but make sure they're not too overloaded with their own offspring to handle yours.

• **Like mind.** You want someone who shares your views on education, religion, and other things that matter to you.

• **Geographical desirability.** Choosing someone who lives nearby is a plus—moving a child after they've just lost one or both parents makes a difficult time even more stressful.

- **One vs. two.** Because of the high divorce rate, if you're inclined to choose a married couple—say your sister and her husband—many estate planners advise naming just one of them or both, contingent upon the fact that they're still married.

Once you've narrowed down your list, you need to ask the person you've selected if he or she is willing to take on this responsibility. This is not the sort of request you want to spring on someone. Do it in person, perhaps over dinner. And should your life change—should you have another child or two, or should your choice of guardian get divorced or fall on hard times of her own—go back and revisit the issue. Run through the questions again and make sure this person would still be your top choice. It's not only legal to change your mind and name someone else, it's perfectly acceptable, as long as you handle it tactfully. Thank the original choice for being willing and explain why you've changed course. Then make sure you revise your will to reflect your new wishes.

The Musts: Durable Power of Attorney for Finances

A durable power of attorney for finances is a document that gives another person the ability to make financial decisions for you if you become incapacitated and unable to do so for yourself. That person can access your accounts and sign your checks in order to pay your bills, buy and sell stocks for your portfolio if necessary, even make $10,000 annual gifts to your kids or grandkids if you were in the habit of doing so yourself. Many estate planners will include a durable power of attorney in part of a basic estate package. Others will charge anywhere from $100 to a few hundred dollars for drawing up the document.

It's well worth having because it can save you, your heirs, and your estate from a costly and harrowing court proceeding over guardianship. Say your older parent, long widowed, becomes incapacitated and as a result his financial life starts to unravel. Bills are going unpaid. Creditors are calling. Without power of attorney, you can't legally handle his finances. Instead, you have to go to court and ask to be named his legal guardian. Not only do you have to make a good case, but if your siblings, for example, want to challenge it, you could be in for a lengthy and expensive battle. And even if you are appointed guardian or conservator by the court, you'll have to report in to the court frequently, filing documents on how assets are performing, and how much money is being spent. People who've been through this process say it's a nightmare. Having power of attorney is the way to avoid it.

Whom should you give this important power to? Most people give it to their spouse or an adult child, a sibling, or a trusted friend. It should be someone who is comfortable enough with his or her own finances to be able to handle yours. If you have no family members or friends whom you trust to make sound financial decisions, you can give power of attorney to your longtime accountant or attorney.

The Musts: Medical Directives

Depending on the state in which you live, you may need one medical directive or you may need two. Let's talk about them separately first. Just as a durable power of attorney for finance gives a person the right to make decisions about your money if you can't do so for yourself, a *durable power of attorney for health care* (also sometimes called a *health care proxy*) gives another individual you choose the right to make medical decisions for you if you can't make them for yourself. A *living will* is the other document you'll want. It tells your loved ones (and the staff of a hospital) how you wish to be cared for in case you become terminally ill and includes instructions about whether you wish to be placed on life support. In some states both of these have been replaced by a single document called a *medical directive*. Hospitals and nursing homes often hand copies of these out and ask you to sign them before you're admitted, but it's better to have handled these matters beforehand. You can get copies from estate planning attorneys, at stores that sell legal forms, and through Choice in Dying, a not-for-profit group, at 800-989-9455.

The Musts: Schedule Regular Estate Checkups

You don't have to schedule an estate checkup every six months as if it were a teeth-cleaning, or even once a year as if it were a physical. Every three years will do. At that point, you'll want to schedule an hour with your estate planning attorney (or make the time to sit down in front of your computer if you drew up your wills yourself). Run through the decisions you made. Are they still appropriate? Are there other assets (or other people) that must be considered? Are you in a position to give some of your money away? It won't take you nearly as much time (or as much courage) as drawing up your plan did originally—that's the good news—but you have to do it to keep your plan up to date.

The Musts: Organize Your Important Papers

As you're going through and making sure you have your basic estate plan in order, there's one other thing you have to do: Clue in your kids or your other primary heirs on where the important documents are. Are they in the top drawer of your desk? Are they in the bottom of your file cabinet? And where's the key to the safe deposit box?

As for what belongs in the desk drawer vs. the safe deposit box, the latter is in fact the safest place you have (it's free of risk from at-home fires and also from tampering—unless you give someone a key). But there are certain documents you may need access to in the middle of the night. By and large, they're also replaceable; in the event of a fire, you could get copies, but you may also want to consider purchasing a fire-retardant safe (there's really no such thing as a fire*proof* one) for home use. Note: Some of the items are on both lists. That's not a mistake. Your lawyer should also have copies of your will, medical directives, power of attorney, burial instructions, and any trusts in his or her office for safekeeping.

Safe Deposit Box (or, as second choice, a fire-retardant safe):

- Deeds and titles
- Marriage licenses and divorce decrees

- Birth certificates
- Home inventory
- Social Security cards
- Stock certificates
- List of bank accounts, brokerage accounts, certificates of deposit, and credit cards (with account numbers and branch locations)

In a Drawer at Home:

- Insurance policies
- Passport
- Tax returns (past seven years)
- Wills and trusts
- Power of attorney
- Medical directives
- Funeral and burial instructions
- List of bank accounts, brokerage accounts, certificates of deposit, and credit cards (with account numbers and branch locations)

One Big Maybe: Living Trusts

During the early 1990s, there was a big brouhaha over living trusts. Some financial advisers and many attorneys (who were, of course, selling these things) were foaming at the mouth about how these "will substitutes" were the solution to every estate nightmare you'd ever heard of, and some you probably hadn't. They were wrong from the get-go. First, living trusts aren't will substitutes. In order to make them work as well as possible, you also need a will. But I'm getting ahead of myself.

Let's talk about what living trusts are and what they do. Unlike many of the trusts we'll talk about in the next section, living trusts are "revocable." That means you have control over the assets in your living trust, which you can change at any time, and that in most cases you are the trustee; you name a successor trustee to do the job if for some reason you can't. The big advantage of a living trust is that any assets you've put in the trust can move to your heirs without having to go through probate, the court process where your will is looked over and decided to be valid. In some states (notably Florida) probate can be a major hassle, taking years to complete, and during those years your assets will be frozen. Nor is the process private: Anyone who's interested can have a look at your will if they're willing to make the effort. If you have a living trust, in contrast, your assets pass privately. Probate can also be costly. The lawyer you hire to shepherd you through may charge as much as 5 percent of the estate. But living trusts aren't cheap, either. These documents cost at least a few thousand dollars to draw up, which makes them more expensive than wills.

The problem with living trusts is that many people believe (or, I should say, are led to believe) that all you need to do is *get* one and then you'll be set. In reality, if all you have is the document, you have nothing. In order to make your living trust work as it's supposed to, you must also retitle all of your assets so that they no longer belong to you, but instead belong to your trust. That way, the trust will have the power to pass those assets along at your death. After setting up your trust, you must also place anything major that you purchase in the trust's name. You also need what's called a "pour-over will" to instruct that any assets you haven't included in your trust be moved into it when you die.

Finally, despite what you hear in advertisements on the radio (these really bug me!), a living trust won't save you one cent on estate taxes. For that, you need a proper estate plan (and a good attorney) to make sure your assets move at your death from your living trust and into the marital and other trusts that we talk about below.

Five Questions to Ask Your Attorney About Estate Planning

1. When should I start planning my estate? "As soon as you have a child, you need a will," says New York estate planning attorney Gideon Rothschild. "Before that, it depends on your assets and if you're happy with the way state law would dictate your estate be dispersed." Typically, if you die without a will, your entire estate will go to your next of kin. In order, that's your spouse, children, parents, siblings, grandparents, and so on. If you're engaged to be married, for example, you might want your fiancé to inherit some or all of your estate. That couldn't happen without a will. Or you may want some assets to go to charity. Again, you need a will to make that happen.

2. Are you the right person for the job? If your attorney is a general practitioner, he or she should be able to handle your estate planning provided your estate isn't too large and your wishes are simple. If that's not the case—if your estate is over $675,000, which means you'll be dealing with tax issues, or if you're trying not to leave assets to the usual heirs—you'll want an estate planning attorney skilled in writing trusts. Their rates are likely to be a little higher, but in the end their expertise will probably save you money. Getting a referral from a friend or colleague is best, but you can search for one at www.estateplanning.com, which maintains a database of estate planning attorneys nationwide.

3. How much will it cost? Just as the cost of living varies from one region of the country to another, so does the cost of lawyering. A basic package—a will, durable power of attorney, living will, and health care proxy—for a nontaxable estate (less than $675,000) might run $500 to $1,500. Estate planning for an uncomplicated but taxable estate between $675,000 and $2 million would likely be about $500 higher. But if you start getting into more complicated trusts—insurance trusts, for example—you're looking at another $1,500 (and very complicated estates—more complicated than we'll get into here—can run ten times that).

Red Flag! If your estate and the trusts you want to establish are simple, you should be able to pay on a project basis, meaning that you pay a predetermined rate for all the work your attorney will do. Only pay your attorney by the hour if your estate is very complex.

4. Will I have to pay estate taxes? You won't, but your heirs might have to pay them out of your estate. The government gives each person a sizable freebie—called the *unified credit*—which currently allows you to pass along tax free $675,000 worth of assets from your estate to whomever you'd like. After that point, assets in your estate are taxed according to a sliding scale that runs from 37 to 55 percent. To determine the value of your estate, total your assets (include property, business interests, retirement plans, investments, and life insurance policies that will benefit a spouse) and subtract your debts. (See below for ways to save your heirs on estate taxes—and, in some cases, to save money on your own taxes while you're still alive.)

5. How can I reduce the tax bill on my estate (or better yet, eliminate it)? If you're over the $675,000 line ($1.35 million for couples) there are things you can do to lower the tax bite, but you'll need an estate planning attorney to help. Things to consider include giving money away (you're allowed to give up to $10,000 annually to as many people as you want with no tax consequences for either party), and putting money into trusts. (See below.)

Red Flag! Beware of any attorney who tries to convince you that a living trust will reduce your tax bill. It won't. They're also expensive to establish—and they don't eliminate the need for the will you probably asked for in the first place.

Beyond the Musts: Estate Planning to Save Taxes

In Chapter 3, we talked about your net worth and how to make sure it was headed in the right direction (up, naturally), by boosting your saving and tracking your spending. For estate planning purposes, you absolutely have to know what your net worth is. As you may

recall, the basic definition is all of your assets minus all of your liabilities. You can get to a specific number by doing the following:
Add up:

- The value of your home and any other real estate
- Your pension and retirement account balances
- Your bank account balances
- Your brokerage account balances
- The proceeds of life insurance plans that will benefit a spouse
- The value of your car(s)
- The value of any businesses you own
- Valuable property (jewelry, art, etc.)
- Anything else of value you own

Then subtract:

- Your mortgage(s)
- Your car loan(s)
- Credit card debt
- Student loans
- Other debts

You don't have to run these numbers to the penny. It's fine to ballpark them. What you're really trying to find out is whether you're worth more than $675,000 (in 2001), if you're a single person, or $1,350,000 if you're a couple. If you're above those levels, you need to read on. If you're not quite there yet, but are quickly approaching those levels, keep going, too.

Here's why you need this information: As we said earlier, Uncle Sam gives each person a huge gift called the *unified credit*. Essentially, this gives each individual person the right to bequeath (either during life or at death) an estate of up to $675,000 free of estate taxes. Money you give away beyond that amount, even at death, is taxed heavily—rates start at 37 percent and climb to 55 percent for estates over $3 million.

The best news I can give you about the unified credit is that it's rising. It's scheduled to top out at $1 million per person, $2 million per couple in 2006. Some people (in fact, some very smart people) use their unified credit during life. More people do so at death. The problem is that many married people don't use it at all.

In fact, they lose it. Why? Because in addition to giving each person a unified credit, the government also allows you to pass *all* of your assets to your spouse at death, tax free. So here's what happens. Say the husband in a couple with more than $1,350,000 in assets dies, passing everything on to his wife. By doing so, he has lost the ability to use his unified credit to pass assets on to his children or other heirs. When she dies, years later, her estate is worth more than $675,000. She can pass along that amount tax free using her own unified credit, but estate taxes must be paid on the rest.

Fortunately, paying at least some of those taxes is avoidable if you use a few tried-and-true estate planning strategies. All of the techniques we'll talk about here are ones estate planning attorneys use to try to whittle a person's taxable estate down to beneath that $675,000 ceiling—or, where very wealthy people are concerned, to the most manageable size possible. If you decide you want to pursue any of these strategies yourself, I wouldn't recommend doing it with software. Find yourself a good estate planning attorney (not a generalist who occasionally does wills, but a specialist) and make an appointment. It's worth the money you'll spend.

Retitling Select Assets (Owning Everything Jointly Is a Bad Idea)

When you buy a house with a spouse or life partner, you typically put both of your names on the deed. Same with your car. Same with the brokerage account you open to invest for retirement. The nice thing about jointly held assets—and the reason some financial planners recommend them—is that when one spouse dies, the assets pass to the survivor automatically. They're not part of the will, so they don't have to go through probate.

The problem with jointly holding all or most of your major assets, as many couples do, is that they'll automatically end up in one set of hands somewhere down the road. That practically guarantees you'll miss out on using one of the two unified credits; so, depending on your assets, you may end up saddling your estate with a big tax bill. Worse, many couples use joint ownership as an excuse not to have a will or other form of actual estate plan. The result of this sort of nonplanning is that when that second spouse dies, all the property goes to his or her relatives in the order designated by the state—not, as you might have liked, to both sides of the family.

Annual Gifts

Here's another of Uncle Sam's freebies: The tax laws allow every person to give up to $10,000 each year to as many individuals as they wish without having to pay gift tax. This means that couples can give up to $20,000 to any person they want—and that one couple can give another couple $40,000 in a single year without paying any taxes whatsoever. (Note: If the couple is married, the spouses can make a joint $20,000 gift; unmarried couples can achieve the same end result, but they need to give two $10,000 individual gifts.) The gifts can of course be cash, but they can also be shares of stock or pieces of a home. And used over time, they can be very, very powerful. Let's say you and your spouse, who've done quite well over the years, decide that you're going to try to whittle down your estate by giving $10,000 each (that's $20,000 together) to your three kids, their three spouses, and their four combined children. That's $200,000 each year. Over a half decade, you could dump $1 million out of your estate with no tax consequences whatsoever. And in the process you could send your grandchildren to private school, even help them put a down payment on a house or two.

Gifts Over $10,000 (Singles), $20,000 (Couples)

One thing people don't often consider—in this flurry to protect their unified credit—is that it may be smart to use that credit while you're still living. Why? Because holding assets in your own estate gives them time to appreciate. The more they appreciate while they're still in your hands, the more taxes will be owed on your own estate *eventually*. And if you *do* want to give away shares of stock that have greatly appreciated during life, while at the same time lowering the value of your estate, it may make sense to consider selling the stock yourself, paying the tax, repurchasing the same shares, and then giving them away. That way, your recipient could sell the shares without owing any additional capital gains and, despite making a taxable gift, you've reduced the size of your estate even more.

Marital (Bypass) Trusts

There are many ways to preserve your unified credit, but this is one of the easiest. It involves hiring an estate planning attorney to draw up two different trusts, one for each spouse. When the first spouse, say the husband, passes away, his will dictates that his trust be "funded"—in other words, that up to $675,000 (the current amount protected by the unified credit) be put into his trust even after his death. While the assets are in the trust, they are managed by someone he chose—preferably someone who will keep his wife's needs in mind. She can collect any income the trust generates and she may also (depending on the wording of the trust) be able to tap into the principal in certain emergencies—for medical reasons, special needs, and even at the discretion of the trustee (which is why you want a trustee who is certain to keep your spouse's best interests at heart). When the wife also passes away, the assets in the trust pass to the heirs, tax free. It's important to understand, however, that marital trusts are among the many trusts on this list that are *irrevocable,* meaning they can't be undone. The risk of putting the money in trust is that if your spouse needs more income than the trust generates, the trustee may not, in all cases, have the power to give her more—or may simply decide not to give her more. That's why you must be sure you both understand the ramifications when you establish marital trusts in the first place.

Trusts for People Who've Been Married More than Once

If you have more than one family—say a set of kids from your first marriage whom you'd like to be your ultimate heirs, plus a second wife you'd like to take care of as long as she lives—then you ought to consider a QTIP trust (or, in many cases, a marital trust along with a QTIP trust). QTIP stands for qualified terminable interest property, and it works like this: When you die, the first $675,000 of your estate moves into your marital trust, leaving the balance behind. Rather than passing directly to your second wife, the leftover balance goes into a QTIP trust from which she gets all the income. She can even get at the principal as long as the executor or trustee deems it necessary (most typically for medical reasons). The point is that the ultimate heirs of this trust, just like the heirs of your bypass trust, are still your kids. If your second wife remarries and has another set of children, for example; or if she has kids from *her* first marriage, you don't have to worry about them vying for your estate. Your kids will remain the beneficiaries.

Insurance Trusts

You probably know who's set to benefit from your life insurance policy. But have you thought about who *owns* it? The question is important, because while life insurance payouts aren't subject to income taxes, if you own the policy you took out on your own life, then it's considered part of your estate—and will be taxed that way.

If your beneficiary is your spouse, no taxes will be paid on the first death—because everything moves from one spouse to another tax free (though you'll want to make sure you have marital trusts established to protect your unified credit). But if you're single, or if the second spouse in a couple dies, things get expensive. The solution is to make sure that you don't own your own life insurance policy, but that instead it's owned by an irrevocable life insurance trust. If you're thinking ahead, you can have the trust buy the policy in the first place. You can name the beneficiary, but the policy will never be part of your estate. Or, if you've already purchased a policy, you can transfer ownership of that policy to an irrevocable trust. Do it sooner rather than later: You have to live three years beyond the transfer for it to be considered valid. If you die before the three years are up, the policy will move back into your estate and will be taxed that way.

Gifts to Charity

Unlike giving to a person, when you give to a charity, you're not limited in the amount you can hand off. One gift that makes a lot of sense: appreciated stock. Here's how it works. Say you'd like to give $10,000 to the American Heart Association this year. You can, of course, simply write a check—and in return, you'll get a tax deduction in that amount. But let's say you also bought 1,000 shares of ABC.com at $10, and they're now worth $100 each. If you sold 100 shares, netting you the $10,000 you'd like to donate, you'd owe capital gains taxes at a rate of 20 percent on your $9,000 gain. Your take would only be $8,200—and you'd have to kick in another $1,800 from your bank account to make up the difference, or sell more stock. But if you instead donate the stock itself to the Heart Association, you'd get the full $10,000 tax deduction. Then the charity—which pays no taxes itself—could sell the shares and keep the entire amount.

If you don't feel comfortable moving sizable assets out of your estate while you're still alive, you can also make a donation by purchasing a life insurance policy and naming the charity as beneficiary. The money you use to purchase that policy is considered a gift to the charity by the IRS, and therefore the premiums are deductible.

Charitable Trusts

If you'd like to remember your favorite charity when you die, as well as your heirs, using a charitable trust can be a crafty, even opportunistic, way to do it. Not only will your favorite cause benefit, but so will you—while you're alive.

You put an appreciated asset, say, shares of stock now worth $100,000 but that you purchased for much less, in trust for a charity you designate. The charity can't take the asset out of trust until you die, but for now it can sell the asset, invest the money, and pay you income at a fixed rate of at least 5 percent for a period you designate—usually as long as you and your spouse live. In return, you get an immediate income tax deduction for the value of your gift.

Here's where it gets a little tricky! The value of your gift isn't the actual amount of your gift, but the amount the IRS believes the charity will ultimately receive, based on your age, the amount of income you're drawing from the trust while you're alive, and projected interest rates. As an example, if you're in your forties and are taking income of 10 percent a year from a charitable trust, your deduction will be in the range of 15 percent of the original gift amount—but it could be twice that for people in their seventies.

The benefit: These trusts can allow you to give more to charity than you'd otherwise feel comfortable with. On that $100,000, for example, you'd typically be able to earn $7,000 to $10,000 a year, often more income than you'd be getting from CDs or some other safe investment. And note: If you're worried that you're giving away your kids' inheritance, there's a way around that, too. Use some of the income that you get from the trust to purchase a life insurance policy on yourself. As we said earlier, don't own it yourself; instead, establish a life insurance trust to own it. Then when you die, your kids will still get the payout.

Charitable Gift Annuities

If you listen to the radio each year at holiday time you'll hear groups advertising charitable gift annuities starting as low as $5,000 and paying you as much as 10 percent a year for the rest of your life. This is different from a charitable trust in that it is a much more commercial product. You purchase the trust directly from your favorite charity (or sometimes from an investment company, where you name the charity), without having to create a complicated trust agreement or pay lawyers. You give the charity money to invest in

SPECIAL GIFTS FROM GRANDPARENTS ONLY

There are certain gifts that only grandparents *can* make to their grandkids, above and beyond (or in lieu of) the $10,000 gifts that anyone can make. And there are a few other kinds of gifts that grandparents may *want* to make, while most cash-strapped parents might find it impossible. For example:

Pay tuition or medical bills outright. You can ignore gift taxes entirely if you pay medical bills or tuition directly for your grandkids. The wrinkle is that these payments, which can be of any size, have to go directly to the college, private school, hospital, or doctor to whom they're owed. They can't go through your kids' or grandkids' hands first. The rule applies only to tuition, not to room and board; but you could give your grandchild a $10,000 gift to cover that.

Make a lump contribution to a college savings plan. State-sponsored college savings plans (529 plans) allow contributions of up to $50,000 in one year, as long as you don't make subsequent 529 contributions for the child for the four years following. The IRS will look at this as if you've made five consecutive $10,000 annual gifts, so you don't eat into your unified credit. The benefit of making a lump deposit is that the money has additional years to grow—that's a nice bonus as college tuitions continue to escalate. Note: If the grandchild for whom you contributed the money decides not to go to college, the funds can be used for the education of a sibling.

Pay off student loans. If you're concerned that making a gift to your grandchildren will hamper their ability to qualify for college financial aid, you may want to wait to make a gift until after graduation. Then, perhaps using annual $10,000 gifts, you can help them pay off their student loans. (If you're afraid you won't be around long enough to see them to the end of their debt, you might want to use a chunk of money to buy an annuity for the grandchild that would begin paying out when college ends. Your grandkids could use that money to pay off their debts—and to get a head start in the world.)

Give stock. By giving appreciated stock to your grandchildren, you could save your entire family on capital gains taxes. Why? Because if you own stock more than a year and you sell, you'll likely be taxed (as long as you're in the 28 percent tax bracket or above) 20 percent on any capital gains. But if you give stock to grandkids over age fourteen who are in the 15 percent bracket when they sell the stock, they'll pay only 10 percent in capital gains. And, if you and your grandkids hold the stock for at least five years in total, the tax on the capital gains could drop to as low as 8 percent.

Name your grandchild as a beneficiary. If you're worried that you won't be around to help a young grandchild with college or other expenses, you can name that child as a beneficiary of a life insurance policy. If you're worried about putting too much money in that child's hands too soon (and you probably should be), stipulate in your will that the payout be put in trust for the child. Then name as trustee someone you're certain will make sure the payout is used for tuition, and not for a trip to Tahiti.

Set up an intergenerational transfer trust. Besides allowing you to leave $675,000 to your heirs, the government allows you to leave an additional $1 million to your grandkids. It's called *generation skipping*, and everyone is entitled to take advantage. But keep in mind, you're allowed to leave $1 million cumulatively to all the members of that later generation—not $1 million to each grandkid. Again, you'll need an estate planner to draw up this document. If you have the money, it's a wise addition to your package.

exchange for a promise to pay you an agreed-upon annuity (usually in the 10 percent vicinity) for an agreed-upon period of time (usually until your death).

Because this type of charitable gift can start as low as a few thousand dollars, it benefits those who want to give to charity but don't have enough money to set up a trust and pay legal fees: It's more like donating directly to the charity. The disadvantage is that a charitable gift annuity isn't as flexible as a charitable trust: You can't contribute property, appreciated securities, or other income-producing holdings (just cash), and you can't appoint your own trustee. Nevertheless, you will receive the same type of annuity return and tax benefits.

Managing an Inheritance

Like a lotto win, those of us who haven't received an inheritance can't imagine it being anything but fabulous. All of a sudden, you have the money to go back to school, to travel the world, to tell that boss you hate to, well, you know. Unfortunately, the folks who've been on the receiving end—particularly of very large inheritances—describe a less-than-wonderful scenario. They talk of guilt over money not earned and uneasy nights out with friends who expect them to pick up every check. They talk of pressure to do well by the money, and not to fritter it away. Adam, who lives in Iowa, inherited a half million dollars at the age of twenty-two. He was so shell-shocked he didn't tell anyone of his windfall for more than a year.

Over the next two generations, according to a Cornell University study, $10 trillion in wealth will change hands through inheritance, an average bequest of $90,000. Some will receive far more, others far less, as Americans live longer and many of them are forced to spend what would have been their children's inheritances on medical care and nursing homes. Nonetheless, it's something to be prepared for.

Inheriting works best if you view it as a two-step process—not simply managing the money or property you receive *after* the fact, but talking about it in the years before. The advantage to planning ahead is that you can discover problems beforehand, giving you an opportunity to solve them. You may find out that many of the issues that appear to be financial—arguments over who gets what, for example—turn out to be emotional. Solving them may mean getting a family counselor involved. Consider the following:

• **Let the dust settle.** You'll probably want to wait a good six months to a year before you make any serious financial decisions.

Stash any money you receive in a safe haven like a money market fund or a certificate of deposit—and do little else. Keep going to work. Keep your spending in check. Why? An inheritance is sort of like winning the lottery. Suddenly you have all this money that you didn't earn. It comes with a tremendous emotional price. You may feel very guilty, or wish that your parent had spent this money on themselves rather than on you. It'll take time to get back to reality.

• **Consider a small splurge.** If the temptation to buy gets to be too great, then go ahead. Just make your splurge a small one, like a great vacation instead of a new condo, or a fabulous new coat, but not an entire new wardrobe. Get the picture?

• **Look at your debts first.** Before investing or spending any money you receive, consider whether it makes more sense to pay down your existing debts—credit card, mortgage, student loan, or otherwise. Look at where you'd get the better rate of return. If your credit card is racking up interest at 18 percent, for example, you'd be hard pressed to top that with an investment return.

• **Hire help.** If you're dealing with more than $50,000 or so (less if you're feeling particularly clueless) you'll probably want to hire a financial adviser, if not to help with the day-to-day management of the money, then at least to get you moving in the right direction. If you're dealing with a much larger inheritance—over $1 million— then you may not want just a financial adviser, but a financial *team* that includes not just an adviser but also a lawyer, accountant, and insurance agent.

• **Find a support group.** Talking with other inheritors can help. The Impact Project (800-255-4903), a group that gives guidance on how to handle a major inheritance or give some of the money away, can help point you in the right direction. Or try the Inheritance Project (804-961-0876), a similar organization, which focuses on people who no longer have a financial need to work.

Giving It Away: Charitable Contributions

Giving money away isn't exactly preserving it for the next generation—but it's preserving it for a cause you deem important. With more than 650,000 organizations vying for a handout, it's not exactly easy to decide which causes to give to. In fact, it's easier than ever for your contributions to fall into the wrong hands.

The Internet can help. It's an excellent tool to help you research charities. Start at GuideStar, www.guidestar.com. It was started as an online registry of IRS Form 990s—the tax form all not-for-profits must file and provide to potential donors upon request. But it goes far beyond that, examining the mission of more than 620,000 charities (at last count), how much money they raise, where that money goes, and who's running them. It also has a great primer on how to read 990s, which, like most tax forms, can be a bit daunting. What GuideStar doesn't do is rate charities. For that, you'll need to go to the National Charities Information Bureau site at www.ncib.org, or to the Council of Better Business Bureaus site at www.bbb.org. Both have a series of criteria charities must adhere to in order to win their approval.

Four Things to Know Before You Contribute

• **Who, exactly, are you giving your money to?** So many organizations use the words "cancer," "heart," and "children" in their names that it's quite possible to get one organization confused with another. Reading a charity's annual report is one good way to get a full sense of what it is and what it does. It's also a good way to make sure your donation is tax deductible. Only those registered with the IRS (excepting religious groups that don't have to register) fall into that category.

• **How is your money being spent?** From a donor's perspective, it's key that as much of your money as possible is being used to fight cancer or battle hunger (or whatever), rather than to raise more money or pay the charity's administrative expenses. To meet the standards of the National Charities Information Bureau, 70 percent of a charity's money must go to "program." Any number above that is a sign of a well-managed organization. You can get these details on the NCIB Web site (www.ncib.org) or by requesting an organization's IRS Form 990. Any group that doesn't hand it over pronto should be removed from your list.

• **Does this donation fit into your giving plan?** A giving plan may sound like something that's only for the rich and famous, but it's not. The idea is to sit down once a year and figure out how much money you'd like to donate for the whole year, and then to take an active role in selecting the recipients, rather than waiting for them to find you. The bonus: When the solicitation calls start to roll in—and they will—you'll have an easier time saying no, because you'll have given already.

• **Is the paperwork in order?** Obviously, one of the benefits of charitable giving is being able to deduct the contributions on your federal income tax return. But you'll need documentation to back up your claim. If you make a donation of $250 or more in cash, you need an acknowledgment in writing from the charity—a canceled check won't do the trick. And note: If you buy a ticket to a benefit, you can't deduct the full price of your ticket—just the price of the ticket minus the cost of the meal and entertainment. If you're giving property away instead, you also need a written receipt, but this time it has to describe what the charity received and include the charity's estimate of the value of the gift. File these receipts away with your tax return in case you're ever audited.

THE BIG THREE: THINGS TO TAKE AWAY FROM TALKING ESTATE PLANNING

1. Far too many people (including plenty of parents) don't have the basic estate protections they need. These include: a will that, if you have children, names guardians for them, durable powers of attorney for health care and finance, and a living will. It's not costly. Having a lawyer draw up the documents will run you, generally, $500 and up. Or you can do it yourself with off-the-shelf software for under $100.

2. How would you feel knowing you were wasting the opportunity to give your kids a $675,000 gift? You might be. If you have assets worth more than that (including your home, retirement plans, and life insurance) and are married, *and* if you and your spouse haven't looked into incorporating a basic marital trust into your estate plan, you probably are. Look into it.

3. Only three things happen to money: You spend it, pass it along to the next generation, or give it away. Most people approach the last item on that list far too cavalierly. Instead, draw up a plan that puts some thought into which organizations you wish to support, and how much you want to give them.

CHAPTER 8

Talking Real Estate

In fall of 1993, my husband, Peter, started angling to flee Manhattan for a house in the suburbs. He was so ready for a backyard and a barbecue he'd talked me into buying one of those electric grills, setting it on the table in our tiny kitchen (which was thankfully next to a window), and cooking a flank steak for company. The kitchen filled with smoke before the meat was anywhere near done. I finished it under the broiler and called a broker the next day.

As it turned out, I was soon wishing I'd made the call even earlier. It took us a while to narrow our search to three towns, two in Westchester County, New York, and another in Connecticut. Then it took time to find brokers we were comfortable with. By that time it was winter and we'd learned we were expecting a child in late July. Now we *had* to find a house.

Some people love house hunting. I did for the first few months. I learned to hate it the day I got a call at work from my Chappaqua, New York, broker. "A house is coming on the market today and it's a really good block so it's going to go fast," she said.

"Okay," I answered. "Can you get us in first thing on Saturday?"

"You don't understand," she replied, clearly annoyed with me. "You have to leave work early so that we can be one of the first ones in the door." We were early, as it turned out, but not early enough. Other brokers had trotted their clients out as well and there was a line of cars down the block. So we sat in her Jeep for thirty minutes with the heater blasting. And when we finally got inside it was, well, just okay. The kitchen was a disaster. It didn't have enough bathrooms upstairs. Oh, and did I mention it was out of our budget? Clearly, with a dozen people freezing their toes off just to get a look, there wasn't going to be any wiggle room. From then on, house hunting was work.

We kept at it every weekend for six months. And in the end we bought a place that wasn't even on our radar screen. One Sunday, when all our brokers said they'd run out of things to show us, we answered an ad for a house in a nearby town. The place was a wreck. The owners, who were in the midst of a messy divorce, had left the place in the care of their triplet sons and their three cats. It reeked. I'm allergic. I would have left without a second glance. But Peter could tell it had potential. It had great light and terrific space and even under a foot of snow a wonderful flat backyard. We bid very low. Negotiated for a week. And all of a sudden, we had a deal. We were going to be *homeowners*.

It quickly became apparent that house hunting was the easy part. It was only once we'd found a place that we started comparing mortgage rates and thinking about things like points and fees, worrying about whether our new home insurance would come through in time to close the deal, dwelling on whether our home inspector would put the kibosh on the whole deal, and coordinating the activities of real estate agents and bankers and lawyers, to whom we were only two more fish in a very big pond.

There's a lot I wish I'd known about the entire process of buying a house before I got started. It's all incorporated into the coming pages. The other half of the chapter is about how to handle the other side of the deal. You may not be ready to sell your home now, but considering that Americans do so, on average, every seven years, it's important information to keep on hand. Even if—like me—you've sworn you're never moving again.

Buying a House: The Homeowner Plunge

The very first thing you must do when you're buying a house is figure out how much you can afford to spend. You've probably heard that you should be spending no more than 25 percent of your take-home pay on housing. Maybe, if you live in a pricey city, someone has told you 30 percent. Those numbers are generalizations. They're assumptions. What actually makes sense for you—given your financial obligations, given the life you want to live—may be much lower or even a bit higher.

A better way to go about making the decision is to see how much a bank will lend you and go from there. In other words, get preapproved for a mortgage. When a bank decides how much it's willing to lend you, it takes many factors into consideration, not just the money you're earning, but the amount you have saved for a down payment, your tax bracket, and current mortgage rates. In a low-interest-rate environment, for example, you can afford more house than when rates are substantially higher. Lenders use a set of detailed equations—for example, they often don't want the total amount you're spending on your mortgage to exceed around 28 percent of your income—that are designed to loan you only an amount you can afford to pay off, and no more. (Lenders don't live and die by their ratios as they used to, but they're still used as guidelines.) Keep in mind: The fact that a bank has decided to loan you, say, $200,000, doesn't mean you have to spend that much. In fact, if you'd like to live a little more leanly, ask your loan officer to state in your preapproval letter that you're only about to borrow $150,000 or $175,000. That way you'll have an out when your real estate agent tries to push you toward a pricier home.

How valuable is going through this process? Extremely. You have to start with your objectives and your goals. A real estate agent doesn't know that you have three kids to send to college or that you're socking it into your retirement plans. All they see is a person who wants to purchase a home. In fact, your budget can be just as unrealistic on the low side as on the high side. Longtime renters need to remember that a mortgage is the last big tax advantage Americans have available to them. You may be able to spend more on your mortgage each month than you did on rent because a big chunk of it—in fact all your mortgage interest up to $1.1 million— is deductible. How big a deal is that? Huge, particularly in the early years when you're paying much more in interest than you are in principal. For a person in the 33 percent tax bracket, this gift from Uncle Sam essentially cuts your mortgage interest rate by one third.

Give Your Credit a Once-over

As you start your house-hunting expedition, you'll simultaneously want to make sure that your credit rating is in tip-top shape. A poor credit rating can boost you from a reasonable interest rate (the ones you see advertised in the Sunday paper) into the stratosphere. In fact, you don't even want lenders looking into your credit files until you've given them a thorough going-over to make sure they're clean.

First, order a copy of your report from one of the three credit reporting agencies. If you find errors, you'll want to see all three. Believe me. In my single days I was once mistaken for another Jean Sherman who had several liens against her property. I got turned down for a credit card as a result and spent hours fighting with the credit bureaus to get them to remove the faulty information. If you've been turned down for a loan or credit card because of something on your credit report, the agencies will provide you with a copy for free as long as you contact them within sixty days. Otherwise, they charge as follows: $5 in Connecticut, $2 or $3 in Maine, free (once a year) in Colorado, Georgia, Maryland, Massachusetts, New Jersey, and Vermont, and $8 in all other states. You'll find the bureaus at:

Equifax: www.equifax.com or 1-800-997-2493.

TransUnion: www.transunion.com or 1-800-888-4213.

Experian: www.experian.com or 1-888-397-3742.

Once you make sure there are no horrendous mistakes on your report, you can also make yourself more attractive by canceling any cards you're not using, and steer clear of making other purchases that would require a lot of inquiries into your report (a blemish in a mortgage lender's eyes). If you've made any big-time credit gaffes in the past few years, explain yourself in a letter to your potential lender. As long as you can show you've gotten your act together, it may be willing to look the other way.

Do Some Independent Market Research

Before you even call a real estate agent, you'll want to get a sense of property values in each area. How do you do that? Start taking the local paper and reading the real estate listings. Keep your eyes peeled for the column (many papers have them) that details how long specific homes were on the market and how much they sold for. Spend several weekends visiting open houses.

By doing this, when you start looking with an agent, you'll have an idea of the worth of what you're seeing. Skipping this exercise makes you putty in a smart agent's hands. Why? Because a savvy agent will try to teach you about value her way. She'll set up each of your shopping days to end with the house that she wants you to buy. First, you may see a three-bedroom, two-bath that's in terrible shape for $350,000. Next, you'll see a house with a somewhat nicer backyard and a kitchen that's just okay for $325,000. And you'll finish with a house that's listed for $300,000 with a great backyard and a dynamite kitchen and bath. Is it a great deal? Maybe. Maybe not. You won't have any idea unless you've done enough homework to know something about the fair market value in this town—which may be quite different from the fair market value in the town just a mile away.

Why You Need a Real Estate Agent

Trying to buy a house alone—without access to the computerized home listings real estate agents have at their fingertips—is like searching for a book in a library with no idea of where it's shelved. You might find the one you're looking for, but only if you're incredibly lucky.

But not just any real estate agent will do. You'll want to join forces with one who's been working in the town that interests you for a good three to five years, who comes highly recommended for his accessibility and resourcefulness. Most importantly, you want an agent who's in the loop—who can point out homes that aren't on the market yet, but might be soon because of job transfers, divorces, undisclosed pregnancies, and so on. Particularly in a busy market, having an agent who can get you in the door first can be a huge advantage.

If you're a first-time buyer, it's also crucial that your agent is patient. You are going to be doing a lot of research on this person's time. You may start out thinking you want a Tudor, because you like the outside, but discover that you don't like the nooks and crannies those houses typically have after all. Or maybe you'll shift gears from old homes to newer ones. Or your price range will completely change. Unless you've hunted for a house before, there's no way to know what you *really* want until you do some serious looking, and you'll do all of that on your broker's time. So make sure the person you settle on is willing to put up with it.

The best brokers (and, as you'll soon learn, the best contractors, painters, plumbers, and nannies) all come from word of mouth. Ask friends who live in the neighborhood of your choice for names and phone numbers, then sit down with these agents to see if there's a fit. At that face-to-face interview, you'll need to sort out exactly what your relationship with this real estate broker would be. Agents wear many different hats these days. Some work specifically for you as exclusive buyer's agents, others work for sellers, and some split the difference (see table on page 192, "Who's Representing You?").

Keep the Next Owner in Mind

As you hunt for a house, you'll have in your mind a list of things you absolutely must have: four bedrooms, two and a half baths, a finished basement to use as a playroom, a decent yard, and big closets (in multiples). You probably also have a list of the things you *want* it to have: a family room off the kitchen, a Jacuzzi for two in the master bath, a den that's secluded enough for you to get some work done, and an island for chopping vegetables in the kitchen. But have you made a list of things the *next* owners might be looking for?

That's right. Since statistically you won't be in this house even a decade, you don't want to buy one that only you could love. What sort of incurable defects should you avoid? The highest priced house in a less-expensive subdivision is bad news, as is being situated at the crux of a busy intersection. Poor floor plans are tough to overcome. And unless you're buying in a community designed for empty nesters, watch out for school districts that have a bad reputation. Alternately, there are some positive factors to look for: Homes at the bottom of a cul-de-sac are a big hit with parents. Those within walking distance to public transportation win raves from commuters. And, if you can find one of the worst houses in a terrific neighborhood with great schools—and you intend on fixing it up—you could make yourself a bundle when you sell.

Making Your Case

In a seller's market—like the one much of the country experienced in the late 1990s—it's sometimes not enough to offer the most money for a house. (Several other buyers may also be willing to meet your price or top it.) You have to prove that your offer is above and beyond in other ways. How can you make that case?

First, get preapproved for a mortgage. This involves going through the same borrowing process as if you'd actually made an offer on a house. The mortgage lender you choose verifies your employment, income, savings, investments, and debts and gives you a letter detailing the amount it's willing to lend you. This is incredibly valuable to a seller because it means that you're for real. It says that you have the money to buy this house, and means that you'd be able to close a deal much more quickly than someone who hasn't gone through the process—and you can close much faster than someone who hasn't gone through this process.

You'll also have advantages if you don't need to sell another property before buying this one, and if you can be flexible about closing dates. But don't go overboard in the hope of making yourself an attractive buyer! Some purchasers make mistakes they live to regret—and pay for—later on. For example, desperate people sometimes waive their right to have a new home professionally inspected as a contingency of the deal. A year later, when the roof turns out to have holes or support beams have to be replaced due to termite damage, they're very sorry.

Making an Offer

Finally, you find it: a home you like well enough to make an offer. But how high should you bid? That depends on a number of variables: How long the house has been on the market. Whether you think it's fairly priced. And how heated the market is in your community.

• **Hot tickets.** When you're shopping in a hot market, you may have to get very creative. That's what real estate broker Amy Grossman did. She was representing her sister and brother-in-law, who had just fallen for a five-bedroom colonial with classic lines on a child-friendly street. The day it went on the market, the offers started pouring in. Grossman made one on her sister's behalf, but it wasn't high enough to stop the frenzy. A few days later the broker for the seller asked for sealed bids including each interested party's "best and final offer."

"My sister, my mom, and I were sitting around my kitchen, trying to figure out what we could do to make my sister's offer stand out," Amy recounts. Finally, they came up with this brainstorm: throw in a week at the family's vacation home in St. Maarten. It was a carrot worth several thousand dollars. Plus, after the hassle of a move, everyone needs a vacation. It worked.

• **Dime a dozen.** If you're interested in a three-bedroom split-level, for example, in a neighborhood where there are plenty of them, take your time and negotiate wisely. Your first bid should be a good 12 to 15 percent below the asking price. That's because most homeowners will be satisfied to sell their properties for 5 to 10 percent below the listing price. And some homeowners will also not accept your first offer. So if your first offer is in this range, it'll be fairly easy for both parties to negotiate into that 5 to 10 percent range and still save face.

• **Leftovers.** Lucky you, you've fallen for a house that's been sitting on the market for several months or longer, maybe even one where the price has already been reduced. While you're strolling through leisurely, pondering changing the wallpaper, the owners are hiding in the kitchen, praying that you're the ones. Take a chance and bid low. Try offering 20 to 30 percent below the asking price. If the owners are so insulted they won't even dignify your bid by making a conciliatory counteroffer, then you'll know you may have to ante up more money to get the negotiations going. You may, on occasion, run up against an agent who tells you that your low-ball bid is too embarrassing to even present to the seller. Be firm. Tell them it's their fiduciary responsibility to do it anyway—if you still have no luck, go straight to the manager of the brokerage firm with the listing.

• **Fixer-uppers.** Nobody seems to want them. If that's the case with a house you're interested in, the ball is truly in your court. The longer a house has been sitting, the lower you can go. Our first offer (our house had been on the market for *three years*) was a full third below the asking price. We ended up buying it for 25 percent less. And if the house is an especially desperate case—if it's been left sitting empty or you know that a rich corporation or a bank has taken it off the previous owner's hands—you can sometimes do even better.

Closing the Deal

It's important to understand how the final stages of this transaction work. There are some regional differences; in some markets you have to write a check in order to make an offer, in others you don't put down a deposit until your offer has been accepted. Once you and the seller have agreed on a price, then you need a team of people to get you through to closing.

Your mortgage lender will hire an *appraiser* (it'll run you about $300) to make sure that the price you agreed to pay for the home is in line with the home's value. If the appraisal comes in substantially lower than your offer, you may not get your loan unless you have enough cash to increase your down payment. (When you hear people say the deal fell apart on the appraisal, this is what they mean.) This doesn't happen often, but it does happen, and for that reason it's crucial to have a clause in your purchase agreement that lets you off the hook. (If you believe the appraisal is out of line, you can also challenge it with one of your own. To find an appraiser in your area call the Appraisal Institute at 312-355-4100 or look on the Web at www.appraisalinstitute.com. You should be aware, though, that this second opinion will also cost you $300 to $600 and that your lender is under no obligation to accept it.)

Depending upon where you live, you may also need a *lawyer* to go over the purchase agreement and represent you at the closing. Look for a lawyer who specializes in residential real estate; even a commercial real estate attorney may not be as skilled at reading between the lines of a residential contract. Friends who've bought or sold houses recently are better sources of real estate lawyers than your broker is. After all, they don't have a stake in seeing your deal go through. Or you can get a referral from your state or local bar association (www.abanet.org). Plan on spending $500 to $1,000 and up for your attorney.

Finally, you must have the place inspected by a professional and *independent home inspector*—preferably a member of the American Society of Home Inspectors. Make sure your inspector is someone who makes his money giving your house the once-over, not one

Who's Representing You?

Although consumers tend to use the terms interchangeably, there's a difference between real estate agents and real estate brokers. Brokers are the people who run the offices; they have tougher licensing requirements and have been through additional classes in subjects like real estate law. They'll likely only get

	WHAT THEY DO
Listing Agent	Represent the seller. Contractually, the listing agent promises the property owner to make his or her best effort to sell the property for as much money as possible as quickly as possible. In turn, the property owner says: "If you bring me an offer acceptable in price and terms, I promise to pay you a commission."
Buyer's Agent	Represent the buyer in a transaction. Exclusive buyer's agents work only with buyers, though today most buyer's agents also work as listing agents on other deals.
Discount Agent	The same thing as listing or buyer's agents, depending on whom they're working for.
Fee-for-Service Agent	The same things buyer's and listing agents do, only on a piecemeal basis. If you want to be listed in the local multiple listing service, you pay one price. If you want your house shown or an agent to run an open house, you may pay an hourly rate.

involved in individual transactions when some problem arises. Agents are the folks on the front lines. They list homes for sellers and show them to buyers. Ninety percent of the time, they're the folks who take you out in their cars. Here's what you need to know to pick the best type of agent for your needs:

How much they earn

Typically, 6 percent on the sale price, which is generally split with the agent representing the buyer. But note: Commissions are negotiable.

Half of the traditional commission, which in most cases is paid by the seller at the close of the transaction. Some buyer's agents may ask you for 1 to 3 percent of the money you expect to spend on a house up front as a retainer of sorts, but that fee is typically refunded at closing. If charging such a fee is unusual in your community, you may be able to negotiate it down or escape it altogether by threatening (nicely, of course) to go elsewhere.

Three to 4 percent of the sale price (split with the agent on the other side of the deal) compared with the traditional 6 or 7 percent.

Getting listed typically runs anywhere from $250 to $500 for six months. Hourly rates of $30 to $50 are fairly normal. But you'll see huge price swings depending on your region of the country.

Who's Representing You? (continued)

THINGS TO KEEP IN MIND

Listing Agent	If your agent brings you an offer at the asking price and, for whatever reason, you do not wish to sell, the agent can sue you for the commission.
Buyer's Agent	Since so many buyer's agents walk both sides of the fence, you'll want to sign an agreement stipulating what your relationship is in this particular case.
Discount Agent	In a buyer's market, discount agents are at a disadvantage. Why? Because when your agent sits down to view the listings on her computer she sees both those houses available and how much commission she'll be paid on each one. A home listed with a traditional agent will pay her 3 percent. One listed with a discounter will pay her 1.5 percent. In a buyer's market—where she has scores of homes to choose from—do you think she'll show you the one that'll pay her less? Probably not.
Fee-for-Service Agent	Selling through a traditional agent would cost you 6 percent of the deal. When you sign a contract with a fee-for-service agent you want to cap costs at that level.

who wants to do the repairs himself. It'll cost you $250 and up to have your roof, heating, plumbing and electrical systems, walls, and windows examined, but the expense is well worth it. Even if your inspector doesn't flag anything that's a deal breaker, he'll leave you

How to find one

Scour your town to see who has the most signs up; ask friends who've recently bought or sold for recommendations.

The National Association of Exclusive Buyer's Agents (800-986-2322 or www.naeba.org).

The Yellow Pages.

The Yellow Pages.

with a veritable road map of all the systems you can expect to fix or replace in the next five to ten years. For a referral you can find the American Society of Home Inspectors at 800-743-2744 or www.ashi.com.

Five Questions to Ask Your Home Inspector

1. A new home is expensive enough. Why should I spend several hundred dollars on you? Precisely because your home is the biggest investment you'll probably ever make, you don't want to go in blind. Don't make the mistake of thinking that you or a friend know enough about houses to avoid an official inspection. There are up to twelve different types of heating systems commonly used in homes and eight types of electrical systems. Chances are, even if you know about one, you don't know them all.

2. At what point in the deal do you come into play? You'll want to line up an inspector while you're shopping for homes. Give yourself time to interview several. There is no home inspector's license in most states, so check references, look in past Yellow Pages to see that they've been in business for at least several years, and ask for a sample copy of an inspection report to make sure it's comprehensive (all a house's major systems should be covered).

Red Flag! If a home inspector tries to talk you into letting him repair any defects he finds, that's your cue to say goodbye.

3. Should I be present for the inspection? A good inspector will prefer it. And so should you—because you'll get a crash course in how your new house works, including where the systems, valves, and switches are located. (Note: If you're selling a house that's soon to be inspected, it's in your best interest to fix any minor problems like leaks and clean up to give the inspector proper access.)

Red Flag! Any home inspector who insists that you *not* be present—or even says you have no reason to be there—probably isn't doing much of a job. P.S. Watch out for inspectors who insist they'll need an entire day. Anything more than three hours for an average (2,000 foot) home means you're dealing with an inspector who's inexperienced, inefficient, or—worse—just killing time.

4. What's included in the inspection? A general home inspection should look at a home's:

- **Exterior,** particularly drainage conditions, exterior surfaces, deck and chimney examinations.

- **Roof,** including the condition of roofing materials and flashing.
- **Interior,** specifically checking out the condition of windows and doors and plumbing fixtures. The furnace and air conditioner should be tested (weather permitting). And electrical outlets and switches should be tested randomly to make sure they're working correctly.
- **Crawl space and attic,** to see that they're structurally sound.
- **Systems,** including ventilation, electrical, heating, and plumbing, which should all be given a thorough checkup.

5. How much will it cost? Depending on your part of the country, prices range from $200 to $400 for an average (2,000-square-foot home) inspection. You may pay more to have your septic system evaluated, for a termite or radon inspection, or to evaluate the conditions of pools, docks, or oil tanks.

Paying for It: Getting a Great Mortgage Deal

If you're smart, you'll start thinking about financing your new home even before you find one. Why? Because not getting the right loan for the right number of years at the best possible rate can literally cost you tens of thousands of dollars over the life of your loan. So clear your head—and your desk—it's time to shop.

Why Choosing a Loan Is Almost as Tough as Choosing a House

Fixed rate or adjustable? Fifteen-year or thirty? With points or without? Mortgages come in as many flavors as Baskin-Robbins. In order to pick the right one for your needs, you first have to understand how they work.

- **Fixed rate mortgages** are fairly straightforward. You lock into a rate and it sticks with you for the term of your loan, whether it's the most common thirty-year loan, or one that you pay off in fifteen.

• **Adjustable rate mortgages (or ARMs)** have more moving parts than fixed rate loans. But if you understand how the most common example, the one-year ARM, works, you'll understand them all. One-year ARMs offer a steeply discounted interest rate in the first year of the loan. (In mid-1999, for example, thirty-year fixed rate loans were running about 7.3 percent, while one-year ARMs were averaging 5.74 percent, though in many years the gap is much greater.) After the first year, these loans start to adjust; they typically move up or down at a rate 2.75 percentage points higher than one-year Treasury securities. But they're not allowed to make that whole leap in the first year; instead, most can move as much as 2 percentage points annually, with a 6-point cap in either direction. One-year ARMs don't really become attractive until they're priced at least 2 to 2.5 percentage points lower than a thirty-year fixed rate loan. The discount taps out too fast.

Assuming you can get a decent rate in the first year, who should be looking at a one-year ARM? People who don't have enough income to qualify for the size loan they need at the higher rate associated with fixed rate loans. They also make sense for people who know they won't be in this home long enough to have to weather the increases (in this case, renting might make sense as well).

• **Hybrid ARMs** are halfway between fixed rate loans and one-year ARMs. These loans stay fixed for the first five, seven, or ten years, then begin adjusting annually. You don't get the same discount as you do with a one-year ARM. But if you know that you're only going to be in your house for a finite period of time, it makes sense to take any break you can get.

How Quickly Will You Pay It Off?

Here's the next question your loan officer will ask: What *term*—or length—loan you prefer. In most cases you'll be deciding between fifteen years and thirty. Financial advisers can argue for hours about this decision. Here's why:

If you borrow money for fifteen years rather than thirty, the lender isn't taking as great a risk, so you'll get a break on the interest rate. In mid-1999 for example, while thirty-year fixed rate loans were averaging 7.31 percent, fifteen-year fixed rate loans were averaging 6.92 percent. That doesn't make your monthly payments lower—after all, you cut the term in half—but they're not double, as you might think. Monthly payments on a $100,000 thirty-year loan at the 7.31 percent rate are $686. Monthly payments on a $100,000 fifteen-year loan at 6.92 percent are $894—$208 higher. The big (make that huge) difference is that by choosing the shorter term, you save more than $86,000 in interest.

Why would financial advisers recommend against that? Because, depending on where they're priced, mortgages can be an inexpensive way to borrow. In addition, mortgage interest of up to $1.1 million a year is still deductible. What that means is for people in the 33 percent (combined federal and state) tax bracket, the government subsidizes one third of your loan. Money you borrow at 7.5 percent is really costing you 5 percent. Financial advisers say you can do better by taking the difference between a thirty-year loan and a fifteen-year loan (that $208 in our above example), putting it into the stock market, and letting it grow for that length of time. And, chances are, you probably can. But you have to ask yourself if you *will*. Be brutally honest here. If you don't have the willpower to invest that money consistently (or if you're not willing to sign up for an automatic investment plan, see Chapter 3), then use the money to pay off your mortgage. The payoff on your home is certainly better than putting the extra money in the bank.

One last suggestion: If the pressure of a mandatory higher payment is too much to contend with, take this informal approach: Send in extra cash with your mortgage payment whenever you're able. Even if you simply send in one extra payment each year on your thirty-year fixed rate loan, you slash the term to twenty-three years.

How Large a Loan Do You Need?

Finally, there's the size of your loan.

• **Conforming loans** are those $240,000 or less. They're called conforming loans because they're originated under a set of guidelines from Fannie Mae or Freddie Mac that makes them similar. As long as they adhere to these guidelines, they can be packaged together and sold as "mortgage-backed securities" in the secondary market, where they're traded like stocks and bonds.

• **Jumbo loans** are those greater than $240,000. Obviously, you don't have a whole lot of control over this category; you need to borrow what you need to borrow. But one thing to understand is that traditionally jumbos have been about a quarter to a half a point more expensive than conforming loans. That gap is shrinking. In some markets it's vanishing. So if you find yourself facing a lender who's telling you otherwise, you'll want to shop around some more.

Where to Shop?

There's nothing like a lot of choices. And when you're shopping for a mortgage—you've got them. It's important to explore the rates being offered by local lenders, through mortgage brokers *and* those you can get from mortgage lenders on the World Wide Web. In fact, you'll want to pit them against each other. Why do you need to go through this time-consuming exercise? Because there are often rate differences of 2 percentage points within a single market. That's a pretty hefty price to pay because you felt like spending an afternoon watching the ballgame rather than doing your homework.

Where to start? A great source is HSH Associates' Web site at www.hsh.com, which can give you a glimpse at rates in your area. Ask friends and colleagues for names of reputable mortgage brokers and sit down with them as well. Mortgage brokers have lost some of their used-car-salesman reputation in recent years—they now make more than 50 percent of mortgage loans—but don't just view them as a form of one-stop shopping. Some have much better deals than others. Finally, get online. The Internet is a very powerful shopping tool. Each site will get back to you with, typically, five to ten rates available in your area. Visit a few to get an idea of the most competitive.

One advantage to using the Web is that it can be blindingly fast. Ellen, a travel consultant in New York City, got a response from eloan.com the day she visited the site: an offer for a 6.625 percent, thirty-year fixed mortgage. "The next day I had a Fed Ex package on my doorstep, including my case number," she says. "Plus they're running a special, so I'm getting back $900 in closing costs."

That's not to say consumers don't have issues with applying for loans via the Internet. One big fear is that by applying to a number of sites, you could hurt your credit score. That's largely unfounded. Recent changes to credit reporting laws say that an unlimited number of inquiries for the same purpose (like getting a mortgage) within a thirty-day period count as only one query. The bottom line: Internet sites are grabbing an increasing share of the mortgage market—one analyst with investment bank Robertson Stephens expects 4 to 5 percent of all mortgages will be completed online within five years—thus driving down costs and increasing competition. You owe it to yourself to take a look.

Paying Points

As soon as you start talking mortgages, you'll find yourself talking *points*. Two different kinds, in fact. *Discount points* are money paid up front to essentially buy down your interest rate. One point—1 percent of the value of your loan—will generally lower your interest rate one eighth to one quarter of 1 percent. Is it worth it?

That depends on where you think interest rates are going. If you believe the country is headed for a recession and rates will be lower down the road, it doesn't make sense to pay points to get a lower rate today. Instead, take the best rate you can get now, then refinance if and when rates do go down. But if you think inflationary times and higher interest rates are coming down the pike, then it does make sense to buy a lower rate.

The most important factor in deciding how many points you'll pay is the number of months it'll take to recoup that investment. Say you're choosing between paying $4,000 in points for a $100,000 loan at 7 percent versus no closing costs for the same loan at 7.5 percent. Your monthly payment on the 7 percent loan is $665.30 versus $699 at 7.5 percent. At that rate it'll take you 118 months—or just under ten years—to break even. At 7 percent, you'll also have paid off more of your interest, so your equity stake will be higher. Should you do it? Certainly not if you're only planning to stay a short time. Or even if you're not sure how long you're staying. Only if this is your forever home should you lay out the money.

Which brings us to the other kind of points: *origination points*. These are administrative fees; a lender may hit you with them to cover its marketing or advertising costs. Watch out: Just as interest rates vary widely, points do as well.

Don't Forget Closing Costs

Including points, your closing costs can total up to 4 percent of your loan amount. That includes a litany of fees (among them about $50 for a credit report, $300 for an appraisal, $200 for document preparation, $20 for flood certification, $50 for recording fees, and $400 to pay the bank's attorney, according to HSH Associates). The total for fees other than points averages $1,200.

You can opt out of practically every one by choosing a no-closing-cost loan. These are particularly popular when refinancing volume is heavy—they're a carrot for mortgage holders who paid points the first time around and don't have the cash to do it again. A no-cost loan should add about one half to five eighths of a point to your rate. Remember, you're not getting anything for free with these, as you'll be giving back the lender the money over time.

One more important note about closing costs. They vary greatly—not only state by state but lender by lender and with the size of your loan. It's crucial as you compare loans that you get a *good-faith estimate* of closing costs on each. It should detail precisely what that estimate includes and it must be in writing. Only then can you compare apples to apples.

Get Your Paperwork in Order

How can you best avoid the headaches, the long phone waits, the paperwork jams associated with getting a mortgage? Organization is key. Take an hour or two to pull together the documents each and every lender is going to want to see. This list from Countrywide, the nation's largest mortgage lender, is typical:

- **Earnings statements** (or proof of self-employment), including your W-2 forms, pay stubs, and tax returns.
- **The contract** for purchase of your home.
- **Debt-related information,** including your credit card numbers (with the address and phone numbers for the banks that issued the cards) and any car loan(s).
- **Bank statements** for the last three months (again, with addresses and account numbers).
- **Canceled checks** or other evidence of mortgage or rental payments.
- **Tax returns** for the prior three years.

Pulling the Trigger—Locking In

When you apply for a loan, you'll need to decide if you want to *lock in* your interest rate. In order to lock, you'll have to pay a quarter point or so, an amount which is typically refunded at closing. When to lock is a crucial question. Trying to time the bottom of the market for interest rates—just like trying to time the stock market—is a fool's game. Even in a declining-rate environment, many people get burned. With that in mind, here are four questions you can use to help you decide when to pull the trigger:

- **Can you afford to lose?** If a jump in rates of a quarter point means you'll no longer be able to afford your house, lock immediately.
- **What's your rate now?** In a refinance situation, if you have an 8 or 9 percent rate, you win whether rates fall to 7 percent or 7.25. If you're already at 7.75, that quarter of a point makes a bigger difference.

• **How is the bond market trending?** Mortgages follow bonds closely—not in lockstep, but closely. In most cases, one bad day won't cause a huge jump in mortgage rates, but if a bad pattern starts emerging (if you hear the CNBC jockeys talking about sell-offs over two or three consecutive days, for example), then act fast. Rates almost always rise more quickly than they fall.

• **Are you being greedy?** If rates have plummeted to thirty-year lows and you're holding out for thirty-one-year lows, you're asking for too much.

Make sure that if you do lock, you get it in writing, that you give yourself enough days to get to the closing table, and that you have all the rates clearly specified.

If you expect rates to fall rather than rise, ask your lender about a *float-down*. That gives you the ability to lock in, then if rates do fall, to relock, typically ten days before closing. Some lenders will give you this gratis, but others charge. It's okay to pay a small sum. Just be sure there are no unreasonable caveats and that you consider how much you're paying in relation to how quickly you expect to get it back. If you don't get a float-down and rates fall, try to renegotiate. On a refinancing where you haven't put up a lot of cash, lenders will often capitulate, knowing that they will lose you otherwise.

When Should I Consider Refinancing?

In the old days (say, a decade ago) refinancing lived and died by the rule of twos: You weren't even supposed to *think* about it unless your current mortgage was two years old, you were cutting your interest rate by 2 percentage points, and you were planning to stay in your house for two additional years or more. No longer. In fact, folks who have stuck determinedly to those strictures in recent years missed out on substantial savings.

Think back to the fall of 1998. Say you were three years into a thirty-year mortgage with a rate of 7.5 percent. You still owed

$200,000 on the loan and were paying $1,398 each month in interest and principal. All of a sudden rates dropped to thirty-year lows. By refinancing, you could have cut your rate to 6.5 percent, dropping your monthly payment to $1,264 and saving you $134 a month. Was it worth doing? It was definitely worth thinking about.

The next step would have been to run the numbers by dividing the cost of the deal by your monthly savings to figure out how long it would take you to recoup your investment. If you expected to stay in the house long enough not only to do that but to save additional money, then it would have been a smart move.

Five Questions to Ask Your Mortgage Broker

1. What are you going to do for me? A mortgage broker is like a middleman between you and, typically, about twenty-five different lenders. He or she can help you shop from a variety of lenders with a single phone call. The broker will then act as your representative through closing.

Red Flag! A broker shouldn't be pushing you toward a particular mortgage program—if he is, chances are his commission on this plan is heads above the rest. Steer clear.

2. How much will this deal cost? Fees vary regionally, but the final tally is generally 3 to 5 percent of the loan amount, including the loan origination fee, closing costs, and other administrative fees. Be sure to ask for a good-faith estimate up front.

Red Flag! Do not work with a mortgage broker who will not give you a good-faith estimate upon your first meeting or one who tries to avoid the question by saying: "We won't know for sure until the deal is done."

3. How do you make your money? It's simple. The higher the rate a mortgage broker can get you to pay over the rate the wholesale lender is charging him, the more money he puts in his pocket. One way to keep a broker competitive is to play him or her off against another broker. That's what Paul, a Connecticut CPA, did. In September 1998, he told two mortgage brokers they were going head-to-head to refinance his 7.5 percent $160,000 loan. In the end, he got locked in at 6.25 percent with one point, saving a half point, worth $800, from his broker's original quote.

4. How much business do you do? Brokers buy loans from banks at wholesale and pass them on to you at retail. The price they pay depends somewhat on the volume they do and the quality of the loan packages they present. You're generally better off with a large operator who runs a professional-looking shop instead of a sole practitioner.

Red Flag! Be careful of any broker who promises you too much too soon. A promise to secure your loan within thirty days is to be believed. A promise of a turnaround in less than a week may very well be broken.

5. Can you guarantee me the best possible deal? Not necessarily. A mortgage broker should be one of the venues you shop when you're looking for the best rate on a loan, just as you should also check out the large banks and the credit unions in town. Note: If you have credit problems—a few late payments on your credit report or a bankruptcy in the not so distant past—a mortgage broker's array of sources will usually work to your advantage.

Moving On: The Best Way to Sell Your House

Here's what happens every spring in my small town (pop. 7,000). The snow melts. The hyacinths pop. Up go the ladders as my neighbors use the weekends to scoop out leaf-filled gutters and repair wayward shutters. Up goes the scaffolding as homes in need get a few new shingles, here and there. And then—with unerring regularity—out come the For Sale signs as move-up buyers and new empty nesters put their freshened-up properties on the market for all to see. It never fails.

What also never fails is that some of those properties move within a week or two while others sit as spring becomes summer and then fall. Often, the differences between those that sell rapidly and those that don't are very slight. A little tweaking, a bit of forward-thinking selling strategy is, in many cases, all it takes to get your house in play.

Get Your House in Shape

You've probably heard the term curb appeal. During our house-hunting months, our agents drove up to several houses that we refused to even walk into. They, quite bluntly, didn't have it. Do you need to invest in a Martha Stewart–inspired landscaping job? Probably not. But you do need to remove the clutter from your yard, pull wayward weeds, repaint those peeling shutters, trim the hedges, and mow. By all means, mow.

Inside, you have a similar task. There's no need to invest thousands in new kitchen cabinets and appliances. But you will want to spend a few hundred giving any walls in need a good coat of Benjamin Moore Linen White. Open all the drapes and shutters while you're at it. Go on a search-and-destroy mission for any wayward clutter. And make sure your house passes the sniff test. A house that smells good, believe it or not, is incredibly welcoming, so make sure you've eliminated any pet or cigarette odors (get your carpets cleaned). And if you're not up for baking cookies whenever you know someone is coming to see the house, sprinkle some cinnamon into a pot of water and let it boil for thirty minutes. That'll clear the air.

If you suspect you have problems with radon, termites, energy efficiency, asbestos, or lead (the latter two are likely in homes that were built twenty or more years ago), you'll want to get the house inspected and have the problems taken care of before you put the place on the market. Each one of these could kill a deal.

Do You Want to Use an Agent?

Real estate agents aren't cheap. In most parts of the country, listing your house with an agent will cost you 6 to 7 percent of the selling price. That money then gets split between the agent you hired to sell your house and the one that brought the buyer to the table. (Or, more accurately, it gets split between the two real estate firms.)

Despite the cost, four out of five people who sell their homes do use real estate agents. Why? Because selling your home isn't as easy as just planting a sign in your lawn. You have to figure out what your property is worth so that you can price it correctly, advertise it, hold open houses, schedule potential buyers (then stay home to show them around), and negotiate your way to an acceptable deal. You may also want to take advantage of some high-tech selling techniques like listing your house on the Internet. Real estate agents can do all of those things for you. Good ones will.

How do you find one who fits your needs? Start with recommendations from friends who've bought or sold recently. Interview at least three, from three of the busiest firms in town. You should insist that each potential agent prepare a market analysis recommending a selling price for your house (make sure you get a look at the recently sold properties on which this recommendation is based) along with a marketing plan. You'll also want the skinny on current selling conditions in your area: How long are properties lingering on the market? How far below the original asking price are they selling?

Don't be wooed by one agent who says he can sell your house at a substantially higher price—or much quicker—than the other folks you're considering. If your house is listed too far above the market, it'll sit (and sit) and you'll get frustrated. Instead, choose the agent who seems to be most realistic about pricing and most knowledgeable about your area. And choose one who's a good personality fit. After all, he or she is going to be underfoot quite a bit as potential buyers wander through.

Going Solo

One out of five homes sold today is what's called in the trade a "fizzbo." The word is derived from the acronym FSBO and it stands for "for sale by owner." The draw is that you save the 6 to 7 percent you'd typically pay to a real estate agent. On a $200,000 house, that's

$12,000 to $14,000, which is substantial. But realize: Doing it your-self can be a huge time commitment.

Goal number one is to figure out how much to list your house for. Watch the ads for homes in your neighborhood, attend open houses, and pay a visit to your town assessor's office to see how much properties comparable to yours are actually selling for. (Alter-nately, you can hire an independent appraiser to do this for you for about $300.) Next, you'll want to advertise the place—by running ads in your local newspapers, sticking a For Sale sign in your lawn, and perhaps paying someone to list the place on the Internet. A well-advertised open house can be a drawing card as well.

And prepare for this scenario: Some potential buyers may show up with buyer's agents in tow, asking if you'll cooperate with them. If you say yes, and unless the buyer has agreed to pay his agent out of his own pocket—which is highly unusual—you'll be on the line for a commission of about 3 percent, which cuts your savings in half. That's just one reason why, according to the National Associa-tion of Realtors (which, admittedly, has an agenda here), half of the people who sold homes on their own say they wouldn't do it again.

How About a Second Home?

Second homes are the country's number one status symbol, accord-ing to a Roper Starch poll. If you're among the 60 percent of Amer-icans who would like to own one, you need to understand that it's a completely different sort of purchase from the first. You'll need to decide how you're planning to use this new property. If you want to rent for part of the year, for example, you'll need one shopping list. If you want a place you can transition into at retirement, you'll need another. The following reasons for buying are top on the lists of today's second home shoppers. Here's what you need to know about each:

• **Preretirement home.** The change, a few years back, in the size of a capital gain home sellers can pocket on their primary residence—to $250,000 for singles, $500,000 for couples—spurred a frenzy in the market for homes to vacation in now, retire in later. If that's your plan, look for an area that's more populated than isolated, with quality health care and a hopping job market. And consider income taxes as well. Moving your residence from a city like Manhattan, where city and state income taxes are steep, to a no-income-tax state like Florida could save you 10 percent in income taxes each year.

• **Weekend getaway.** Biding your time is the key to looking for a second home to use exclusively on weekends. Why? Real estate agents say weekend homeowners aren't motivated sellers. Most had no pressing need for the money they sank into their second home originally. As a result, they can hold until they get their price. That said, a certain amount of nervousness sets in when traffic vanishes at the end of tourist season. In many hot weekend areas, you'll see price dips of up to 20 percent when properties listed in the summer haven't sold by fall. Of course, when it's your turn to sell, you don't want to have to twiddle your thumbs. So be sure to buy in an area where tourism trends are positive. Check with the local chamber of commerce to see that occupancy rates in local hotels and new hotel construction are both strong.

• **Rental property.** According to the American Resort Developers Association, Americans vacation two weeks a year, one week at a time on average. Add that to the fact that insuring a not frequently used, remote vacation home costs significantly more than insuring the same property for full-time use in a neighborhood *and* that paying someone to watch over things while you're absent runs $35 to $50 a week. All of a sudden, that empty bungalow is an expensive proposition. As a result, many people become part-time landlords. The IRS rules in this area are complicated, but you'll fall into one of three basic categories: Use the house for more than fourteen days a year or more than 10 percent of the rental period and it's a residence; the amount of expenses you write off are capped at the amount of income you take in. Use the house for fourteen or fewer days a year or less than 10 percent of the rental period and it's a rental property; you're not limited in the amount of expenses you can write off. Finally, rent fewer than fifteen days a year and Uncle Sam gives you a freebie; you don't have to report the income. Keep in mind: While you're clear on what you want in a vacation home, what prospective tenants want may be a different story. Being on the water is a plus, as is being a short walk from town. And amenities like cable, VCRs, and state-of-the-art barbecues can often make or break a deal.

THE BIG THREE: THINGS TO TAKE AWAY FROM TALKING REAL ESTATE

1. The time to start preparing to buy a home is six months to a year before you put yourself in the marketplace. Figure out what you can truly afford to spend (not based solely on what you can borrow, but also on what living there will cost). Give your credit report a once-over. And get preapproved for a loan.

2. Whether you're buying or selling, choose your brokers wisely. Make sure you understand who they're working for, who's paying them, and how much. (Helpful hint: If you do a lot of the early legwork yourself by shopping online, you ought to get compensated for it.)

3. Choosing a mortgage is almost as important as choosing a house. Be certain to survey the landscape of adjustable and fixed rate loans to find the right product for your needs—then shop everywhere for the best rate: online, local banks (big and small), credit unions, and mortgage brokers. Even small rate differences can mean a huge amount of money over thirty years.

CHAPTER 9

Talking Spending

Jim, a forty-three-year-old airplane restorer living in New York City, may not have been born to shop, but he was trained for it from a very young age. When he was a boy, his father, a manufacturing executive, took Jim with him to Paris on business. Dad led son into the lobby of an ultraposh, ultra*expensive* hotel, then asked for the manager and began to bargain.

"I could keep an apartment in the city, but I'd prefer to stay here five or six weeks a year," his father explained. "The only thing is, since I'm giving you that much business I don't expect to pay the full nightly rate."

"What would you be willing to pay?" the manager inquired.

Jim's father thought for a minute, then named his price: precisely half the going nightly rate. Noticing the manager's hesitation, he sweetened the deal by offering to pay for his first year's worth of stays up front. That did it. "Remember, Jimmy," his dad said as they headed for the exit, "everybody negotiates."

Jim not only remembered, he's put that philosophy to use in countless ways throughout his life. Two years ago, he had about

$100,000 in one of his brokerage accounts, against which he wanted to take a $10,000 loan. But before he opened up a margin account with his current brokerage firm, he did some hard-core research on interest rates using one of his favorite tools—the telephone. "I made about thirty phone calls to brokers who offered rates ranging from as high as 11 percent to as low as 6.5 percent," he says. In fact, telling them up front he was shopping for the best rate helped immensely. The reps on the line didn't feel the need to go through a big sales song-and-dance. Ultimately, he went with PaineWebber at 6.5 percent, which saved him thousands over the life of the loan.

Even more recently, he was in the market for a car. After sifting through a number of car magazines as well as *Consumer Reports*, he decided on a mid-level sedan. He had a handle on dealer cost. He was fluent in his options. But instead of driving from one dealership to another, he faxed about two dozen dealerships. His goal: to find the cheapest possible deal. Again, it worked. After talking to several of the most promising respondents over the phone, he got an offer of $200 over invoice price. Excellent.

I like to think of myself as a pretty good shopper—I thoroughly research my purchases, I tend not to buy on impulse, and I have a knack for buying clothes at the end of the season when they're on sale—but even I took a few lessons away from Jim, particularly that last one. On the other hand, sometimes it's hard not to get so involved in the hunt for the best price on a dishwasher, swing set, or pair of leather loafers that you forget that the time you spend shopping is a valuable commodity, too.

Shopping well, *spending* well, falls somewhere in between. It means learning to buy what you need, avoid what you don't, and tell the difference. It means learning to do enough research that you get the best possible price while not compromising on your time. It means learning how to recognize the signs of buyer's remorse before you make a purchase in the first place (believe me, they're there).

We'll talk about the biggest mistakes people make with their money, according to research by some of the country's leading behavior experts. Then we'll focus on how to avoid making them,

using the Five Questions to Ask Yourself Before You Buy Anything—which you can (and should) apply to a $59 pair of shoes as
well as a $30,000 SUV—and the Four Golden Rules of Shopping
(these rules are what my mother taught me). And we'll talk about
the best ways to approach Internet shopping—and what you need
to look out for. Finally, here are some tips on making some of your
most common—and costly—purchases.

Avoiding Overspending

Elyse, one of the reporters who helped me research this book, and
her husband, Barry, were out recently shopping for a desk for their
home office. They spent two full afternoons on their quest, even paying a baby-sitter, so that they could give it their full attention, when
finally they hit upon a beautiful one. It was made of cherry wood,
practically heirloom quality. At $1,600 it cost more than they planned
on spending—but after so much time and effort, they simply bit the
bullet and handed over their Visa card to give the store a deposit.

Wouldn't you know, the next day a friend happened to mention
to Elyse that she had a spare computer table. Its price tag was
slightly better: It was free. Elyse checked out the piece and it was
not only functional, it was even a better fit for her space than the
desk. She decided to take it. But when she went to stop the ship-
ment of the desk, she learned there would be a $70 cancellation
charge. That was annoying. She didn't like the idea of spending $70
for *nothing*—who would?—so her mind started to scramble. She remembered that, in fact, there was a $125 lamp in the store that she'd
also liked, so she asked the sales clerk if the $70 could be applied
to *that* purchase. It could. But there would be a $35 delivery charge
for that item. Elyse agreed. In fact, she was relieved.

But what actually happened here? Did Elyse save $70 by not
paying the cancellation fee? Or did she waste the money she spent
because she bought another piece of furniture she didn't really
need? "The larger savings on the desk completely wiped out any
commonsense thoughts about the fees I proceeded to pay on the

lamp," she says with a shrug. "In fact, that lamp wasn't necessarily the best deal to begin with—but it had a lot of appeal considering I was faced with spending $70 and getting nothing in return."

This is exactly the way most people spend money. We run into the supermarket for milk and eggs and come out fifteen minutes later with two full bags of groceries. Why? *We were hungry.* We head into Old Navy for a couple of pairs of pajamas for our kids and emerge with an entire wardrobe. Why? *It was on sale.* We run to CompUSA to check out the prices on the latest PCs so we can use that information to shop around and return home with a new machine in the back of the minivan. Why? *We were afraid it wouldn't be there tomorrow.*

How can we avoid making mistakes like these? Two ways:

The Studied Approach

For two decades now, business school professor Max Bazerman, most recently teaching at Harvard, has been marveling at the often ridiculous decisions we make about our money. When the stakes are highest, we make the most mistakes, he says. "I'm shocked at the number of people who'll spend a Saturday afternoon going to three different grocery stores in order to save $7, but will then blow $30,000 because they don't do their homework when they buy a house," says Bazerman. He spoke with me about some of the mistakes people make most often. Just being aware of them should help you avoid them.

• **Being unprepared.** Most people don't do enough prep work before they make big decisions. Car buyers who hate the process, for example, will just bite the bullet and buy something, rather than spend ten minutes on the Internet to find the exact dealer cost of the make and model they're looking for.

• **Ignoring what others are thinking.** Whether you're involved in buying a house, a car, or a stock—or negotiating for a raise at work—ask yourself what the person on the other side of the deal is thinking. It puts you in a much better negotiating position.

- **Acting on impulse.** Particularly when it comes to your money, it's important to make rational decisions. Do you really want to jump to buy the latest in computers, for example, just because they're flying out of the store at lightning speed and you're afraid they won't be there tomorrow? Or would you be better off figuring out how this particular machine fits into your life? Perhaps you don't need all that power and could save a bunch by buying last month's model.

- **Butting heads.** Most people head into negotiations convinced that what's good for the other side is automatically bad for them. In truth, there's often a middle ground that has benefits for both parties. Think about a car negotiation. Perhaps you've asked for a lower price than the salesman is able to cough up. What happens? You can—and should—try shopping around some more, but don't give up on the fact that this salesman may be able to satisfy your needs in some other way: Perhaps he can offer a terrific financing deal? Maybe he can throw in the first month or two on a lease for free.

My Mother's Approach: The Four Golden Rules of Shopping

I've come to realize in life—as in money—there are two very different kinds of intelligence. There's book learning, which is nice to have. But there's also common sense, which I believe (particularly because I've been around enough people *lacking* it) is even more important. These are four rules of shopping that my mother lives by. She rarely put them into words, but I've watched her my entire life and these are the things she *does*. They are huge money savers.

- **Make a list.** Here's what happens when you have a list. You can run into the grocery store (or wherever), scurry down the aisles for the items you need, and get out having spent about what you'd planned on. Without a list, you're lost. You buy everything that looks good, spend more than you'd planned on, and end up with items you really don't need. Plus, shopping with a list isn't just a money saver, it's a time saver. It keeps you from having to run back to the store the hour before your guests arrive for a dinner party because you forgot the olives the recipe called for.

• **Don't procrastinate.** While it's true that waiting to buy that pair of loafers until the end of the season when they're 50 percent off can save you a bundle, procrastinating usually doesn't pay when it comes to shopping. That's something my mother has always understood. She buys the plane tickets for her trips as soon as she puts them on her calendar, so that she can either use frequent flyer miles or capitalize on the cheapest available fare. She subscribes to the magazines she wants to read rather than paying the more expensive newsstand price. And she really loads up at the supermarket, so that she rarely needs to "pick up a few things" at a higher-priced convenience store.

• **Work the phones.** When I'm shopping, whether for a hotel room, new carpeting, or a bunch of flowers for Valentine's Day, I work the phones like crazy. Why? Because I'm the daughter of a woman who understood that taking some time to call around saves you money. Here's how my mother books a rental car. She calls the 800 number and asks for the rate. Then she asks a series of questions that sound something like this: "Can you do better? Do you have a corporate discount? How about an AAA discount? Is there a better rate on a larger car or minivan? And if we're there over a weekend? How about if we take it the entire week?" For an upcoming family vacation she booked her own car and then phoned me: "Now, don't book your car directly through the rental agency," she told me. "If you book it through the hotel, you get a much better deal." How did she know this? She kept someone on the phone for a good ten minutes until she figured it out—and saved each of us more than $100 in the process.

• **Wait a day.** This might be the best one on the list. The next time you're in a department store, holding a super pair of black pants in your hands that you think you *have* to have, stop. Think. Don't you have three pairs in your closet just like them? Do you really need another? If you're wavering, put the item—whatever it is— on hold. If you still absolutely, positively have to have it tomorrow, it'll still be there. But you'll probably decide you can live without it.

Our money habits are probably not innate. But they're with us from a very young age. If your kids hear you talking about prices on everything from airfares and hotel rooms to birthday party entertainment, they're going to get the message. We live in a haggle economy. You're not going to do better price-wise unless you ask.

Five Questions to Ask Yourself Before You Buy Anything

Okay, so let's pretend you're standing in Williams Sonoma with your fingertips on the carafe of the latest Krups coffeemaker. It's sleek and stylish. Fits in nicely with your all-white kitchen. At $189, it seems a little expensive but not all that over-the-top. So, what do you do? If you said, "Buy it!" you haven't been paying attention. Asking yourself the following questions about this purchase—and any other—will clue you in as to whether you want to head to the checkout. Or not.

1. Do I know the fair price of this item? No matter what you are buying, you could be overpaying. What's more, the fact that one model costs more than another does not ensure that it's better quality. You need to know what an item should cost so that you're not enticed by some kind of gimmick. This is particularly the case on rarely purchased things such as a crown for your tooth or a new roof for your house.

2. Am I too emotionally involved in this purchase? Home buying and buying at auction (online or off) are two areas famous for people overpaying due to emotional reactions. Often people realize that and can focus on the more practical side of those deals. But did you know you could be just as emotionally attached to that trendy shirt at Banana Republic? So says Takira K. Hira, Ph.D., professor of Human Development and Family Studies at Iowa State University. In a 1999 report published in the *Journal of Family and Consumer Sciences* she found that self-worth had a lot to do with the amount of money people felt comfortable spending—and *not* spending. In general, she noted, people with low self-worth are more inclined to shop without plans, buy things they can't afford, and have secretive spending habits.

3. Do I really need this? One of the biggest spending mistakes is buying something you won't use. If you have an exercise bike or a treadmill at home gathering dust, you understand. Aside from having too lofty New Year's resolutions, people also waste money buying items simply because they are on sale; or they buy in bulk for the better price and wind up giving stuff away or throwing it away.

Red Flag! Make sure you compare unit costs at warehouse clubs with those at your local supermarket. There are times when bigger isn't necessarily cheaper.

4. How well do I know this product? Just as you shouldn't blindly trust a brand name, you shouldn't trust just one source's review of a product, even if the source is *Consumer Reports* or another of your favorite magazines. Get at least one more expert opinion. And finally, don't pay for features that you don't need.

5. Am I using the Internet to shop smartly—or just to shop? No doubt there are many unbelievable deals to be found shopping on the Web. But caveat emptor: Such giveaways and promotions are there for one reason—to draw you in. As anyone who's ever surfed the Net for a couple of hours can attest, cyberspace can be a tough world in which to control yourself. To get the most out of the Internet, use it for comparison shopping and research that will point you in the direction of the best online deal for whatever product you're looking for.

Red Flag! Make sure you take the value of your time into account. Spending two hours to save $5 isn't a wise move, when you could be making much more than that by putting in some extra time at work.

Shopping on the Internet

Before we move on to how to shop for some specific items, let's talk a minute more about Internet shopping strategies. I'll admit up front,

I love Web shopping. I use it to actually buy clothes for the entire family, groceries, toys and other birthday gifts, and cosmetics. It works well whenever you know precisely what you're getting, less well when you don't. For example, I've used it to load up on basic GapKids clothes for my two children—turtlenecks ($4.99!), T-shirts, mittens. But I wouldn't use the Internet to buy them shoes; those have to be properly fit. I might have to return them once they arrived and that can be expensive and time-consuming. But I don't have concerns about giving my credit card over the Internet as long as the site is secure (look for an s after the http, or a little lock in the lower-left-hand corner of your screen) and has a decent privacy policy (read it!). A few other things to keep in mind:

• **Watch shipping costs.** Just as with catalogue shopping, Internet shopping can save you time—but it can also cost you when it comes to shipping. Make sure you include shipping and handling when you're comparing prices between sites (particularly as sites try to win your business, some throw in shipping for free). And if you think whatever you're ordering might end up going back to the site, factor in return shipping as well.

• **Look for seals of approval.** One of the things that's both advantageous and frightening about shopping on the Web is the access it gives you to merchants not in your area (great if you're looking for your favorite saltwater taffy from Atlantic City). But you need to be sure that the person selling this item to you is legit. So scroll to the bottom of the site's front page and look for a BBB icon; that means it passes muster with the Better Business Bureau. Also look for a BizRate.com icon or link. BizRate is like the Zagat guide of Internet shopping. Consumers rate stores they've shopped in for things like customer service and shipping and BizRate compiles those ratings so that you can look at them before you buy.

• **Keep records.** Just in case something goes haywire with a purchase, you ought to have a paper trail. Make sure you print out the confirmation you receive at the end of your order as well as any e-mails the site sends you noting when your package will be (or has been) shipped. Then save them until you've not only received and checked over the merchandise, but until the charge shows up on your credit card and you know for certain that it squares.

 • **Note return policies.** Returning items purchased online isn't the bear that many people think it is. According to one report from Forrester Research, 90 percent of sites that have actual stores will allow you to return merchandise in person rather than paying to mail it back. Still, that's something you want to know up front. And in the case of pricey electronic equipment, you also want to note if there's a restocking fee—a charge of sometimes $50 to $75 just for putting the item back in the warehouse.

Getting a Good Deal On:

Cars

It makes sense that cars come first in this section. Next to your house, you'd probably be hard pressed to name another single item that costs as much. There are two big questions you need to ponder when it comes to your next car purchase. First—do you want to buy or lease? And second—how do you get a good deal? Let's tackle them both.

Buy or Lease?

Before you get enticed by a fantastic-looking lease deal, you need to understand how a lease works. When you lease, you pay for the depreciation (decrease in value) during the time that car is in your possession. That amount is the difference between the price you pay (called the *capitalized cost*) and the car's worth at the end of the lease (the *residual value*). The smaller the gap between those figures (and the lower the interest charge), the lower your monthly payment. So when a company wants to move cars, it reduces interest rates or raises residual values.

There were a few years in the late 1990s when leasing looked incredibly attractive. Residual values were being kept ridiculously high. But when those leases expired, leasing companies discovered that a car wasn't worth a 68 percent residual value, for example, but

58 percent. As a result, the incentives to lease have been scaled back. But it's still the right call for some people. How do you know if you're one of them? Ask yourself these four questions:

- **How many years will I have this car?** If the answer is three or less, you're better off leasing. At four you could go either way. More than four, buy.
- **How many miles do I drive annually?** If it's more than 15,000 you ought to buy. Leases are usually figured on mileage of 12,000 to 15,000 a year. Drive more than that and you'll pay an additional 10 to 15 cents per mile. Ouch!
- **Do I take good care of my car?** Be honest. If you're the kind of person who never misses an oil change and avoids curbs at all costs, you'll be fine when it comes time to return your leased car. But if not, buy. Otherwise, you could find yourself looking at a hefty bill for "excessive wear and tear."
- **Do I use the car for business?** If yes, you may want to lease. When you buy a business car, the IRS limits the amount of depreciation you can write off. If you lease, you can write off up to your full monthly payment.

Negotiate Like a Pro

Whether you buy or lease, you then need to be prepared to negotiate. It's not always easy. (Remember my Durango?) Here's what you need to do:

- **Get a handle on costs.** The very first thing you have to do is get a grip on the dealer's cost (also called the dealer invoice price). You can find these on the Internet (try edmunds.com) as well as in a number of books. Once you have that number, decide how much above it you're willing to pay. Several hundred is a good starting point on the most popular models. On luxury cars, you'll have to pay $1,000 to $2,000 over invoice. Sometimes more.
- **Put yourself in the driver's seat.** The best thing you can do before you walk into a dealership is have a loan approval in the bag. Even if you decide to go with manufacturer-arranged financing be-

cause it happens to be a great deal, you don't *have* to. Which means you can just name your price and see if the dealership will meet it. Get all offers you like in writing and don't jump at the first one that seems to be in your range. Make sure you shop at least a couple of other dealers to see if you can beat it.

• **Consider going used.** There's no better deal on the planet than a good used car, with a solid warranty, that you drive into the ground. Used cars started outselling new cars in the late 1980s and continued to do so through the 1990s. It makes sense. By the time a car is two years old, it's depreciated by about 60 percent—and yet it has only about one third of its lifetime miles. The advent of manufacturers' certified warranties, with 100- to 120-point checklists that must be satisfied before a car leaves the showroom (again), made them even more attractive. These warranties cover cars either for an additional year or two or up to a preset mileage cap. If you're thinking about buying used, they're something to look for. But be certain you know what entity is behind the warranty, and precisely what it covers.

Dining Out

A few years back, fashion writer Hal Rubenstein wrote a series of restaurant reviews for *New York* magazine. At the end of one of his stories he tossed in a nugget about how he took the time to double-check his last dozen restaurant tabs and found that nearly half of them were wrong. Shocking? You'd think so, except that Americans don't typically think of the money they spend in restaurants as typical purchases. We don't fight as hard to get our money's worth.

We should. Every year the average American household spends nearly $2,000 dining out, according to New Strategist Publications. And as we work longer hours leaving us less time to cook, I have no doubt that number will head skyward. That's reason enough to approach dining in a restaurant as any other consumer experience. I'm not saying you need to haggle over every item on the bill; just to make sure you know where rip-offs are likely to lurk.

• **Specials.** Beware of servers who push specials that aren't written anywhere. It's not unusual for them to be more expensive than every other item on the menu. Simply ask how much they are as he lists them. After you ask a couple of times, he'll get the idea.

• **Bottled water.** Before I started writing about money, I harbored some fantasies of writing about food—and to that end, spent a semester in cooking school. One thing I learned is that bottled water (along with egg dishes and coffee) is a huge profit center for restaurants. Beware of a place that starts pouring and doesn't stop.

• **Wine.** Be certain the bottle you order is the bottle you receive. Sometimes less expensive varietals are substituted for pricier versions. Sometimes a restaurant will cavalierly substitute a less expensive year but still charge you the higher price. Pay attention to what you order, and if there's something wrong with a bottle, don't hesitate to call the sommelier over for a second opinion or to simply send it back.

• **Tips.** More and more restaurants, it appears, are blowing it when it comes to service these days. Sixty-two percent of complaints received by the Zagat Survey are about service; only 10 percent are about food. I was in a restaurant with a party of six over the summer of 1999 when the waiter unceremoniously tacked his own 20 percent gratuity onto the bill. Had this been the restaurant's policy (duly noted on the menu or anywhere else) I wouldn't have been annoyed. But there was no such policy. So we complained to the manager, who apologized profusely. And I'll never go back. Tips are your prerogative. If you feel as if service was lacking, you don't need to feel it's a must to give your server a full 15 to 20 percent. However, if there was a problem with the meal that wasn't your waiter's fault, he or she shouldn't be penalized. (See more on tipping in other situations in Chapter 11.)

Home Repair

As the real estate market boomed at the end of the 1990s, home renovation contractors—you know, the ones who stopped returning your phone calls—reaped the rewards. Yup, they were swamped.

And as a result, their prices soared. So did the waiting time for their services. In fact, home improvement firms, big and small, were having such trouble finding good help they started offering employees a litany of unusual benefits. My Plumber, in Fairfax, Virginia, for one, started bringing in manicurists and masseuses for its staff. At times, the situation may seem grim. But it isn't hopeless. Five tips to help you get the job done right:

- **Know what you want.** Before you sit down with a contractor, list exactly what you want your project to include. Put things you must have (your needs) at the top of your list, and those that aren't such necessities (your wants) below, so that you can get a base rate for the project and add on incrementally.
- **Get three bids.** You'll never know if you're getting a good deal unless you ask several contractors what your project will cost. Be sure to ask each to bid on the same job (use your needs-and-wants list as a guide); otherwise you'll never get an apples-to-apples comparison. And make certain anyone you consider has the proper liability insurance (typically $500,000 to $3 million). Your contractor should be willing to show you an insurance certificate, but they tell me no one ever asks.
- **Put it in writing.** Once you've chosen a contractor, get all details on paper. Include what will and won't be done (such as protecting the property around the job site); specify materials to be used down to the brand of paint; and settle on a start and estimated completion date. Any changes to the original contract through the course of the job should be put in writing and initialed by both parties.
- **Gauge the payoff.** There are two places in the home that give you the biggest bang for the buck—new kitchens and new baths. According to *Kitchen and Bath Business*, an industry publication, both of these generally return close to their full investment in one year (as long as you don't go completely crazy) and continue to boost your home's value thereafter. Other features you might want to add, particularly to older homes, are those that buyers expect in newer homes: a family room (off the kitchen if you can manage it), and master bedroom *suite* (with dressing rooms). Everything should

be bright, airy and open; dark wood was for the 1970s. Other additions—like a home office—don't pay off as often because not everyone will use them.

• **Pay in chunks.** Pay your contractor only as the job progresses. Usually, that means one third up front, another third when the job is half completed, and another chunk at the end. Try to hold back at least 10 percent until the punch list of odds and ends to be taken care of by the contractor is complete. And be sure to build in a financial buffer. If you have friends who are renovating, you've heard horror stories about how much more than the estimate the job is costing. Even if contractors stick to their guns in terms of materials, two things can throw a job into a financial free-for-all. First, contractors don't have any clue what's behind your walls. Damaged pipes, misplaced wires, and other structural problems all can be very expensive to fix. It may pay to let a contractor hack a hole in your wall simply to take a look (as long as you know you're going to be taking it down eventually anyway). The other factor that jacks up the price is your mind. Start changing it in the middle of a job or asking for extras (especially those "and while you're there . . ." kind of extras) and it's going to cost you.

• **Don't let small jobs go.** Letting routine maintenance slide can be incredibly costly later on. For example: Poor roof drainage can cause basement leaks and damage to your walls, carpet, and floors. All told you could spend $1,500 to $2,000 to fix the problem. But you could save yourself the trouble in many cases by cleaning your gutters regularly (or paying a handyman $50 to do it for you). Likewise, rotting windows can cost $1,000 to $1,500 to replace, but you may not need to if you make sure that they're properly caulked.

Pets

I recently spent $175 to cure an ear infection. I don't know that I would be writing about it if the ear infection were my daughter's. Then again, even if she had it in both ears—as is often the case—I would have forked out $15 at the pediatrician and another $10 at the pharmacy for amoxicillin, and been done with it. Not this time though. The ear infection was my dog's.

We got our dog, Pavlov (my husband, Peter, was a psych major in college), in the summer of 1998, strangely enough the same time several of our friends got puppies of their own. Over the last few years our conversation has veered toward the surprisingly high cost of pet care. At one point, we were spending $40 every three weeks for a giant-sized bag of premium dog food, about the same every three months for Lyme disease prevention serum (we live in a deer-filled zone), $25 a day for pet sitting if we were away. And I'm not even going to tell you the cost of fixing the newly upholstered sofa that the dog ripped trying to unbury a bone that was stuck underneath. We love her—no doubt about that. But I don't need to spend more than necessary on her care. And neither do you. So:

• **Skip the superpremium foods.** Because of competition from superpremium brands, many supermarket brands have really improved in quality. Just be sure that any food you buy has been developed in accordance with protocols set by the AAFCO, a not-for-profit government group that develops pet food guidelines. It'll be reflected on the label.

• **Invest in preventive care.** According to the American Veterinary Medical Association, pet owners spend more than $11 billion annually on pet health care services—about $200 per year per pet—making that the biggest pet expense overall. What figures into that number? Annual checkups, vaccinations, heartworm pills, flea and tick treatments, and so on. What many pet owners don't understand is that preventive care—good nutrition, dental hygiene, plenty of fresh water, vaccines, and regular physicals and exercise—can mean the difference between pet bills that run hundreds of dollars annually, and those that run thousands, particularly as your pets age.

• **Consider pet insurance.** Some people won't go beyond a certain point in paying for their pet's health care. But a huge number—78 percent according to a study published in the *Journal of the American Medical Association*—think of their pets as children and expect their pets to get the same level of medical care as everyone else in the family. If you're among them, pet insurance is probably a good idea. Some insurance plans work like traditional indemnity health plans; the insurer covers 80 percent of medical bills after a deductible is met. Others are like preferred provider organizations (PPOs); you pay an annual fee, then receive a discount off veterinary bills. Look for brochures in your vet's waiting room. Some doctors have even established their own insurance plans.

• **Invest in training.** Obedience training runs anywhere from $40 to $100-plus an hour (less if you take a group class) but it can be well worth the expense. A dog that tears up your yard, chews on your furniture, or—yes—rips a hole in your couch can cost you much more than that. My dog's in-house expenses ran $300-plus. I could have purchased a semester's worth of obedience training for that.

Phone Service

Whether you're shopping for long-distance, regional, or cellular service these days, you ought to be following the same basic methodology. You need the answers to three questions.

• **How much do you talk?** If you pull out your last three bills, and average them, you'll have a basic idea.

• **When do you do that talking?** Do you talk business hours—essentially weekdays between 9:00 A.M. and 5:00 or 6:00 P.M.? Or do you talk nights or weekends?

• **Where do you call?** Are all your calls essentially local or regional? Are most of them long-distance, but domestic? Or are you a big international caller—and if so, where specifically (as in country) do you call?

Once you have that information, you can use it to shop for the best deal in any type of phone plan. I'm not going to recommend any specific phone plans here; they change so rapidly, I have no doubt they'd be obsolete in the short time it took this book to make it into print. Instead, here are a few general guidelines:

• **Call your own phone company first.** Call customer service and ask them to "audit" your bill. Essentially this means, look at my calling habits and tell me if I'm on the cheapest plan for me. If you spend more than $25 a month on long distance, it's crucial to be on some sort of discount plan, despite the fact that these often come with monthly fees in the $3 to $5 range. If you spend less than $25 monthly, you may not want a plan, but instead will want to use one of the dial-around services (you'll know them because they start with 10-10) each time you place a long-distance call. Often, just the five to ten minutes it takes to make this call can slash your bill by a significant amount.

• **Then shop around a bit.** If you still think you can do better, call the other phone companies. Don't limit yourself to the biggies— smaller carriers can provide similar service often at much cheaper prices. You can find a list of carriers at the Web site of the not-for-profit Telecommunications Research and Action Committee, www.trac.org. Note: If you're a big international caller, you have to compare rates for calling each country specifically.

• **Don't sign a long-term contract.** If you're asking a cell phone company for a free or cheap phone (or even a very low rate), chances are that company is going to ask you to sign a one- to two-year contract in return. Be careful. If you haven't used a cell phone before, you likely have no idea how many minutes you'll really use. You may sign up for a package with very few minutes and use a lot, only to be charged for those extra minutes at extremely high rates.

• **Think about cutting the cord.** It may be in your best economic interest for your cell phone to be your only phone—particularly if your usage justifies a package where minutes are ten cents or below. Often you get features like voice mail, call waiting, and caller ID that can be pricey with basic long distance for free.

Travel

Here's the thing about shopping for travel: If you don't shop around, either by doing it yourself or pressing your travel agent to come up with "something better," you're almost certain to get ripped off. The trick, particularly with airfares, is understanding a bit about how they work, so that you can get the lowest ones going. The same is true for finding a decent rate on a hotel room—even for renting a car (remember my mom?). Here are a few of my favorite strategies:

Airfares

• **Ask for the lowest fare.** Sounds simple, I know. But when you call to book a flight, if you don't ask for the lowest available fare, you're not going to get it. Then ask if there are any promotional fares kicking in soon. If there are, ask if there's a way to hold a seat at that lower price. Finally, reserve your seat and say you'll call back to pay for it. Then head over to the Web and see if you can do better on a site like Travelocity.com.

• **Shop early, shop often.** You can save significantly by purchasing your tickets at least seven to fourteen days before you fly—and by staying over a Saturday night. Yes, the reservationist will tell you these are nonrefundable, but you can exchange them for a small fee and use the money for travel in the next one to two years (policies vary by airline).

• **Try a consolidator.** Consolidators are companies that take large blocks of seats off an airline's hands, then sell them at a discount— to you. You still fly on the airlines whose names you know (as opposed to charter flights, where you typically don't). But while you can save a third or more on your ticket price, you won't have as many flights from which to choose. It's easy to find up-to-date lists of consolidators—for both airfares and hotel rooms—on the Web using just about any search engine.

• **Become a courier.** If you're traveling light, think about becoming an airline courier. In exchange for a big discount on a ticket, you give away the right to check your luggage to a courier service (you can bring a carry-on bag). The pros: The prices, but they're not all bottom-of-the-barrel—you need to compare courier rates with the bargains you can come up with yourself. The cons: Inflexibility. You typically have to leave from a major U.S. city, and though you'll have a choice of international destinations, they won't be limitless.

• **Use your miles.** According to *Inside Flyer* magazine, 75 percent of all frequent flyer miles go unused each year. Big mistake. As long as you're taking the time to earn them, you ought to use them—and use them wisely. Don't blow a lot of miles to book a flight that would be inexpensive anyway. Rather than save $200 on a round-trip ticket, you might do better by transferring your miles into a hotel program that would get you two or three free nights. Note, too: If you're close to hitting the mileage needed to qualify for an elite level of a frequent flyer program, make the effort to cross the line. It often comes with more free upgrades, and bonuses on miles earned.

Hotels

The basic price on a hotel room is called the *rack rate*. That's what you get when you call and book a room without asking for added discounts. How do you avoid it?

• **Call the hotel directly.** If you press the reservationist a bit—and it usually pays to call a reservationist at the hotel itself, rather than one manning the toll-free number for an entire chain—you shouldn't have to pay it.

• **Speak your mind.** Ask for corporate or group discount if you work for a big company or belong to a group like AAA. If you're staying Friday or Saturday night, ask for a weekend discount or a weekend package (often these come with freebies like continental breakfast).

• **Phone your travel agent.** Check the prices you find yourself against those your travel agent can get you. Travel agents often book through hotel brokers who buy blocks of rooms at cut rates, so they may be able to offer you better prices. Or, if you're willing to do some additional research, you can try these brokers yourself (hotelnet.com on the Web is one large one).

• **Be loyal.** Finally, if you travel frequently, pick one chain, join its loyalty program, and stick with it. My brother Eric, who travels constantly for business, is a Marriott loyalist. Every time we go away on a family vacation he gets something for free—it may not be his room, instead it may be his rental car or some other perk, but it often comes from the nights he's spent with Marriott.

Shut Up, Already: Financial Information to Keep to Yourself

Here's how the scenario typically goes. It's nine at night. You're dozing off in front of *Frasier* and the phone rings. You answer, suspecting it's your mother (she's so predictable) but no. It's the AAA collection agency. The impatient guy on the other end of the line wants to know how soon you'll be able to pay the $5,000 you owe to First United Capital One Bank USA Visa.

"Excuse me," you stammer. "I think you've got the wrong number. I don't have a card with First United Capital One Bank USA. And I certainly didn't charge $5,000 worth of stuff." But the guy's not backing off. He's got your number. In fact, that's not all he has. He has your name, address, date of birth, and your Social Security number. You've been a victim of identity theft.

According to the Privacy Rights Clearinghouse, some 400,000 people a year have their identities stolen. Sometimes it's done the old-fashioned way: A thief slips your wallet out of your purse or jacket pocket. Other times it's more covert: Pirates case your mailbox for fresh preapproved offers of credit. They sift through your garbage for credit card receipts you toss. Even better, they case your doctor's garbage where new patient applications, thrown out after the information has been entered into the computer system, lie just waiting to be taken. It's not only a big problem, it's a growing problem. Incidences of identity theft have been climbing 140 percent annually since 1992.

If it happens, your liability, thankfully, is limited. On a stolen credit or debit card, you'll owe no more than $50 max. But the cost in your time can be enormous. To say identity theft blotches up your credit record is an understatement. It can take months if not years to clear your good name. That's why it's important to do what you can to protect it in the first place. Some steps:

• **Clean out your wallet:** We carry around far too much identifying information. You shouldn't be toting your passport, birth certificate, credit cards you're not using (if you haven't used them in some time, close the accounts), and most importantly your Social Security card. Your Social Security number is key for an identity thief. If someone gets ahold of it, they can use it to apply for credit or other loans in your name. There are only a few valid occasions to give it out: when you're applying for a job, doing your taxes, or involved in a stock or other financial transaction. In most other cases the person asking for the number wants to use it for identification purposes. Ask if they'll substitute another number instead. Even states that use Social Security numbers as driver's license numbers are often willing to make a switch.

• **Get off mailing lists:** Preapproved credit applications aren't the sort of documents you want to leave lying around the house (or the garbage for that matter). Most of these come from mailing lists generated by the three major credit reporting bureaus, Trans Union, Equifax, and Experian. The good news is you can get off these lists with a single phone call to 1-888-5OPT-OUT. (If you want to get back on these lists, a phone call to the same number will accomplish that as well.)

• **Choose smart passwords:** Even if a thief gets his hands on your ATM card, chances are he won't be able to use it unless you've chosen an obvious password. So stay away from your name, date of birth, address, phone number, and the last four digits of your Social Security number. Instead, pick something that's easy for you to remember but would stupefy a thief: the name of your first-grade teacher, the license plate number of your first car. A combination of letters and numbers is best.

• **Check your credit report:** Identity theft goes for months in some cases because the victim has no idea it's happening. The best thing you can do to keep tabs on your identity—the only thing, in fact—is to check your credit report frequently. The Privacy Rights Clearinghouse suggests twice a year. For details on how see Chapter 2.

> • **Act quickly, if it happens:** If your identity is stolen, report it immediately to the three credit reporting bureaus. Ask to have a victim's statement added to your file, so that any future applications for credit will have to be verified by you. Report it to the police and make sure you get a copy of the police report to show to credit card companies in case they ask. If there has been fraudulent activity on your own cards (rather than just those that the thief has applied for) cancel every one and get new cards and account numbers. Stop payment on checks you have outstanding. And get new cards, PIN numbers, and account numbers for the ATM as well. Only change your Social Security number in the most severe of situations—if your name has become associated with bad checks and credit. It's a record-keeping nightmare. If you go this extra step, it's up to you to let your financial institutions, employers, the IRS, creditors, and the credit bureaus know of the change.

THE BIG THREE: THINGS TO TAKE AWAY FROM TALKING SPENDING

1. Making smart spending decisions requires more commonsense (even old-fashioned) wisdom than anything else. To keep yourself on the straight and narrow, make lists, do research on the phone before you hit the stores, and if you're not certain whether you really want something or not, put it on hold for a day and give your decision some time to settle.

2. Internet shopping may be the next big thing, but it can also be a huge waste of time—and a pocket drain. Make sure to watch shipping costs, look for seals of the Better Business Bureau (and similar organizations), note return policies, and keep a paper trail of all your transactions.

3. Next to your house, your car is likely to be your biggest purchase. Be certain you understand the decision to lease or buy. And don't even start talking to a salesman until you know what *the dealer* paid for the car.

CHAPTER 10

Talking Money with Your Investment Team

I recently spent several hours on the phone with Denise, a Florida woman who says that money was the *only* contentious issue in her recent divorce. Denise, a mother of two in her mid-forties, says she and her husband had no problem deciding to sell their house, sharing custody of their children (he took the kids on weekends), or dividing up their belongings, 50-50. But when it came to their cash and stocks—some of which he'd brought with him to the marriage—they tried and failed to reach an agreement, mainly because Denise's ex insisted she was trying to claim too large a share of their assets. Several months and a few thousand dollars in legal bills later, Denise's attorney suggested bringing in a different kind of pro: a financial planner specializing in divorce, known in the business as a "divorce planner."

In just twelve hours, and for less than $2,000, the divorce planner they selected untangled their mess. How? He ran two sets of numbers showing the division of assets. The first depicted only the couple's marital assets, and the second showed all of their assets. The comparison demonstrated that the 50 percent of marital assets

Denise was requesting was only 35 to 40 percent of the couple's total net worth. Result: The pie charts made Denise's ex-husband feel more comfortable. All of a sudden they had a deal.

There are many different kinds of financial planners—literally dozens. Some are generalists who can advise you on everything from buying insurance to building a portfolio to buying a car. They are often a part of your life for years, if not decades. Other sorts of planners, like divorce planners, are specialists. They're hired to perform a specific function like working out the details of a divorce or simply getting you started financially, and after that you may never see them again.

Choosing a financial planner is a job in itself, partly because the government doesn't regulate the financial planning industry. The bottom line is that anyone—licensed or not—can call themselves a financial planner. Insurance agents, full service stockbrokers, lawyers, and accountants, as well as people trained specifically as financial planners, do it all the time. There are planners paid by commissions, some who make their money on fees, and others who do both. And all of these folks are likely to come with a slew of different designations behind their names. Many of these titles have been created by the financial planning industry, but none is regulated. So if they seem to have been invented to confound you, don't worry, you're not the first person to feel that way.

Despite the confusion, choosing a financial planner isn't a decision you can afford to take lightly. The advice you get from a planner carries a lot of weight, considerably more than the research you do on your own in the library or on your PC. Almost 60 percent of the people who hold mutual fund shares have, at some point in their financial lives, consulted a financial adviser, according to a Spectrum Group/PSI Global survey. And when they did, that adviser's recommendation was three times more likely to spur the purchase of a particular mutual fund than information gleaned from any other source.

In the following pages we'll talk about all the different sorts of planners you're likely to run across and what you can expect to get from them. We'll discuss their fees, their experience, and how to check them out before you put them on your payroll. Then we'll move on to the other important person (or in many cases these days, company) you need in order to have a fully functional financial life: a broker or brokerage firm. Should you work with a full service broker or a discounter—where you're most likely to get personal service—or are you better off with a deep discounter or an online broker, where you'll save a pretty penny but receive little to no hand-holding at all?

As we head into these pages, one caveat. Always remember that this is *your* money you're dealing with. No one is going to be as careful with it as you will. So read every statement you receive in the mail. Let members of your financial team know that you're paying attention. Call them with questions, and point out even minor errors. Speak up when things aren't being handled in a way with which you feel comfortable. You may even learn enough that you decide to take on some of the management tasks yourself.

What Is a Financial Planner?

Financial planners are folks on a mission: to help you assess your goals, and then figure out how to reach them. What you get from financial planners is akin to a financial physical. You'll be asked about what prompted your visit in the first place, as well as your financial past and what you want for your future. Planners will not only look at your investments, but your savings, debts, insurance, taxes, even your estate plan—all with an eye toward developing a written plan that makes sense in all of these areas, as well as weeding out mistakes you may have made previously. If you're making taxable investments when you should be concentrating on tax free ones, a planner should spot that error and point out what it's costing you. If you have too much life insurance and not enough disability coverage, a planner should bring that to your attention as well. Above all, a planner's focus should be on the process and not on selling you particular products.

The major difference between financial *planners* and the law-yers, accountants, and others who give you financial advice is that the planner's work is *comprehensive.* Health, marriage, divorce, kids. It all factors in when a planner is looking at whether you have enough life insurance, the adequacy of your assets, your overall fi-nancial picture. Most people hire financial planners on an ongoing basis. They see them several times early on to develop a financial plan and set it in motion, and then a couple of times a year for a checkup. But it's also possible to hire a planner as a sort of short-term therapist, to help you figure out a specific problem, like how much you can afford to spend on a house or how best to invest for college. Or, if you *think* you're doing well managing your money on your own, but want to be *completely sure,* you can hire a planner for a few hours to give your finances a once-over.

For these shorter-term questions, a specialist who doubles as a financial adviser may work just as well as a comprehensive plan-ner. The adviser may not be as qualified to give you a holistic view, but may be perfect at helping you focus on one part of your financial picture. There are times when an accountant, for exam-ple, may serve every one of your needs. But trying to figure out whether you've got enough life insurance for your growing family probably isn't one of them. Likewise, if you're struggling with in-heritance issues or trying to set up trusts for your kids, you want to talk to an estate planning attorney; but you probably don't want to rely solely on his or her investment advice. Nor should you as-sume your stockbroker knows how much disability insurance you need.

How Is Your Financial Planner Paid?

One important distinction among planners is how they get paid. As a journalist, I tend to rely on "fee-only" planners as sources because I don't think they'll push particular products on my readers. But as a consumer, I don't feel as strongly. In fact, I think that—particularly when you live in an area where there are only a few planners to choose from—you should pick the planner with whom you're most comfortable and who has the best track record rather than limiting yourself to the two or three fee-only planners in town. In order to make sure you don't overpay the planner, ask each one you interview to estimate the costs of fulfilling his or her plan. In the case of a fee-only planner, take into account charges you're not actually paying to the planner, such as brokerage or insurance commissions, as a part of the overall plan. That way you'll be comparing costs on an apples-to-apples basis.

What Do Their Designations Mean?

To read the laundry list of letters behind a planner's name, you'd think they spent decades in school. That, unfortunately, is often not the case. Certified divorce planners, for example—while they come armed with software that can be truly enlightening—took a two-day course followed by a four-hour exam. But they had other credentials (many were already planners, some lawyers, some accountants) to start. Here are some of the designations you'll often see:

• **CFP** (certified financial planner). Given by the Certified Financial Planner Board of Standards, this is the oldest and best known of financial planning designations. It requires a college degree (including a financial planning curriculum), three years of financial planning experience, passing a ten-hour, two-day comprehensive exam covering more than 100 financial planning topics, and thirty hours of continuing education every two years (including two hours in ethics and professional responsibility).

• **ChFC** (chartered financial consultant). This designation is given by the American College in Haverford, Pennsylvania. Recipients must have three years of business experience, take ten courses in topics including financial planning and taxation, and pass an exam for each course. ChFCs who started the college after 1989 must also take thirty hours of continuing education every two years; for others, it's optional. Because the American College was started by the

How they work	
Fee-Only Planners	Fee-only planners charge purely for advice. You pay them by the hour (typically $100 to $300) or by the plan (anywhere from about $1,000 to $5,000) and in return you get guidance.
Commission-Only Planners	As the name suggests, commission-only planners make their money when you buy an investment or insurance product from them.
Fee-Based Planners	These planners charge both commissions and fees. They may work as fee-only planners for some clients, and commission-only planners for others, depending on the client's preference. Or they may charge a fee for developing the plan and then charge commission for buying the products to set it in motion.
Wealth Managers	Wealth managers (sometimes called money or asset managers) design and manage investment plans for their clients. In return, they receive a percentage (which shouldn't be more than 2 percent) of the assets under management. (Note: The more you invest, the lower your percentage should be.)

Pros	Cons
The fact that they're not selling you any specific products makes them more objective. They're not tempted to put you into the mutual fund or insurance policy that pays them the heftiest commission, because they're not earning any commission at all.	Fee-only planners get paid whether or not you implement their suggestions. They don't have the same financial need to push you until you actually put your money to work. Plus, there aren't nearly as many fee-only planners nationwide as there are planners who get paid by commission; finding one may prove to be a challenge.
The upside is that because the planner doesn't make dollar one until you start putting money into the plan, he or she is more likely to make sure that you actually implement the plan.	Selling products means a loss of objectivity. Commission planners often won't, for example, put you in no-load (no sales charge) mutual funds, because they won't earn a commission from the fund company.
The fees you pay are likely to be lower than those with a fee-only financial planner—in fact, in some cases you'll get a break on the commission as well.	As with commission-only planners, you have to wonder if you're being pushed to buy the products that are best for you—or into the products that pay the planners most.
More than the other planners on this list, wealth managers take you out of the loop. They manage assets on a discretionary basis—which means you give them control. For people who don't have the time or inclination to manage their own money, this can be a huge plus.	It can also be a risk. Whenever you give up control of your assets, you need to make sure there's a system established to allow you to monitor the goings-on in your portfolio, to make sure that your assets aren't dwindling away because of poor performance.

insurance industry, graduates tend to be insurance agents and focus heavily on insurance as a key part of any financial plan.

• **NAPFA** (National Association of Personal Financial Advisors) member. This is not a designation, but it might as well be. If you feel strongly about going the fee-only route, you'll want a planner who belongs to NAPFA. The tough membership requirements include a peer review of a financial plan. Consequently, more than 60 percent of planners who apply to get into the organization are denied. It's not surprising that one in five NAPFA members shows up on *Worth* magazine's annual list of the country's 250 best financial planners.

• **PFS** (personal financial specialists). Certified public accountants who wish to specialize in financial planning can apply for this designation from the American Institute of CPAs. Applicants must have done at least 250 hours of financial planning each of the prior three years. They must pass a six-hour comprehensive exam and follow up with seventy-two hours of continuing education every three years.

• **CDP** (certified divorce planner). The Institute for Certified Divorce Planners in Boulder, Colorado, has certified some 500 CDPs since 1993. Applicants take a two-day course in tax, pension, and alimony issues, and then must pass a four-hour exam.

• **CMFC** (chartered mutual fund counselor)/**CFS** (certified fund specialist). Both of these designations, the first from the National Endowment for Financial Education, the second from the Institute of Certified Fund Specialists, are tailor-made to instill confidence that the bearer has a lot of experience helping clients choose mutual funds. In order to qualify for both, advisers take a home-study course, and then must pass an exam.

Checking Up on Your Planner

You've no doubt heard the horror stories: Older people who've had money siphoned from their accounts. Life savings gone. Accounts churned into nothingness. It pays to be as careful as possible. Hiring a financial adviser isn't like hiring a plumber. Anytime you give someone access to the workings of your financial life, you're putting yourself at risk. So despite the fact that your best friend is hugely devoted to the planner you're considering hiring, do yourself a favor and check him or her out.

• **Financial planners.** Ask your planner for a copy of Parts I and II of the ADV form. This is the form he or she filled out to register with the Securities and Exchange Commission or your state's securities agency, and it contains information about the planner's educational background, professional experience, compensation, and disciplinary history. He or she is required by law to give you Part II, which provides details on how—and by whom—the planner is paid (keep your eyes open for payments coming from financial services companies whose products your planner happens to be pushing). Part I, which contains a planner's disciplinary history, isn't required to be given to you, but be wary of any planner who won't gladly hand it over. You can also get a copy of Part I from the SEC (800-846-2722 or www.sec.gov) for planners managing more than $25 million or from your state's securities commission for those managing less than $25 million. The North American Securities Administrators Association (888-84-NASAA or www.nasaa.org) can give you the phone number of your state securities commissioner. Finally, the Certified Financial Planner Board of Standards (888-CFP-MARK or www.CFP-Board.org) can tell you if a CFP has ever been publicly disciplined by the board. This is also where you'd go to lodge a complaint.

• **Insurance agents.** The National Association of Insurance Commissioners (816-842-3600 or www.naic.org) will direct you to your state insurance commissioner, who in turn can check to see if a particular financial planner is licensed to sell insurance or has any insurance violations.

• **All of the above.** The National Fraud Exchange or NAFEX (800-822-0416 ext. 33) offers a one-stop background check on brokers, financial planners, real estate agents, trust advisers, and other financial professionals. The cost: $39 for the first person checked; $20 for each person thereafter.

What Do You Get for Your Money?

The traditional output from a planner's office is a thick, comprehensive report, detailing what you have, what you want, and what you need to do in order to get there. But some planners have discovered that these imposing documents are a waste of time. First, they scare people. Some people react to seeing their entire financial life laid out for examination by retreating. Many react by shoving it in a drawer. Some don't even take the time to read it. And that makes the entire exercise a waste of money—and time.

"I mail someone a report, I can't see whether or not they understand what I'm saying—or if they agree with it," says New York–based financial planner Gary Schatsky. "That's a problem, because part of what I'm selling is advice, but part of it is comfort. Very often, I might express a piece of advice very clearly, but if they don't understand it or agree with it, I haven't made them comfortable with it, so I've failed."

Schatsky's solution has been to abandon the thick document except for clients who insist on seeing it. Instead, he gives a few hours of discussion accompanied by a two- or three-page summary. "That," he says, "my clients can digest."

Regardless of what kind of report you receive, the important thing is to know from the beginning how the whole process will unfold. That includes knowing how many visits you'll have to make to the planner's office before you'll get your initial plan. How many times will you see the planner each year? What will you be charged for those visits? I know of financial planning clients who were peeved when the planner phoned *them,* unsolicited, to discuss insurance, then billed the clients for an hour of his time. You'll want to know: Is talking on the phone part of the program? Will my planner call me, or vice versa? What will I pay for those calls? In this transaction—as in just about every business deal—managing *your own* expectations is critical to being a satisfied customer.

Five Questions to Ask a Financial Planner

Here's an e-mail I recently received:

I'm fifty-six years old, female and single again (widow). I read financial reports and of course everything sounds like Greek to me. Every piece of advice I pick up says to invest in individual stocks and in mutual funds. The last time I talked to a financial adviser the first question he asked is: How do you want to invest your money? If I knew, I wouldn't have been there. I would like to find somebody who could tell me which mutual funds and which stocks to buy. Does that sort of person exist? Please, any help would be appreciated.

I wrote back telling her that it sounded to me as if she fell into the wrong financial planner's hands. A planner who was doing his job well would have stopped long enough to look at her entire financial situation in order to help her figure out how she *should* have been investing her money. Then he or she should have directed her to some specific investment choices. Do these careful, detail-oriented planners really exist? Of course they do. Finding them is a matter of pulling together a list of planners who come highly recommended. Ask friends or colleagues who have financial situations similar to your own, or the other financial pros on your team—your accountant or estate planner, for example—for recommendations. If you can't think of anyone you know personally to call for advice, you can search the Web sites of the National Association of Professional Financial Advisors (www.napfa.org), the International Association for Financial Planning (www.iafp.org), or the Financial Planning Association (www.fpanet.org) for one in your area. Once you've got three or four names, then you need to conduct a series of informational interviews, preferably face-to-face. Any planner who isn't willing to make time to do this is a planner you should avoid anyway. Here are the questions to ask:

1. What qualifies you to do this job? You're looking for a combination of factors in this answer. First, significant experience (I know planners have to cut their teeth on someone, but I wouldn't work with a planner who had been at it for less than five years).

Second, an explanation of their specialty. Planners who were stock-brokers first may emphasize your portfolio over your life insurance; those who are CPAs may focus on your taxes, with stock picking or insurance planning coming second. Both of those things are fine, as long as their strengths coincide with your focus. Pay attention to the designations following the planner's name (you can use them to check the planner out; see above).

2. Tell me about your current clients. The best response is that the planner works with someone who sounds a lot like you, in profession, in income level, in family status. When I was working as a freelance writer, I used an accountant who seemed to be dealing with every third freelancer in town. He knew precisely what I could—and could not—deduct on my tax return, because he understood my work and lifestyle. I had full confidence in his recommendations. That's not to say most planners couldn't study enough to deal with a situation they haven't seen before. You just don't want to be the test case.

3. How do you get paid? In the previous pages, we discussed the different ways planners are compensated. Every one of those compensation methods is acceptable, as long as the planner's willing to tell you about it—in writing—before you start doing business. You also want an estimate of what the planner believes doing the work for you will cost (ask that it be broken down into start-up costs and ongoing costs so that you'll know what the relationship will cost you over, say, a year). *Red Flag!* If a commission-earning planner asks for discretionary power (the ability to buy and sell for your account without specific permission for each transaction), watch out. By granting this blanket permission, you give him the ability to churn your account, that is, to execute transactions simply to pad his pockets with commission dollars!

4. Tell me about your investment philosophy. While it's true that a planner should take his cues regarding the amount of appropriate risk from you, it's also true that most have their own ideas about what does and doesn't constitute "a lot" of risk. You'll need to get very specific in your questioning here. Ask if there are certain stocks or funds that the planner believes should be a part of every portfolio. Ask about what *asset allocation* (the ratio of stocks to bonds to cash) the planner thinks is appropriate for you. You're trying to make sure that you and the planner have the same ideas in mind.

Red Flag! Beware of a planner who seems to be trying to make your life too easy by essentially taking you out of the loop. No matter how much you trust your planner, you should want to see all account statements and to sign everything relevant to your money.

5. I'd like to check you out before we start to work together; can you provide me with references? Am I going to find anything disturbing on your record? Okay, so that's two questions. They're both important. If you've worked your way through this book, you already know that I'm a huge believer in references—and not only getting them, but calling them (you'd be surprised how many people only go halfway!). Sure, it's possible that the planner will give you the name of his three best friends. But it's also possible that those three friends, when called, won't give you the pat answers your planner expected. As for the background check: Ask what organizations a planner is regulated by and call them to make sure there's nothing in his or her disciplinary history that you find disturbing. If your planner also sells stocks, he or she must be able to provide you with a copy of Form ADV (see "Checking Up on Your Planner" above).

Financial Counselors: Hand-holding in Money 101

If you feel like you're starting from square zero financially—instead of square one—even the thought of visiting a financial planner may seem daunting. How can you possibly talk about investing to help reach your goals when you're not sure of the basics: how to budget, how to save, how to pay off your debts? You may be embarrassed that even though you seem to the outside world to be competent and organized, your financial life is in total disarray. And perhaps you're unwilling to show how little you've thought about your money to a professional who seems to do little else.

You're not quite ready for a financial planner. But there's a new breed of practitioner to know about. They're called financial counselors. And their mission is to teach you the basics—from how to balance a checkbook to how to choose a credit card—then meet with you on a regular basis to help you develop a budget, then to make sure you're paying your bills on time and not overspending. They don't want to be your financial planner; instead they view themselves as shorter-term teachers. Once you've accomplished enough to move on to a planner, most financial counselors will refer you to one they respect.

The only problem with financial counselors is that there aren't nearly as many of them as there are financial planners. You won't find a listing in your Yellow Pages, but you can get a referral by contacting the Association for Financial Counseling and Planning Education at 614-485-9650 or by visiting their Web site at www.afcpe.org for a referral. Counselors typically charge $60 an hour and up.

Planners Specializing in Divorce

Divorce planners are a fairly new breed of financial planner, but their numbers are growing. The Boulder-based Institute for Certified Divorce Planners has certified some 500 financial planners, accountants, and attorneys as CDPs since 1993—more than 200 of them in 1999 alone. They focus on the specific tax, pension, and alimony issues that hamper most divorce negotiations, using software to project how proposed settlements will change the net worth of one or both spouses twenty years out. After they're certified, CDPs work not only as consultants but as expert witnesses, whose goal is to get a judge to mandate an equitable split.

If you're going through a divorce, you may want to consider adding a CDP to your payroll (you can call the institute at 800-875-1760 for a referral).

Choosing a Broker

June 30, 1998, started out like any regular Tuesday for Lois, a good friend of mine and an active investor. She finished her morning coffee, sifted through the newspaper, and turned on CNBC in time to hear the head of the arbitrage department at CIBC Oppenheimer explain why he believed Cabletron Systems was an attractive—and very likely—acquisition target. His logic: The company has so much free cash in the bank, a buyer could use the surplus to practically finance the sale. It was almost a freebie.

That sounded interesting to Lois, who flipped on her PC and surfed to her online broker. She watched the stock for a bit after the open—to be sure investors were taking the story seriously—and at 10:00 A.M. with the offering price at $12⅚₆, she placed a market order to buy 5,000 shares. Then she waited.

And waited. Two minutes went by and she started to get nervous. "Waiting more than thirty seconds for confirmation is a little unusual," she explains. After four minutes, she was annoyed. And by the time six minutes had gone by, the price was ¼ point higher and she was seething. "That was $1,500 to me. It was already real money," she says. Unfortunately, it wasn't over yet. It took nine minutes for her broker to fill her order, and when it did the price was $13⅚₆. Total cost of the delay: $4,200.

Lois wasn't exactly sure what to do, so she fired off an e-mail asking someone in customer service to look into the problem. The reply that came twenty minutes later explained that a large order— more than 130,000 shares—had come in around the same time as hers, causing "a huge order imbalance that influenced the price of the stock." That didn't put any money back in her pocket, so she probed further. She called a friend on the trading floor and told him the story. He offered to pull up the "time and sales report," the Exchange's official record of trades, including their size and the exact price of the shares at the time in question. The report was incredibly enlightening: It was true that a huge trade had occurred simultaneously with Lois's at $13⅚₆. But what the firm hadn't told her was that three minutes earlier—and six minutes *after* she'd placed her order—4,300 shares traded at $12¾. And that wasn't all. Two minutes before that, 3,500 shares traded at $12⅝. And a few minutes before that, a few hundred traded at $12⅟₁₆.

This time, fully armed, she picked up the phone, called her brokerage firm, and got her account representative on the line. He also pulled the time and sales report and his response was immediate. "We need to fix this," he said. "We'll make it right." A week later, the company had done exactly that. It filled her entire order at $12⅟₁₆ and waived the commission for good measure.

The unfortunate fact is, with trading volumes regularly pushing the envelope, problems like this one aren't all that uncommon. Worse, the culprits are difficult to pinpoint. So many variables are involved in trading—the exchange, the price of the stock, the time of day, and whether or not a broker makes a market in the stock— that no one can ever honestly say "I deliver the best executions." So it boils down to this: You need to keep your eye on your transactions—or be willing to pay someone to do it for you.

When you're looking for a broker, you have four distinct choices. From the most to the least expensive they are: full service brokers, discount brokers, deep discounters, and online brokers. What differentiates them is the advice they'll provide you. Full service brokers will call you with stock ideas, and back up this advice with reports from their firm's equity research department. They'll keep an eye on your picks and let you know when they think a stock is likely to tank and they believe you should sell. Discounters do less of this. Deep discounters do nothing of the kind. And while there's typically plenty of research available on the best online brokerage sites, it's up to you to go digging for it.

Here's a more in-depth look at the four categories, so that you can pick the one that's right for you. You may even want to choose two different kinds of brokers for different purposes. I believe that full service brokers should be paid for the stock ideas they provide you with. That seems only fair. But if you've done the research yourself and decided to buy a particular stock, I don't see any reason to pay a hefty commission when you could place your order on the Web for as little as $8 to $15. The nice thing about the way the brokerage world is shaping up is that you may be able to have both of those things in one account at one firm. Merrill Lynch and the other full service brokers of the world are quickly coming around to the fact that they need an online component—and need to charge you lower commissions for using it.

Finally, a couple of suggestions about getting started. First, any brokerage firm you're considering should have SIPC insurance. The Securities Investor Protection Corporation (SIPC) covers you if your brokerage account fails, if your broker steals assets, or if your brokerage house loses track of assets your records show that you own. You're covered for up to a half million dollars (that's $100,000 in cash and $400,000 in other assets).

If you're signing on with an individual—a full service broker/account representative at a brokerage firm—you also want to know that *person* has nothing to hide. To get a report on any broker you're considering using, call the National Association of Securities Dealers at 800-289-9999.

And finally, whether you're thinking of changing brokers or opening your very first account, don't deposit every last cent you have immediately. Open your account with the minimum dollars required and try it out over a few weeks to make certain you're happy with the service and execution of your trades. Only once you're satisfied should you give a broker 100 percent of your business.

	WHO THEY ARE	WHAT THEY DO
Full Service Brokers	The Merrill Lynches and Morgan Stanley Dean Witters of the world. They typically have branch offices in your town where you can pick up literature on just about any stock you're interested in.	Full service or "traditional" brokers, as they're often called, not only direct you into specific investments, but help you put together a portfolio that's suitable for the amount of risk you want to take at each stage in your life. Some, who also function as financial planners, will go even further, helping you buy the right amount of insurance for your needs, doing basic estate and tax planning, and monitoring your investments on a day-to-day basis.
Discount Brokers	The big names in this category include Waterhouse Securities, Charles Schwab, Quick & Reilly, and Fidelity, among others. As with full service brokers, they'll often have branch offices in your town.	Most of them will provide written research, but not the same hand-holding as a full service broker. Only for an additional fee will they take on additional financial planning tasks. But they can certainly execute trades as well and as quickly as any full service broker. And it's important to note that the line between full service and discount has started to blur—Schwab and Fidelity have both started offering a fuller range of services in recent years, but at lower prices than traditional, full service firms charge. Keep that in mind as you shop around.

RESEARCH	INITIATIVE
Historically, this was the reason you paid more for full service brokers. It was their job to recommend stocks to you as a result of research generated by their firm's highly paid (and hopefully highly qualified) analysts. And, to be fair, research is still these firms' number one advantage. But thanks to the Internet, much of this research isn't proprietary anymore. Any Web surfer with a few hours to spare and a fast computer can find volumes of information on just about any stock or other investment. The questions are: Do you have that much time? Are you willing to do the work? And will you be able to interpret the research once you dig it up?	Your broker should call you not only with ideas for stocks you may want to purchase, but if he or she sees a problem with a stock in your portfolio (if the firm's analyst lowers its recommendation from buy to hold, for example, or if there's negative news about the stock) and you ought to consider selling.
Some research to help you make your own decision is often available. Waterhouse, for example, provides reports from Standard & Poor's and Morningstar (for mutual funds) for free or a small fee.	Yours. It's up to you to pick the stocks you want to buy and make the call to purchase them. Likewise, it's on your shoulders to monitor those investments so you'll know when it's time to sell.

	WHO THEY ARE	WHAT THEY DO
Deep Discount Brokers	The names you may know in this category include Brown & Co., Olde, and National Discount Brokers.	You won't actually have a broker assigned to you if you go with a deep discounter; instead, you'll get a phone number that you can call to initiate a trade. Whoever answers will typically call your account up on a computer and do your bidding. It's important to know that some deep discounters trade a full range of products, including mutual funds and bonds, while others are simply *stock* brokers.
Online Brokers	Some of the big ones are E*Trade, NDB, SureTrade, Ameritrade, Datek, and MSDW (formerly Discover).	These online firms offer you the opportunity to place your own trades over the Internet. Once you've opened an account with NDB, for example, whenever you want to buy shares, you can log in, place an order for the number of shares you'd like, specify your buying price, and wait for your confirmation to pop up. If you're buying at the current price, your order should be confirmed in a minute or less.

Talking Money with Your Investment Team □ **255**

RESEARCH	INITIATIVE
Typically, not much. Some of the deep discounters may have online arms where you can check out their research offerings on your own.	As with discount brokers, yours alone.
Depending on the online brokerage firm you chose, there's tons of material available—from annual reports to Morningstar reports to research from brokerage firms to message boards, where individual investors help each other with stock suggestions (tread carefully!). In some cases, you have as much access to research material as you would if you went with a full service brokerage—or more. The difference: It's up to you to find what you want, read it, interpret it, and decide if you think it has any value whatsoever.	Yours.

FINDING A GOOD ONE

Full Service Brokers

With more than a half million brokers to choose from in this country, you'll want to make an educated decision. That includes pulling together a list of quality candidates recommended by friends and the other professionals on your team (like your accountant and lawyer). Narrow the list by making sure each one has no history of complaints from clients with the NASD. Then make the final call by interviewing at least three face-to-face. Ask what the person would do with your money, what sort of stock-picking methodology he or she follows, and how he or she generates ideas. Get a handle on how much the relationship will cost you. And don't ignore your gut. The most important thing to figure out is whether your ideas about risk are in sync with each other.

Discount Brokers

First, make sure any firm you consider is trading the full menu of products you'd like to buy. Full service brokers, as you'd expect, trade just about everything, but with the reduction in price comes a reduction in services—some discounters don't trade foreign stocks, for example, and others don't trade derivative products like options. You also want to make sure you're dealing with a broker that is at the top of its game in terms of service. There are loads of ratings of discount brokers done every year by magazines like *Money* and *Smart Money*—check them out before you open your account.

PRICE	POTENTIAL PITFALLS
Full service brokerage commissions start at about $70 for a 100-share purchase and go up from there. Commissions are typically based on a percentage of your purchase (or sale) price, so they vary widely.	Some say high commissions—both for buying and selling—encourage brokers to overtrade, whether or not the transactions are in a client's best interest. And, as SEC chairman Arthur Levitt has warned investors, you should make sure that your broker isn't pushing certain stocks that are on his own (or his firm's) agenda—for example, stocks in a company for which the brokerage firm happens to play the role of investment banker.
Commissions are about one third those of full service brokers. Schwab, for example, charges $29.95 and up per trade; Vanguard charges $20 and up.	It may not be as cheap as it seems. Note the prices say "and up." That's because different trades on different exchanges have different pricing schedules. Pay attention.

FINDING A GOOD ONE	
Deep Discount Brokers	There is no reason that a deep discounter should execute your transactions any differently (faster or slower, for example) than a full service broker. Again, broker surveys in personal finance magazines will point you toward the good ones.
Online Brokers	There are dozens of online brokerages, some of which you've never heard of. Finding the right one for you means taking the time to visit at least a few sites, to see what they're offering in terms of research, how their pricing compares to other sites, and how comfortable you feel with the interface. Is it simple? Can you pull quotes easily—and the research to go with those stocks? Does the site enable you to monitor the investments you own with the touch of one button—and those you're thinking about owning with another? You also want to know how satisfied its current customers are. Again, magazines do annual online brokerage surveys, but you can also get evaluations of different online trading firms on the Web, from sites like Gomez.com.

THE BIG THREE: THINGS TO TAKE AWAY FROM TALKING MONEY WITH YOUR INVESTMENT TEAM

1. You may have all the necessary skills to manage your money; the bigger question is whether you will actually spend the time doing it. If not, putting a financial planner on your family payroll is a great way to make sure that the necessary decisions get made—and to take a huge weight off your shoulders.

2. That said, you have to be very careful about hiring one. Just about anyone can call themselves a financial planner—that's why you see brokers, insurance agents, accountants, and members of just about every profession with a tie to your money doing it. Go about hiring one with as much care as you would a contractor to

PRICE	POTENTIAL PITFALLS
Deep discounters typically charge a flat fee—$15 to $25—for a NASDAQ or New York Stock Exchange–listed trade of up to 5,000 shares.	Watch the hours of operation—some deep discounters only operate from nine to five.
At $8 to $15 a trade (typically), it doesn't get any cheaper than this.	Sites may get jammed and shut down. This doesn't happen frequently, but it does happen. So be certain that your firm has sufficient 800 number access to enable you to trade in an emergency. (Note: Some of these firms also have discount or deep discount arms. If you decide you need to talk to a broker to complete a transaction, you'll usually pay rates similar to those at the discount or deep discount firms described above.)

do a major renovation on your house. Get referrals. Check references. Conduct informational interviews. Get a sense of cost. And make sure your idea of risk jibes with that of the person you hire.

3. You'll also need to choose a broker. You can hire a full service broker who will provide you with plenty of research and stock recommendations, or you can go with a deep discounter who will simply execute your trades. The difference in cost is great, but you're only *really* saving if you're going to do the research yourself.

CHAPTER 11

Talking Money with Your Family and Friends

I had a girls night out with Gail, one of my best pals, who recently headed to the altar. "I gotta tell you," she said as we split a thin crust pizza with fresh mozzarella and chunks of provolone, "this married money thing is weird."

"What do you mean?" I asked her.

"I'm used to knowing exactly what I have coming in and being responsible for everything that I spend. I'm used to being in control," she said. "But with two people depositing paychecks, withdrawing cash, and charging on the same credit card, it gets a lot more confusing."

A few months back, for example, they had a vanishing bank balance problem. Gail and her husband, Stu, have an informal system for investing. They let money accrue in their checking account. When the balance tops the amount they need to cover their monthly bills, they transfer a lump sum into their money market account. And when the balance in their money market account goes a few thousand above their emergency cushion comfort zone, they invest the extra in their index mutual fund. It's simple, easy to under-stand—and it usually works.

But on this occasion, when Gail took cash from the ATM she no-ticed their balance was higher than usual, so she transferred a few thousand to their money market account. A few days later, Stu went to the machine to deposit *his* paycheck. Remembering how high their checking balance had been, he immediately put the entire amount into the money market account, without bothering to even look at the checking account. Neither of them told the other what they had done.

So a few days went by. Several bills, which they'd wisely set up as automatic debits to avoid the hassle of writing checks, were paid automatically by the bank. And when Gail returned to the ATM the next week to get some cash, she panicked. There was practically no money there. "I'd just assumed Stu had deposited his paycheck. I had no idea what happened," she says. It didn't take long to call him at the office and figure out what had transpired, but that feeling—of not knowing where your money is—is distinctly uncomfortable. Particularly for someone who for a good decade or so has known exactly where every penny was.

"I'm used to being in control," she confesses. "If the credit card bill is a little high, I used to be able to know that it was because I bought too many books at Barnes & Noble, or because I had four friends with birthdays that month and I bought them all dinners, so I could rein it in a little."

That's not so easy when two people are playing the game. Par-ticularly if, like my friend, you've mingled all your money. The so-lution: Stop assuming. Start talking. (And make sure you write *everything* down.)

Throughout this book we've focused on the knowledge and skills *you* need to become a better manager of your own finances. You know what questions to ask before you pick a mutual fund. You've cut your auto insurance rate by a third.

But here comes the truly tough part. Often, it isn't just *you* that you're dealing with. Sometimes other people have their fingers in your finances—your spouse, your parents, your kids. Or maybe you're involved in theirs. How do you make sure that your husband is on the same page when it comes to saving for a new car? Or that your kids learn enough about money so that they'll become financially independent at a reasonable age (rather than continuing to rely on you for handouts)? How do you come to understand what your parents want from their money as they age, so that if there comes a time when you have to manage it for them, you can do so in accordance with their wishes? You have to talk about all of those things.

Easy? Absolutely not. Possible? Definitely. But you have to work at it. Money is so symbolically loaded with other meanings—for some people it's love, for others it's power, for some it's self-esteem, and for many others it's a combination of all of those things. So be patient. Don't expect yourself to get to a resolution the first time you broach the subject. It's going to take a little time.

In this chapter we'll take a look at talking money with the most important people in your life: your spouse (or life partner), your parents, and your kids. In each, we'll talk about where the money problems typically begin, and how you can avoid them. We'll also go through topics it's important to touch on with each; with your kids, for example, a major portion of the challenge is teaching them about money so that they'll become fiscally smart teens, then adults.

Finally, I've included a section on the etiquette of money. I can't tell you the number of e-mails I receive asking me how much to spend on wedding gifts, or how to nicely tell your dinner partner (who ordered a $25 entrée) that you don't want to split the check because all you had was a salad for $7.95. Here, the answers:

Talking to Your Spouse (or Life Partner)

Money is the biggest source of arguments in a marriage—that's a fact that has been documented numerous times, among them in studies from Citigroup, *Worth* magazine, and PREP, the Prevention and Relationship Enhancement Program. California-based financial planner Victoria Felton Collins, author of *Couples and Money*, says it's the driving factor in divorce a whopping 90 percent of the time.

The problem with the way couples handle money in a marriage usually extends back to the time they were dating.

In fact, therapists say it's harder to talk about money than it is to talk about sex. Why? In part, it's because talking about sex—in the safe sex era—has gotten easier. Talking about money hasn't. But just as we learned to ask about condoms and HIV testing, we can learn to ask about spending habits, financial goals, and credit card debt. It's a matter of diving in. And for that, it helps to have a bit of a script (at the very least you need a good opening line). Here's how to get off on the right foot.

How to Start Talking

• **Find a neutral time.** It's best to talk about money when money is not the issue. If you start talking while you're paying the bills or after your spouse has just purchased something you thought was a little too extravagant, your discussion is going to degenerate into an argument. You're better off talking about money issues over breakfast or during the commercial breaks on *Friends*.

• **Give a little to get a little.** This is a trick reporters like me often use. We'll serve up some fact on our own lives to get our sources to similarly open up, a strategy that works really well with a spouse as well. Explaining how *you* feel about a particular money issue will encourage your partner to do the same. You want to talk about who pays for what. You might begin: "I think it's really nice that you paid for dinner the last couple of times we went out, but I need to know how you feel about that. Are you the kind of guy who feels good paying for women, or do you feel like it's a burden? Because I'm perfectly comfortable with picking up the check, too."

• **Know where you stand.** It's important to be honest with yourself about how *you* feel. It may be hard to have a relationship with someone with major debt problems if you've paid every bill on time and in full your entire life. You may have mixed emotions about letting a date/spouse pay your way—part of you may enjoy being taken care of, while another part wants to maintain some independence. You can't be up front with your partner if you're not willing to be up front with yourself.

• **Bring in a third party.** If you can't get yourself to start a financial conversation, sit down with a counselor and ask him or her to help you sort out your issues. That person could be a money therapist, but also a compassionate financial planner or member of the clergy. Many churches and synagogues now offer financial planning courses as part of their preparation for marriage.

Opening Lines

• Sometimes you just need something to say to get the ball rolling. Try: *"Growing up, I don't remember my parents ever talking about money. How was it in your house?"*

• *"I got a raise today—and I want to make sure I don't spend every last dime. Let's talk about some ways I/we can be sure to save it."*

• *"These student loans are driving me nuts. Do you have them, too?"*

• *"My friend Joan just inherited $40,000. I think my Aunt Margaret may leave me some money someday."*

• *"Do you have renters insurance?"*

• *"That vacation we want to take is pretty expensive. Let's talk about how we can put together the money."*

Merging Your Finances: Dos and Don'ts

Here's my take on merged finances. I think married couples ought to do whatever *both* partners are comfortable with. That means if one person feels as if they want to maintain some separate assets, the other ought to respect that, and they should have not one set of bank and brokerage accounts, but three: yours, mine, and ours. You may want to do this for tax reasons anyway. If you put all your assets together in both names—and don't do other estate planning to compensate—you (or your heirs) may end up paying more taxes than you otherwise would. If you go with a three-account system, you'll need to decide up front who contributes how much to the ours account, and what that money is going to cover. I like a system in which partners kick in amounts proportionate to their salaries. If you make one third more than your spouse, for example, you contribute one third more to the house account and vice versa. If one of the spouses doesn't work, that doesn't eliminate the possibility of having three accounts. Have the working spouse's paycheck directly deposited into the house account, then schedule regular transfers into the his and hers accounts. What else do you need to do to make your relationship financially compatible? Here are some things to keep your eye on.

• **Track your spending.** You know the old saying, two can live as cheaply as one? It's not easy. Perhaps two can spend the same amount as one on rent. But when it comes to food, gas, utilities, evenings out, unless you know what you have going in and what you have going out, it's going to be hard to save one dollar.

• **Agree to disagree.** Once you come up with spending and savings goals (and guidelines), it's not a good idea to micromanage each other's spending. Nothing breeds hostility faster than a spouse who seems cranky every time you blow a few bucks. Establish a dollar amount above which you have to talk about a purchase before either one of you makes it.

• **Designate a bill payer.** Financially, as in just about every other way, opposites attract. That means one of you is going to be better at the day-to-day management of your household finances (and therefore, probably more willing to do it) than the other. It's okay—preferable actually—for one partner to be the writer of checks and payer of bills. What's not okay is for the other partner to abdicate completely. Keep in mind that 90 percent of women end up on their own financially at some time during their lives. If you've never paid the bills, balanced the checkbook, and so forth, you're going to be lost. So make sure that at least once or twice a year you swap responsibilities to make sure that you know *how* to do it—or at the very least, that you sit down and do it together.

• **Keep separate credit cards.** Each partner should have at least one credit card in his or her own name. This is how to make cer-

THE PRENUP QUESTION

Only about 5 percent of couples heading into marriages actually sign prenuptial agreements, but more probably should. You should consider one:

- If you're bringing significant assets into a marriage.
- If you have your own business.
- If you have family money.
- If you have kids from a prior marriage.
- If you are expecting a major inheritance.

If you go this route, make sure your agreement covers in the case of divorce or death: how to divide property each of you brought to the marriage, how to divide property you acquire after the marriage, how your assets will be divided, how your debts will be handled, and whether each spouse has any financial responsibility for the other's children from previous marriages.

Most importantly, in order to hold up in court, a prenup needs to be *fair.* That means each of you needs to have his or her own attorney when the agreement is being drawn up, and all assets and liabilities need to be disclosed. And don't wait until the day before you head to the altar to talk about this. You don't want a court to later say you pressured your spouse into signing.

If you married without a prenup, but feel you should have had one—particularly if those feelings are causing a strain in your marriage—consider a post-nuptial agreement. As with a prenup, this is the drawing up of a financial agreement that, hopefully, will bring you sufficiently together on your finances to allow you to stay married. Again, you need separate lawyers.

tain you have a separate credit history. That's crucial. If you get divorced or if your spouse dies, it's the only way to insure you'll be able to get a mortgage, home equity loan, or even other credit cards. And note: Joint cards with both your names don't do the trick.

Five Questions to Ask Your Spouse to Get Your Goals in Sync

1. Are you willing (really willing) to have this conversation? It's not uncommon for someone to be totally uninterested in financial matters. But make sure that they're willing to get interested. If you're both interested in money, you need to sit down and discuss a division of labor: Who will pay the bills? Who will pick the stocks? Are you going to handle it jointly? Or do you want to hire someone to do it? *Red Flag!* If your spouse answers no to this question, make sure he or she is perfectly willing to allow you to take care of all the financial matters in the family, no questions asked.

2. What do you want from your money? A pretty simple question, yes, but one that often doesn't get asked at all. The answers define your life. At what age do you want to retire? Are you dead-set on having a thirty-foot yacht by age forty-seven, or a place on the slopes by age fifty? Do you want $500,000 in your 401(k) before you'll even think of slowing down or is your magic number $1 million? If you're having difficulty putting your goals into plain English, hiring a financial planner can help.

3. What size family are we going to have? Perhaps you're a young couple planning to have kids, perhaps you already have one or two young ones, or maybe you're even further along that road. Whether your children are two or twelve, you have to plan ahead financially for each one of them. Do you want to foot the bill for their college education? Or did working your own way through school make you a stronger individual and so you want that for your kids? Will you want to raise them where you're currently living? Or is a new neighborhood in the cards? And what are your views on inheritances? Do you want to leave them something when you're gone? Or are you of the "die broke" mentality? You need to talk about all of these things—and more. Why? See question No. 4.

4. How should we invest our money? You need the answers to question No. 3 in order to answer this question. You also need to know how strong your partner's stomach is. If one of you is conservative and the other craves risk, that may create substantial tension when it comes to investing. Communication is key: Talk to each other before you make investing decisions. Understand, also, that what you're really talking about when you're discussing your investment strategy are your priorities: Do you want to live the good life now and have less for retirement? Or would you rather be frugal now and have a larger nest egg?

5. How much financial privacy do you want? There's no right answer here. You can opt for total financial disclosure, and completely merge your financial lives, or you can each keep some of your money in separate accounts. But agree on a methodology up front.

Talking to Your Parents

According to a Phoenix Fiscal Fitness survey from early 1999, almost half of adult children with a living parent hadn't discussed financial issues with that parent—and a full third said they had little to no knowledge of their parent's financial situation. Yet 35 percent believe they'll support that parent financially at some time in the future.

Noelle, a thirty-something mother of two, knows how that feels. She's the only one of her five siblings that lives in the same small town as her mother and her grandmother. Already, she's providing her grandmother with financial support—not by giving her cash handouts (she's worried the money would disappear) but by paying for groceries, or footing bills for the upkeep of her home. Now she's afraid she'll be in the same situation with her mother. "My mom has no savings," she says. "She's deeply in debt. She owns one original art print that's probably worth a few thousand dollars, but that's it. She's already cashed out her pension from the bank where she worked." Noelle doesn't even want to think about what would happen if her mother ever became disabled or injured. Instead, she's focusing on taking care of her own family—her husband and three kids—researching their best investment options, making sure they have enough life insurance. She knows they're all long overdue for a multigenerational family powwow. And that her siblings ought to be involved as well. She just doesn't know how to make that happen.

Legally, of course, parents have no obligation to tell their kids anything about their money. More than likely, too, they grew up in an era where discussion of money was even less common than it is today. That's why it's probably going to be up to you to open the door. This is an area where you need to tread lightly. Head into a conversation like this with too much force and your parents may think you're trying to move them toward a nursing home, or worse, that you're just after their money. That's not only true if your parents have assets, but even if, like Noelle's, they don't have much of anything at all. What's the best way to do it?

- **Use your situation.** If you're visiting a cemetery, it's a good opportunity to say, "I really need to talk to you about what happens if you're not here anymore." If you're home for the holidays, ask your parents to take you by the hand and show you where the important papers are, just in case.
- **Use the experiences of others.** Say to your parent: "My friend Suzy's father just passed away and she's really worried about her mother's finances; it made me wonder whether you and Dad had done any planning."
- **Use the news.** The next time tax reform is in the news, use that to open the door. For example: "I just read about a proposal to get rid of estate taxes entirely. What do you think of that? Would that make a difference in how you're planning?"
- **Use your own planning.** Explain to your parents the steps you and your spouse are going through yourselves. If you're open about your own finances, it'll make them feel more comfortable about being open with theirs. Say: "I'm drawing up my will, and I was wondering if you'd take a look at it." Or, "Mark and I just set up marital trusts to save the kids from having to pay taxes on our estates. Do you and Mom have those?"
- **Use pencil and paper.** If you can't bring yourself to open your mouth, then write a letter. Send your parents an article about people who didn't have these conversations and the mess that ensued.

Or just put on paper how you feel, then stick it in the mail before you have time to censor yourself.

Five Questions to Ask Your Aging Parents About Money

These are the points you need to cover when you finally sit down and have this all-important money conversation with your parents.

1. Are all your legal documents up to date and signed? Most parents will say, "Yes. I have them," but their forms are frequently inadequate. When Mom and Dad say yes, it may mean they have a will, but it's twenty or thirty years old, and a power of attorney that they got at a drugstore. Old fill-in-the-blank forms, and even old attorney-drafted forms, do not offer nearly the options that new ones do. So ask your parents to *show* you the documents, and to have an attorney look them over if they are not recent.

2. What plans have you made for when you can't take care of yourself? Hopefully, your parents have signed powers of attorney and selected someone to manage their end-of-life decisions, but often even these simple steps aren't taken. Many older parents assume they'll take care of each other—or that you'll take care of them—without broaching the subject.

Red Flag! Don't allow your parents to gloss over this issue with an "It's all taken care of" type of answer. Make them get specific.

3. Have you planned a strategy to make your money last the rest of your life? Though your parents may think they have enough money to last them, many expenses, including long-term care and medication (up to $600 a month) often aren't considered. As difficult as it may be, if your parents don't have enough to last them for the rest of their lives, that's something you need to know—because of the effect it'll have on your finances. Seeing a financial professional can help—but make sure the person is of your parents' choosing, not yours.

4. Where is your money invested? It is quite possible that they have assets that are not yielding close to what they could be, because they haven't been updated in years. Look for large sums of money in a low-interest account—or the other extreme: $100,000 invested in stocks that are too risky. Your parents may also be underutilizing their property holdings, for example, by living in a space they could profit from by renting it out.

5. What are your wishes and concerns? This is a very general, open-ended question, but critical to ask. Ask your parents to share their feelings now, or sometime soon. Are they going to need your help in any way? Is there anything on their mind about their future? Common worries include not having any money left over for their kids, or worse, dying with debt. Often, too, parents are more concerned with what their legacy will be than with paying the bills right now. It's up to you to help them prioritize.

Red Flag! If your parents won't talk to you, then find someone with whom they will open up to join you so that you can get this important conversation rolling.

Financial Planning for the Seriously Ill

Frequently, it's a serious or terminal illness that spurs parents and their adult children to talk about money for the first time. That's unfortunate, not only because of all the extra baggage involved in this conversation, but because tactically, it complicates matters. The difference between the financial strategies that make sense for a healthy person and those that make sense for someone sick or dying can be enormous. Here are some of the strategies that you'll want to consider. Some of them make sense not just for an older parent, but for a person in their peak earning years.

• **Make sure your estate plan is up to date.** That not only includes your will, but also your medical directives. A living will tells a doctor or hospital how you wish to be treated if you can no longer breathe on your own. A health care proxy gives another individual the right to make health-related decisions for you, should you become incapacitated. You need both, as well as a durable power of attorney, which gives another person the right to make financial decisions on your behalf.

• **Buy credit card life insurance.** Financial reporters like me like to make fun of credit card life insurance. We routinely put it down as one of the worst possible deals on the horizon. If you're seriously ill, however, you want to grab as much as you can get if you have credit card debt. If you look closely at your credit card statements, you'll probably find an offer to buy a life insurance policy which will pay off up to $10,000 of credit card debt if you die. As life insurance policies go, these are always far more expensive than basic term life (which is why the financial press disparages them). But they work for the very ill because they don't require a physical exam. One cautionary note: These policies typically have a six-month preexisting condition exclusion, so only buy them if you're certain to live that long.

• **Buy hospital indemnity coverage.** Another policy I'd usually trash, but not in this case. AARP (American Association of Retired Persons) and other organizations market hospital indemnity policies that typically pay $100 to $200 for each day you spend in the hospital (and more for days in intensive care). If you know you're likely to be hospitalized for a lengthy stay, having a policy like this can mean a steady stream of income for you or for your family. Again, there's often a preexisting condition exclusion, in this case usually three months.

• **Switch jobs.** Yes, it sounds drastic. But if you've been diagnosed with a potentially serious illness but expect to remain well for a while, now may be the best time to think about trying to find a job that offers better health, disability, and life insurance coverage. When you change jobs, the first thirty days are typically considered an open enrollment period, which means you can get on these plans without a medical exam. Before you make a switch, however, make sure that you convert any group life coverage you have under your current employer to an individual policy.

• **Continue to fund your retirement contributions . . .** When you're very sick, your impulse is going to be to stop making contributions to your 401(k) and other retirement accounts—after all, you may think you're not going to make it to retirement. That's not a wise decision. If you work for a company that matches your contributions, any money they kick in is essentially free, and if you leave work due to a disability you'll often become 100 percent vested in your employer's portion of that match.

- **. . . while not withdrawing that money immediately.** You'll also want to resist the urge to withdraw your retirement money as soon as you leave the workforce. You won't incur a 10 percent penalty if you have to withdraw funds because of a disability, but you will be taxed on the income at your current rate. Chances are, though, your tax bracket will be lower next year. So if you can wait a while, more of your savings will end up in your pocket.

Talking to Your Kids

Marc, a father of two in his late thirties, grew up never thinking much about money. Lectures from his parents about saving—about stretching a dollar when necessary—weren't part of the family program. That turned out to be unfortunate. He was halfway through his first semester of college when he realized he'd already blown through most of the money he'd set aside for the entire year. There went his free time. Marc flipped burgers at McDonald's and clerked at a local grocery store so that he could afford to stay in school.

Then a few years after college he got married. Interestingly enough, he found himself with Carol, a woman who's his financial opposite. For her, saving and planning seem to be innate, he says, and so with her taking the lead they began building a nest egg. It wasn't easy for Marc—there were weeks when he felt his paycheck burning a hole in his pocket—but she held firm and he stuck with it. And today, they save 20 percent of their income, and invest the money in mutual funds and individual stocks.

When they started a family seven years ago, Marc—who's now a stay-at-home dad—hoped that their kids would inherit the money genes from Carol's side of the family. No such luck. Every time he took Josh, now seven, or Meg, four, into a toy store, there would be a bout of begging for this toy or that. He'd say no and the kids would start tearing up. Occasionally, they'd have a tantrum.

So when Josh was five, he introduced the concept of an allowance. Josh had to work for it. If he brushed his teeth, completed his homework, and put away most of his toys, he'd earn $4 a month. Originally, that money went into a piggy bank. But when Josh started asking questions about his parents' bank account and got wind of a concept called interest, he wanted to have one, too. So Marc set up a faux account, with a 5 percent interest rate, using Quicken on his home computer. One benefit of Marc's program is that because his kids know they have the means to buy things for themselves, crying in store aisles has become a thing of the past.

Marc and Carol's kids are off to a solid start—which is a good thing. Most are not. According to the Phoenix Student Fiscal Fitness survey, few kids age twelve to twenty-one understand even basic financial terms. Only 12 percent could define the word "budget." Kids themselves seem to understand that they're lacking—two thirds say they don't know enough about money, according to the American Savings Education Council.

With credit cards being offered to kids as early as high school, student loan debt on the rise, and more adult children living off their parents than ever before, it seems crucial to make sure that your children get a solid financial education. The job falls squarely on your shoulders. (Only one out of ten kids receives a personal finance education in school.)

It's best to start early. Kids start to understand the connection between money and spending around age three (my own kids got it when I started to let them use the gumball machine at the grocery store). So that's when you can begin with small lessons. Start by showing them the difference between what a dollar buys at the candy counter and what you can get with a quarter. Let them pay and explain why you get back change. Carry on a running dialogue with your kids—"this orange juice is on sale," "these cookies are a better value because you get twice as many for the same price," and so on—as they're sitting in the basket of the grocery cart. Try to have a toy cash register in the house so that they can play store.

As your kids approach kindergarten and first grade, start introducing money-related board games. You can go out and buy some specifically designed to teach your kids about money, but traditional games like Monopoly Jr., where you lose when the money runs out, work fine. And make sure when you say no to your children's request for pricey purchases—like the $60 sneakers my son was after—you explain *why* you're saying no: that the family only has so much money to spend and that it needs to be used for food and school supplies and things you really *need* before you can choose to spend it on things you *want*. A few other suggestions:

Ages Five to Twelve

• **Make payday routine.** Some families don't believe in giving allowances, but I do, with certain restrictions. I think an allowance should come like a paycheck, on the same day each week, so that kids can begin budgeting mentally. You may, for example, say no to all requests for candy in the drug or convenience store. But a child with an allowance will know that he can pay for his own treats once a week. I don't believe in paying for good grades or for anything else that is the child's responsibility as part of the family (making his bed, tidying her room). Often parents will start with 50 cents or $1 in kindergarten or first grade and give a raise of 50 cents or $1 each year. On average, nine- to ten-year-olds get $3.50, eleven- to fourteen-year-olds $5. But it really depends on what you expect your kids to pay for—at ages six to eight, they might be expected to pay for their own trading cards, for example. At ages ten to twelve, admissions to movies might be expected to come from the allowance. But if you expect your kids to put part of their money away for college each week, or to give a certain percentage to charity, you'll probably want to give them more.

• **Don't overdo it.** If you give your child too much financial responsibility—and too much money to go with it—you may regret it later. Before you start asking your son to pay for school lunches out of his allowance, for example, think about what you're going to do when he blows it all on video games over the weekend. Will you bail him out? If so, that's teaching the wrong lesson, and he'll probably do it again.

• **Enable them to earn more.** When your kids are trying to buy something really expensive, sometimes an allowance won't do the trick. Consider paying them to do chores you might pay outsiders to do: weeding the garden, shoveling the sidewalk, ridding the upholstery of pet hair. You could also try offering matching dollars. Tell your child that you know saving is hard, so to help you're willing to match each dollar he or she is saving for a particular big-ticket item. (P.S. Then you have to let them buy what they want without disapproving.)

• **Expose them to basic banking.** Many banks still have low-minimum passbook savings accounts (seniors insist on them, but they're perfect for kids), which allows you to start talking about interest and how money grows. Once their piggy banks are stuffed, take your kids to the nearest branch and help them fill out the paperwork to open an account. Then encourage them to deposit birthday money and other major windfalls.

• **Let them stumble.** The best way to teach wise spending habits is to let your kids make their own money mistakes. They can learn on their own what it feels like to throw away money on something foolish—but they'll never get there if you insist on approving all of their purchases.

The Teenage Years

Once your children hit their teens, they'll be making many of their own money decisions. According to research from Channel One, teens spend nearly $100 billion annually, more than $4,000 each on average. Much of that money is going to movies, CDs, and Starbucks, but older teens in particular are also socking it away for cars and college. How do you make sure yours are handling their money wisely?

• **Make a decision on allowance.** When teens need money, today as always, they have three basic ways to get it: They can get a job, ask their parents, or wait until allowance day rolls around. A

$5 a week allowance is still the primary source of cash for kids in sixth and seventh grade (and a close second for those in eighth and ninth), according to a *USA Weekend* study. But most high school kids work for their money. As long as your kids can handle their schoolwork, I'd encourage that. How? By giving them only enough for the bare necessities and insisting they earn the rest. Their part-time jobs run the gamut from flipping burgers to designing Web pages, yet gender still plays a significant role. Girls are six times more likely than boys to earn their money baby-sitting; boys are twice as likely to foot their bills with yardwork and other household chores.

• **Pay your teens to help you save.** Financial planner Dee Lee always hated clipping coupons, so she gave the job to her kids. When they were small, she assigned them to clip coupons for items the family used on a regular basis. "Then we split the money," says Lee. "Half would become theirs and half would go to a charity of their choice." Another strategy: Pay your teens to help input the family's receipts and other expenses into Quicken or whatever personal finance software program you're using. Again, it takes a tedious exercise off your hands—and your kids learn what things *really* cost in the process.

• **Teach your kids about stocks.** When my nephew was bar mitzvahed at age thirteen, we aunts and uncles got together and bought him a starter stock portfolio with a few shares of several stocks we thought he might be interested in. Then we opened a custodial account with an online trading firm and gave him the passwords so he could manage the money himself. The trick here is to hold your child's hand for at least a little while. Pick stocks you think your kids might be interested in (Disney, McDonald's, sports teams). Then show them how to follow stock prices in the newspaper or on the Web. And be sure to make the stock market part of your dinner or breakfast table conversation. You'll be surprised at how fast they pick these concepts up.

• **Bankroll an IRA.** If your children are wage-earners, they're eligible to contribute up to $2,000 each year to an IRA. (If they don't earn $2,000, they can only make contributions up to the level of their earnings.) Now, I'm not suggesting that you force your children to put their hard-earned cash away for retirement (unless they're designing Web sites and pulling in some truly big bucks). At least some of what they take home ought to be discretionary. But you may want to make an IRA contribution for them. The money they sock away when they're young teens is far more valuable than those dollars they put away once they hit their mid-twenties and early thirties simply because it has more time to grow.

Talking to Your Friends: Money Etiquette

In May of 1999 I flew to Chicago to tape an Oprah show. The subject: money and manners. It sounds innocent enough. It even sounds lightweight. But in fact, the people in the audience—mostly women—brought tough questions and issues with them. They wanted to know how much to spend on wedding gifts. How to deal with splitting checks at dinner. What to do about friends who didn't pay back loans. The good news is, there are now *rules* in this area. There are basic money etiquette guidelines, some of which have been around for eons, others are newer-fangled innovations. Here are my answers to the questions I'm asked most often.

How much should I spend on a wedding gift? That depends on how well you know the person (you'll probably feel like digging a little deeper when your only niece is at the altar compared with the child of a co-worker) and how much you can afford. A gift isn't meant to break you. If you give much more than you can really stomach financially, you'll resent it. Then, what's the point. In general, wedding gifts these days range from about $50 to $250. For example:

• If you're just out of school and on a budget, but the bride or groom is a close friend. Whatever you spend, make sure your gift is from the heart. Try dropping $40 or $50 on a beautiful picture frame. Even better, spend $30 but blow up a great picture of your friend and her fiancé for the inside.

- If you're a well-established professional with no money problems, but the groom is a colleague you don't know well. In heavy-spending big-city circles, there are people who'd spend $150 at Tiffany's. In other areas, $75 would suffice. In either case, if you don't know the couple well, buy from the registry.
- If you're very successful and the bride is your only niece. This is the time to go all out. Throw a shower if you're able. Ante up for a place setting of silver if you can afford it (they can be hundreds of dollars) or china if you can't. It's not unthinkable to spend $300-plus in some circles, but in most cases that's excessive. Typically anything around $150 is very generous.
- If you're bringing a date to the wedding. While it's nice you've been invited to bring your own dancing partner, it doesn't mean that you should be spending more on a gift. Likewise, the conventional wisdom that the money you spend on a gift should cover the price of dinner is ridiculous. You are not buying a ticket. Again—spend what you can afford—and don't even think about asking your date to chip in.

Remember, you can always spend less by giving more of yourself. One of my most treasured wedding gifts is two silver serving pieces from a great-aunt who is homebound. She didn't spend a dime on them—she picked them out of her personal collection, wrapped them in an old stationery box (which I still have), and shipped them off to me.

How about the other big occasions: bar mitzvahs, confirmations, and so on? These are definitely smaller-ticket occasions than weddings, though they've seen some gift inflation through the years. The range is fairly large: Spend on a gift or give $25 to $100 (or more) depending on what the going rate is in your area and how well you know the child. Savings bonds still work as gifts, but I prefer shares of stock. Choose well and you'll have little trouble beating savings bond returns.

Is giving cash appropriate? Sometimes. It works when you're giving to a person younger than you are by a generation—nieces, nephews, and the children (even adult children) of friends. It's not fine for your contemporaries. Writing a check to a college buddy, for example, feels more like charity than it does a gift. If you don't have the time—or the confidence—to select an actual object, gift certificates are a fine alternative no matter what age the person is.

What do I give at a shower? Unless you've received advance notice that there's going to be a money tree, giving cash is a no-no. Gift certificates (particularly for anything that pampers the bride) are fine, however; just be sure the amount on the certificate will actually buy something (a $15 gift certificate to a salon where the cheapest manicure is $20 is thoughtless) and that you've covered any tips and tax. How much you should spend, again, varies geographically. The going rate is $25 to $35, which will easily cover a great cookbook, a few special utensils, or a fabulous corkscrew and a bottle of wine to go with it. (Likewise, at a baby shower, $25 to $35 will get you a great picture frame or receiving blanket.)

It seems like my kids are invited to two or three birthday parties a weekend. How do I afford this? I'm right there with you. And my friends Oskar and Carla, parents of four in Atlanta, have it worse. They've solved the problem by setting a present cap. "You can get away with $10 for each child under the age of five or six," says Oskar. "After that, you have to spend $15 to really get something substantial." My secret is to buy in bulk. Recently, for example, I found a great paint-your-own-umbrella kit marked down from $15 to $9.99. I bought six.

How about giving cash to kids? No question, today's kids appreciate cash. For small children, age five to ten, a $5 bill is plenty. Once they hit the double digits, send $10. And for kids who are dating and driving, $15 to $20 is a substantial sum.

My friends always want to split checks—but that's after they've had a $27 steak and I had an $11 plate of pasta. What do I do? The key is to broach the subject up front, when you're ordering. Just say: "I'm trying hard to stick to my budget. Would it be okay if we all just pay for what we order?" Then do it. The other small eaters around the table will be noticeably relieved.

Because I make more money than my friends, they always expect me to pay. Do I have to? No. But if you've made a habit of paying in the past, you have to clear the air. One nice way to do it is to pick up the tab for the last time, simultaneously warning your friends that next time they should bring their wallets. Say: "I'll get it this time. Next time, it's someone else's turn."

The Lowdown on Tipping

Believe it or not, I am sitting in a hair salon as I launch into this section on tipping. How appropriate, because when Tony finishes styling my hair, I'll reach into my wallet and give him a 15 to 20 percent tip. (Generally, it's 20. Today, it may be 15 because he was ten minutes late.) We tip our hairdressers without fail. But there are so many other service professionals about whom we're not so sure. If Tony owned the hair salon, then he wouldn't get tipped. Or would he? And how about the person who shampoos your hair or checks your coat? Start adding up all these potential tips and they can make even a cheap blowdry a much more expensive venture. Here are the answers to your tipping questions, plus a guide to help you determine who should get what.

If I tip consistently, do I also have to give a gift at the holidays? If you have a standing appointment with a service professional (a weekly massage or manicure), then it's a nice gesture to give something extra at holiday time. Usually the cost of one appointment will suffice. That extra week's pay is also the correct gift for a cleaning person or baby-sitter (most of whom much prefer cash to a material gift). If you live in a doorman apartment building, you'll probably notice that a list of the names of doormen and porters mysteriously appears in early December. That's so you don't forget anyone—and also so you can spell each one's name correctly if you choose to tip in check form. But they much prefer cash. How much? About $30 to $50 per person, more if you live in a luxury building.

Do I tip extra if a gratuity has already been assessed? That depends on how much of a gratuity has been assessed. If room service tacked on 15 percent, but a waiter was particularly helpful, it's fine to up the amount to 20 percent. Note: Particularly for parties of six or more, restaurants are starting to tack on tips themselves. Pay attention, or you could mistakenly tip twice.

What should I do if the food or service was poor? Don't wait until after your dinner (or massage or round of golf) is complete to point out the problem to your server. Tackle it midstream, then give them a chance to correct it. If they do, you should still give a decent tip. If they don't, then you have to decide how much of the problem was their fault and penalize them accordingly.

When should I try to butter up a maître d'? The best time is when you're leaving a restaurant where you'd like to be remembered. Give him $10 to $20 with a handshake. That way, you're doing two things at once, giving the maître d' a tip for service you just received and insuring that he has a good look at your face and your name for the next time around.

Who gets tipped—and how much? Here are some basic guidelines to follow in rewarding good service:

Barbers and beauticians—15 to 20 percent

Bartenders—15 to 20 percent

Bellhops—$1 to $2 per bag

Cappuccino jockey—the change from your latte in the counter jar

Chambermaids—$2 per day (more for a suite)

Coat checkers—$1 per item

Concierge—10 percent of the cost of the Broadway tickets he gets you; $5 for making a dinner reservation ($10 if you couldn't get in yourself)

Cruise staff—$2.50 to $3 per day for your steward and dining room waiter, half that for your busboy (assuming tips aren't included)

Doormen—$1 for hailing a taxi, $2 to $5 for unloading the car, depending on how much stuff you have

Headwaiter/maître d'—$5 to $10 for a special table

Golf caddies—15 to 25 percent of greens fees

Manicurists—15 to 20 percent

Massage therapists—15 to 20 percent

Parking attendant—$1 to $2

Restroom attendant—50 cents to $1

Room service waiter—15 percent of bill (make sure it's not already included)

Server at counter—15 percent

Shampooer—$2

Skycap—$1 per bag

Sommeliers—15 percent of the wine bill

Taxi driver—15 percent

Tour guides—10 to 20 percent of the cost of the trip upon its conclusion

Usher (at a sporting event)—$1 to seat you ($5 to $10 if you're moved closer to the floor or field)

Waiters—15 to 20 percent

THE BIG THREE: THINGS TO TAKE AWAY FROM TALKING MONEY WITH YOUR FAMILY AND FRIENDS

1. It's not easy to talk about money—but it gets more comfortable the more often you do it. And it's so important. If you don't broach the subject with your spouse, your aging parents, and your kids you'll regret it down the road.

2. To make it easier on yourself, approach each conversation with a few talking points. Some could be conversation starters (opening lines), others could be items you need to get through for specific reasons. Then don't leave the room until you've tackled them.

3. If you need help to get going—and you very well might—you can always hire help. Financial planners (compassionate ones at least) are often up to the task, so are therapists who help couples and singles deal with money problems.

Dear Reader:

The world of personal finance is always evolving. This is fortunate (it certainly keeps me from getting bored) but it is also frustrating. Between the time this book went to press and the time you picked it up, I guarantee there were new bells and whistles added to financial services products, changes in consumer protection laws, and a host of other twists in the world of money (need I say *Internet?*), none of which, of course, are covered here.

Sadly, there is nothing that I can do about that. But I do have an idea about how to deal with it: Use the technical suggestions in this book where you see fit. But try to go a step beyond as well, absorbing the principles of *Talking Money*. Then apply them to your life not just as it stands today, but as *it* changes.

Best of luck!

Jean Chatzky
December 2000